S0-AZX-255

The Korean Peninsula

Published in cooperation with

the Center for Strategic and International Studies,
Washington, D.C.,

and

the Korea Institute for Defense Analyses, Seoul

The Korean Peninsula

Prospects for Arms Reduction
Under Global Detente

EDITED BY

William J. Taylor, Jr.,
Cha Young-Koo, and John Q. Blodgett

Westview Press
BOULDER • SAN FRANCISCO • OXFORD

This Westview softcover edition is printed on acid-free paper and bound in library-quality, coated covers that carry the highest rating of the National Association of State Textbook Administrators, in consultation with the Association of American Publishers and the Book Manufacturers' Institute.

All rights reserved. No part of this publication may be reproduced or transmitted in any form or by any means, electronic or mechanical, including photocopy, recording, or any information storage and retrieval system, without permission in writing from the publisher.

Copyright © 1990 by the Center for Strategic and International Studies

Published in 1990 in the United States of America by Westview Press, Inc., 5500 Central Avenue, Boulder, Colorado 80301, and in the United Kingdom by Westview Press, 36 Lonsdale Road, Summertown, Oxford OX2 7EW

Library of Congress Cataloging-in-Publication Data
The Korean Peninsula: prospects for arms reduction under global
    detente / edited by William J. Taylor, Jr., Cha Young-Koo, and John
Q. Blodgett.
    p. cm.
Includes index.
ISBN 0-8133-8148-7
    1. Arms control.   2. Detente.   3. Korea (South)—Foreign
relations.   4. Korea (North)—Foreign relations.   I. Taylor,
William J. (William Jesse), 1933–   . II. Cha, Young-Koo, 1947–
III. Blodgett, John Q.
JX1974.K74   1990
327.1′74—dc20   90-12939
                                                                     CIP

Printed and bound in the United States of America

The paper used in this publication meets the requirements
of the American National Standard for Permanence of Paper
for Printed Library Materials Z39.48-1984.

10   9   8   7   6   5   4   3   2   1

Contents

PART THREE
Arms Control in Korea: Issues and Prospects

Introduction and Overview

Amos A. Jordan

There can no longer be any doubt that the course of world history has been fundamentally and irreversibly redirected since 1985. Although the political epicenter of change has been Europe, the dynamics that triggered this change are global and its ramifications will affect—for better or worse—the quality of all human life on our planet. This is because the political upheaval of our time is impelled by emerging economic, technological, social, and environmental dynamics that strike to the heart of the human condition. We are privileged, in the final years of this millennium, to set a stage for the next—liberated, to a degree, from the shackles of outmoded ideologies and inhibitions.

The challenge to public policy in all world societies today is to interact in reshaping the amorphous clay of the past into an integrative new model for the future. The key words here are "interact" and "integrative." For the time has passed—presumably forever—when any nation can pursue a destiny outside the warp and woof of the new global fabric.

The purpose of this book is to superimpose that new fabric onto a regional issue of cardinal importance to world peace and to U.S. interests in one of the world's most dynamic regions. The Korean Peninsula is an arena in which the old ideologies continue to collide. There remains a real danger that the collision will become violent. The issue addressed in this volume is whether the new East–West atmosphere of detente and arms reduction can smother the sparks of conflict on this peninsula and perhaps illuminate the path to a Korea reunified as a democratic state.

The contributors to this book are U.S. and Asian experts of acknowledged authority. Their combined conclusions, although not always identical, are summarized in the final chapter. As the reader will observe, the tone of this book is largely optimistic. Time is on the side of peace. North Korea and its intractable dictator, Kim Il-Sung, are increasingly isolated. The inspired initiative of South Korean President Roh Tae-Woo of meeting with Mikhail

1

Gorbachev in San Francisco on June 6, 1990, led to a spectacular result—the establishment of full diplomatic relations between North Korea's adversary and its long-time military supporter. Even China, which is closest to Kim in ideology, in 1989 conducted nearly $3 billion worth of trade with South Korea—four times as much as its trade with the North.

Even as Kim watches his old friends lured away by the attractions of South Korea's infinitely more vibrant economy (and by the urgent need for improved economic ties with the West as a whole), he is besieged with forthcoming overtures from old foes. South Korea tries, and tries again, to engage Kim in a constructive dialogue. Japan has offered diplomatic recognition in return for a more moderate North Korean stance. Kim must be aware that the United States and its friends will find ways to reward a North Korean standdown.

North Korea has long remained isolated from the changes now taking hold throughout the Communist world. Will all these new pressures force political change and a new strategy in Pyongyang? If so, will the direction be toward accommodation or violence? These are the questions, among many others, that are addressed in this book.

To set the stage for the chapters that follow, we need a common understanding of the new global dynamics that have evolved since 1985 and what they could portend for the Korean Peninsula.

Woodrow Wilson once wrote that history is but the lengthened shadow of great (not necessarily good) men. To a certain extent, the cold war of the past 40 years was the lengthened shadow of the paranoic Joseph Stalin, and today's dramatic movement toward global detente in considerable part is the lengthened shadow of Mikhail Gorbachev. Nevertheless, there is a great deal more to history, including the cold war and global detente, than the character and abilities of Stalin or Gorbachev. Although Gorbachev has been the first Soviet leader to fully recognize how essential genuine detente is for the Soviet Union, the forces behind that recognition are much larger than Gorbachev and his policies.

The most fundamental force pushing the Soviets toward detente has been, and will continue to be, the pervasive failure of the Communist economic and political system. In decades past, the combination of political totalitarianism and economic centralization, which has been the hallmark of the Soviet Union's version of Marxist socialism, was able to mobilize that nation's human and material resources and apply them in an adequate manner. Through extensive, rather than intensive, methods of production, underpinned by ideology and repression, the Soviets and their Marxist neighbors were able to achieve acceptable, even respectable, levels of growth until the last decade.

With the waning of ideology as the revolutionary generation faded away and with the growing consciousness of peoples throughout the Soviet empire of the shortcomings of their system, a profound malaise settled over the socialist world. The inadequacy of a centrally planned command approach to economic life became painfully clear in the latter 1970s and 1980s, as the Soviet and satellite economies grew more complex and diversified. In particular, the inability of a command economy to innovate and to exploit technology became an increasingly important brake as economic growth came to depend more and more on the diffusion and application of science and technology. Compounding and contributing to these dismal economic results have been the growing nationalist and ethnic troubles in the non-Russian republics of the Union of Soviet Socialist Republics (USSR), along with alcoholism, inflation, corruption, and a general decline in civic morale. As these difficulties mounted, productivity slumped and gross national product (GNP) growth rates fell to to very low levels in the 1980s.

For the leaders of the Soviet Union, the growing disaffection of its peoples and the stagnation of its economy have carried an additional danger, namely, that the country will lose its superpower status—indeed, to use Gorbachev's own words, that it will descend into the ranks of a "Third World country." Losing the superpower competition with the United States would not only mean the end of the extended Soviet empire, but might also mean that the cohesion of the Soviet Union itself would be put at risk.

Reform of the required depth and breadth requires, at a minimum, an easing of international tension sufficient to permit a redirection of resources away from defense and increased attention to internal matters. Going further, the Soviets need a sufficient warming of relations with the West to stimulate an inflow of trade, investment, and technology. From these imperatives were born *perestroika, glasnost,* and "new political thinking."

I stress these deep roots of the emerging global detente to emphasize the forces beyond Gorbachev's personality that will press detente to persist and deepen over time, even if President Gorbachev himself should falter or fail. The West has wanted genuine detente all along; now the Soviet Union desperately needs it.

The longer detente persists and the broader its reach through arms control arrangements, through revised political relations between the Soviet Union and its former satellites, through enhanced economic relationships with the capitalist world, and through institutionalization of political reforms within the Soviet Union, the harder it will become to reverse detente.

The observations I have just made about detente are not intended to signify that global peace is imminent. There will still be many opportunities for conflict throughout the world. Even shorn of its East European empire and under continuing economic pressure, the Soviet Union will still possess a major nuclear arsenal and large, well-armed conventional forces. It will continue to try to ensure that its neighbors accommodate its fundamental international interests. It will attempt to maintain its superpower status and global reach through a modernized strategic nuclear force, a strong blue-water navy, and allies in such places as North Korea, Vietnam, and Cuba. Wherever it sees an opportunity to extend its influence or diminish Western influence at little risk and low cost—for instance, through the provision of sophisticated arms (of which it will have increasing surpluses)—it will do so, particularly in Third World areas where economic strain and social and political turbulence are likely to present unlocked doors.

Such behavior does not depend on Gorbachev's success or failure. My own judgment is that Gorbachev's complete success is out of the question and his complete failure unlikely. *Perestroika* confronts deeply entrenched difficulties. Yet—in spite of queues for food and consumer goods, enormous budget deficits, repressed inflation, shortages of managerial and entrepreneurial talent, and worker disgruntlement and unresponsiveness—continuing, serious efforts at reform of some kind will proceed, either under Gorbachev or a successor. Hence, the East–West detente that supports reform will very likely continue as well.

During the earlier short-lived and shallow detente at the end of the 1960s and the start of the 1970s, U.S. leaders made plain to the Soviet Union that detente could not be selective, that is, the Soviet Union could not decide that it would enjoy the benefits of detente in some places and subject the United States to the costs of confrontation in others. Leonid Brezhnev seemed to concur, and the famous 1972 agreement on the "Basic Principles of U.S.–Soviet Relations" resulted. That agreement stipulated that both sides would exercise restraint and endeavor to calm conflict around the globe. In spite of the agreed principles, the Soviet leaders promptly began escalating tension by supplying arms and advisers in such trouble spots as Angola, Ethiopia, and Nicaragua. These actions and other examples of Soviet bad faith—most noticeably, the invasion of Afghanistan at the end of the decade—spelled an end to the first chapter of detente and ushered in the U.S. military buildup of the early 1980s. It seems likely that current Soviet leaders will not repeat the errors of that earlier period. Still, we cannot be sure and must move cautiously.

Before tracing some of the implications for Korea of the emerging U.S.–Soviet or, more generally, East–West detente, let me reflect briefly on the growing Sino–Soviet detente and the apparently shrinking Sino–American detente.

The current, relatively warm state of Sino–Soviet relations has taken more than two decades to develop. You will recall that the Sino–Soviet alliance of the 1950s gave way in the early 1960s to distrust and, by the end of that decade, to sizable, open hostilities.

In the 1970s, fearing Soviet aggression and encirclement through Soviet treaties and arms supply relations with North Korea, Vietnam, and India, the Chinese sought detente, indeed active political cooperation, with the United States. That Chinese political cooperation with the United States was in large part accomplished by the normalization of relations with the United States in 1979. It was further strengthened by the common opposition of the United States and China to the Soviet invasion of Afghanistan at the end of that same year.

With the Reagan military buildup of the early 1980s, which the Chinese viewed as shifting the superpower balance back toward the Americans, China was again prepared to change its stance on detente. By the mid-1980s, in Deng Xiaoping's words, the danger of Soviet hegemony had receded and China could adopt a policy of equidistance from the Soviet Union and the United States. China, Deng said, had no interest in playing a Soviet or American card in the triangular diplomatic game; indeed, it had no intention of being a card player at all. Of course, in practice "equidistance" meant equidistance with a clear bent toward the West because China would receive economic help with its modernization and because the West posed little or no military danger.

To make equidistance more than a slogan, China needed to normalize relations with the Soviet Union, relations that had been broken off since the early 1960s. Because the Soviet Union was even more eager to warm up the relationship, China took the position that normalization could proceed only if the Soviet Union would meet three Chinese preconditions: reduction of Soviet military forces along its borders, withdrawal of Soviet forces from Afghanistan, and withdrawal of Vietnamese troops from Kampuchea. In the case of the withdrawal of Vietnamese troops, the assumption was that Soviet influence in Hanoi was sufficient to mandate withdrawal.

With the fulfillment, in whole or in part, of these preconditions by the Soviet Union, normalization proceeded and was sealed by Gorbachev's visit to Beijing in May 1989. Both nations have a stake in moving beyond normalization to cooperation; therefore, in the absence of some unanticipated adversity, the Sino–Soviet relationship will continue to warm and—within limits—to strengthen in the 1990s. For each country, these limits depend critically on the other's domestic troubles: The Chinese are deeply worried about the spread of Gorbachev's political reform, and the Soviet leaders are distancing themselves from the Tiananmen crackdown and its repressive aftermath.

During 1989, while Sino–Soviet relations were blossoming, U.S.–Chinese relations were withering. The faltering of Chinese economic reform, beginning in the latter part of 1988, and the student demonstrations, beginning in April of 1989, produced an understandable reaction in China, which was sensitive to critical views by outsiders. In May, as the student demonstrations intensified, the People's Republic of China (PRC) government attempted to limit the interaction between students and outsiders and began to severely criticize Western media coverage.

With the brutal Tiananmen Square crackdown in early June came strong public criticism of the Chinese government from around the world, particularly from the United States. Calls by the U.S. Congress for economic sanctions against China produced strong reactions in Beijing, even though the actual steps taken by President George Bush were relatively mild.

The welcome given in the West to refugee leaders of the demonstrations and the U.S. embassy sanctuary given to dissident physicist Fang Lizhi resulted in even more Chinese hostility toward outside critics. Although China's leaders insisted that they were continuing on the path of reform and opening to the outside, the execution of some protest leaders and the bitter attacks against critics further weakened relationships with the West, especially the United States. In a tit-for-tat response, the U.S. Congress then made economic sanctions a matter of law.

By the late autumn of 1989, many U.S. leaders were attempting to halt the deterioration of Sino–American relations. Henry Kissinger's view that "China remains too important for America's national security to risk the relationship on the emotions of the moment" was a typical reaction. Indeed, if China does not engage in a wave of further executions or other major human rights violations, it seem likely that by early in the 1990s both sides will be seeking reconciliation. Restoration of meaningful Sino–American cooperation and a resumption of the military supply relationship, for example, will take longer, perhaps to mid-decade and could be delayed indefinitely if the struggle to succeed Deng Xiaoping should turn out to be bloody—which is not altogether unlikely. The recent PRC decision to resume student exchanges, however, is an encouraging sign.

China, as well as the Soviet Union, has a substantial interest in restarting its growth. In 1982, when the last Chinese census was taken, there were nearly 1.1 billion people; by the year 2000, it is estimated that number will have grown by about 250 to 300 million—in other words, in less than two decades, China will have added more people than the United States now has. To cope with this massive increase, which is occurring despite the continuing government policy of one child per couple, and to deal with unemployment and underemployment figures in the hundreds of millions, China simply must grow and modernize. Whether Jiang Zemin will finally prove to be Deng Xiaoping's successor or not and whether it takes two, four, or six years to get firmly back on the path of modernization, China's leaders are bound to pursue that course and will, accordingly, be seeking outside trade, investment, aid, and technology from the West.

The United States, too, wants China to grow. It is clearly in the interest of the West for China to be modernizing economically and liberalizing politically, for China to be focusing on internal development rather than adventures abroad, and for China to be providing a check on lingering Soviet power. A weak, politically repressive, unstable China is an undesirable strategic and economic partner for the West. In terms of regional political and strategic stability, too, it is in the West's interest that China not be preoccupied with national strain and strife. Such a China would be less able to help resolve the Kampuchean tangle or to ease tensions on the Korean Peninsula.

In short, in East Asia as well as in Europe, the West has a stake in successful reform of Communist societies. Furthermore, Marxist states in both regions have a stake in continuing detente with the West and in drawing the economic benefits that can flow from such relationships.

Reflecting on the implications of the emerging global detente for Korea specifically, it is important to be clear that the Korean Peninsula is part of the West. Its fate and political, economic, and security interests are inextricably tied to those of the West as a whole. Therefore, the positive conclusions just reached about the value and likely durability of global detente and about the strength of the forces behind it apply specifically to Korea. Similarly, the conclusions about the temporary setback in China's relations with the West arising from the repression at Tiananmen Square also apply to the Republic of Korea (ROK). This is true not only because of the ROK's global position as a part of the West, but also because of its regional position and rivalry with North Korea.

PRC–North Korean relations, which had been decaying as China proceeded with economic and political reforms and while North Korea resisted such efforts, have improved since Tiananmen Square. It is noteworthy that North Korea has been the only Asian country to support Beijing's crackdown. There are, of course, limits to the new warmth between Beijing and Pyongyang, but even a shallow improvement increases Kim Il-Sung's ability to maneuver between its two giant Communist neighbors.

Conversely, although the PRC has tried to continue to strengthen its growing economic ties with the ROK after Tiananmen, those efforts have inevitably suffered somewhat with the restriction of China's private sector. Moreover, there is also at least the short-term danger that relations between the United States and China will continue to deteriorate, thus inhibiting the South Korean relationship with one or the other, or both. Still, it seems unlikely that these possible setbacks will prevail over the continuing drive on the part of South Korea and China toward greater cooperation over the long run.

Turning back to the implications of U.S.–Soviet detente for the Republic of Korea, let me add a few thoughts. One significant, near-term consequence of the new U.S.–Soviet detente will be deep reductions in the U.S. defense budget. The Bush administration has announced that the 1991 fiscal year defense budget will be substantially lower than projected earlier, and Secretary of Defense Richard Cheney has ordered each branch of the military to submit stringent budget-cutting proposals for the next few years. Personnel will be one of the first areas reduced, and the army and air force are likely to lose several divisions and air wings over the next three to four years. For various reasons, these cuts will fall first on U.S. troops stationed overseas, primarily in the European theater, in the context of the Vienna negotiations on conventional forces, but inevitably also in Asia and on the Korean Peninsula.

A small reduction in the number of U.S. troops stationed in South Korea, which may begin as early as the end of 1991, should not provoke undue alarm in Seoul. Such a measure will not mark a lessening of the U.S. commitment to the Republic of Korea, nor need it be the first step in a unilateral, total withdrawal of the U.S. presence. A small cut in U.S. ground forces, which makes sense militarily in light of the vast improvement in South Korea's defense capabilities, should be viewed as an opportunity to ease tensions on the peninsula and to promote further dialogue with North Korea. In fact, given the strong probability that such force cuts will occur, the South Korean government should begin thinking now about how this situation can be turned to its advantage.

The Soviet Union will continue, indeed is likely to intensify, its effort to improve its security and economic position in Northeast Asia. It is clear that the Soviet leaders view their country as at a disadvantage in the region, compared with the United States and its allies. Despite the Soviet Union's massive investment over the past decade in regional military forces and increased diplomatic and economic efforts, it will continue to remain at a disadvantage unless it can somehow turn the emerging global detente to its advantage in Asia.

Certainly, the leadership of the Soviet Union—as well as that of the United States—will continue to place priority on Europe. Starting with Gorbachev's 1986 Vladivostok speech, however, Soviet policymakers have clearly been trying to strengthen their political and economic position and to reap the benefits of detente in the Far East, as well.

Specifically, Gorbachev has tried to engage the United States in arms control arrangements and confidence-building measures in the region that would take the pressure off Soviet resources and increase the likelihood of the flow of trade and investment in the development of Siberian resources. In particular, the Soviet Union has sought to constrain U.S. naval power and to find a formula that would secure the Soviet submarine-launched ballistic missile (SLBM) bastion in the Sea of Okhotsk in the context of naval forces limitations. It has also attempted, although half-heartedly, to find a way to defuse the Northern Territories issue with the Japanese—and to obtain Japanese economic help in the region in exchange for limited concessions. If the Soviets could succeed in weakening U.S.–Japanese military cooperation through these various initiatives—and especially if they could obtain Japanese help in developing Far Eastern provinces—the Soviets would significantly improve their regional position and become a larger factor in Seoul's calculus.

Parallel with the Soviet initiatives just cited, the Soviet Union has also been reaching out recently to the Republic of Korea, primarily through unofficial economic inducements and personal and cultural diplomacy. The opening of full diplomatic relations between Seoul and Moscow through diplomatic establishments will be a watershed. These initiatives are also intended to contribute to the easing of tension on the Korean Peninsula by inducing the United States to take parallel informal initiatives with respect to North Korea. The pressure is now on the Bush administration to consider recognizing and exchanging ambassadors with North Korea. If Pyongyang were amenable to this, it would send the strongest signal yet that Kim is ready to negotiate in earnest.

My central conclusion is that the emerging global detente provides a favorable environment for realizing the Republic of Korea's national objectives. Taking advantage of that favorable environment will require a steady hand by the leaders in Seoul, backed by an informed citizenry throughout the Republic. I have no doubt that both the enlightened leadership and public support will be forthcoming.

PART ONE

The Global New Detente
and the Korean Peninsula

1

Global New Detente:
Historical Perspectives

Robert Martin

> Decoding [today's international] environment is extremely
> difficult. Everything is in flux.[1]
> —*Admiral William J. Crowe, former chairman,*
> *U.S. Joint Chiefs of Staff, at his retirement*

At the eve of a new decade, the international political system is indeed in a state of flux. There is a juxtaposition of events in several of the most important arenas of international relations, any of which alone would be considered revolutionary in its effect on the world order. Trends in Soviet foreign policy and domestic trends in the Soviet Union and other Communist states raise hopes of the end of the cold war, the independence of Eastern Europe, and a general reduction in military confrontation around the world. Meanwhile, the United States' budget deficit and continued unfavorable balance of trade have made the United States an international debtor for the first time in this century, raising questions at home about its large expenditures on behalf of global security and abroad about a perceived decline in U.S. power and will.

There is a growing (but not yet universal) belief around the globe that the utility of military power in international politics is declining and that economics and technology are rising in importance as elements of national power. This trend and others are making arms control in both its nuclear and conventional dimensions more feasible and attractive as a means of achieving a stable military balance at a lower cost. At the same time, sophisticated weaponry has become widely available to those engaged in the drug trade and other criminal activities, as well as to smaller nations and revolutionary groups. This new weapons trade has blurred the distinction between low-intensity warfare and high-intensity crime and has increased the propensity for the use of force at the lower end of the conflict spectrum.

These trends and perceptions are part of the setting for a new, rapidly developing global detente that some have already described as the end of the cold war. Whether the phenomenon merits such a description is a matter of much more than academic importance. If nations are to adopt good policies, they need to understand first what the policies must address. Policies based on perceptions that turn out to be incorrect to a significant degree can threaten the very survival of nations.

Democratic societies in particular are at risk in being premature in their reactions to perceived opportunities to reduce military expenditures. Alternative needs for resources are immediate and compelling. It is very tempting to argue, "If the cold war is in fact over, let us reap the benefits now by cutting back military expenditures and reducing the cost of our alliance commitments."

Unfortunately, the cold war is not yet over. Many of its most dangerous features remain largely unchanged. In Europe, the North Atlantic Treaty Organization (NATO) and Warsaw Pact forces armed with nuclear weapons remain in readiness. In the United States, the Soviet Union, China, the United Kingdom, and France, strategic arsenals remain poised. Strategic weapons continue to be modernized, even as Strategic Arms Reduction Talks (START) negotiations look for ways to reduce their numbers. In Asia, Soviet occupation forces remain in their postwar locations in Japan's Northern Territories, and a Stalinist dictator installed by Soviet occupation forces still looks south from Pyongyang with unrenounced dreams of a reunited Korea under his rule.

It is, at best, premature to declare the cold war over. It is also dangerous. Deterrence based on military strength remains important. We do not know the limits of Soviet tolerance for the changes taking place in Eastern Europe. Hard-line Communist leaders in North Korea, East Germany, and China are seeing the very basis for their claim to power eroded by the revolutionary changes taking place in the Soviet Union, Poland, and Hungary. Deemphasis of military power and external threat are not characteristic of those who perceive themselves as beleaguered and alone.

At the same time, it would be tragic to be presented with the opportunity to end the cold war and fail to recognize it. If we are not yet at the end of the cold war, are we at least at the beginning of the end? It is the contention of this author that we are.

The Global Confrontation

To assess the significance of the new global detente, we need to look at the evolution of the global confrontation it purports to replace. Identifying significant changes in the fundamental elements of that confrontation would support the assessment that the new detente is more than a temporary breathing space in an unending struggle between the Communist powers and the rest of the world.

Revisionist arguments to the contrary notwithstanding, the origins of the global confrontation lay in Joseph Stalin's opportunistic use of the Soviet Union's postwar position to expand the area of Soviet control and in the adoption of the strategy of containment by the Western powers to stop it. The addition of Eastern Europe to the Soviet empire, the occupation of North Korea and the Japanese Northern Territories, and the 1949 triumph of the Chinese Communists added territory and peoples to the Communist bloc that, it was claimed, was riding the tide of history to inevitable triumph over the capitalist nations.

This claim and its ideological underpinning made the Communist expansion a revolutionary challenge to world order. Vladimir I. Lenin had contended that the struggle between capitalism and socialism is the central feature of international, as well as domestic, politics. Stalin advanced the argument that the forces of socialism and the forces of capitalism were two camps locked in an unrelenting struggle for supremacy and that the socialist camp would inevitably win.

When Communist expansion in Europe became stymied by the execution of the containment strategy, by West European recovery that limited the support of national Communist parties, and by the formation of NATO, the Soviets and the Chinese turned to Asia and the Third World to try to break the wall of containment. Joseph Stalin approved the 1950 invasion of South Korea by the Soviet-armed forces of the north. When that attempt also resulted in a stalemate, Moscow and Beijing began to support national liberation movements to continue the spread of communism. They were aided in the 1950s and 1960s by many Third World revolutionaries who were attracted to the Marxist–Leninist development model and to the Communist Party as an instrument of mobilization and control. Communist aid—directly or through surrogates—to insurgent movements, such as the Algerian rebels in the late 1950s, associated them with the forces of nationalism against the remaining vestiges of colonialism.

Soviet military and development aid established political relationships that led to military access in such far-flung locations as Egypt and Syria (1955), North Yemen (1957), Indonesia (1958), Guinea (1959), and India (1961).[2] China, on a lesser scale, in the 1950s and 1960s also assisted insurgency movements in Southeast Asia and provided both military and development assistance to several African nations. One of the Communists' most important successes, however, came as a windfall after the Cuban revolution when Castro, rebuffed in his overtures to the United States, turned to the Soviets. The Soviet Union provided weapons to Cuba free of charge beginning in the early 1960s. In 1962, Soviet attempts to take advantage of the Cuban relationship by placing missiles there led the United States and the USSR to the brink of nuclear war.

In the early 1960s, other recipients of Soviet military aid included Ghana, Iraq, Mali, North Vietnam, Somalia, Sudan, and Tanzania. Throughout the 1960s and 1970s, the Soviet navy gained access to ports in Algeria, Egypt, Ethiopia, India, Iraq, Libya, Mauritius, Mozambique, Somalia, South Yemen, Syria, and Yugoslavia. Cuba, of course, remained a major base, and access to Cam Ranh Bay and Da Nang in Vietnam provided a major staging facility in Southeast Asia after the fall of Saigon to Hanoi.[3]

Military aid was more than a trade-off for access. It also became a form of intervention, with the Soviets or surrogates supplying arms in Third World conflicts in which U.S. interests were at stake on the other side. These included the Middle East War (1973), the Vietnam War, Ethiopia (1977–1978), India (1971), Angola (1975), the Sino–Vietnamese conflict (1979), and insurgencies in Nicaragua, Zimbabwe, the Western Sahara, Chad, and South Yemen.[4]

The extension of the two camps' confrontation into the Third World made the confrontation global. Marshall Shulman describes the early recognition of this challenge by the United States:

In the early postwar years and up until the partition of Germany after the Berlin Blockade of 1948–49, Europe was the central territorial concern in the East–West competition. As Europe became relatively stabilized after the partition, attention shifted to the Third World as the battleground. Nikita Khrushchev, in refuting Chinese charges of the loss of revolutionary zeal by the Soviet Union, affirmed Soviet interest in and support of "National Liberation Movements," and it was this flagging of Soviet intent that led President John F. Kennedy to see the "strategic importance" of the civil war in Vietnam. . . .[5]

Almost from the begining of the cold war, the Yugoslav refusal to toe the Stalinist line and the Sino–Soviet split belied the idea of the socialist camp as a monolithic bloc controlled from Moscow. Nevertheless, the continued adherence of China to the central tenets of the "two camps" view of the world and its aggressive support for Communist insurgency movements offered little relief from earlier perceptions of the revolutionary character of the socialist camp. The issue was who should direct the world socialist movement; the capitalist camp remained the enemy for both the Soviets and the Chinese. Both continued to express a belief in the inevitability of war and the inevitable triumph of world socialism. The conflict between the two nations somewhat reduced the threat the Soviet Union and China posed to others. The continued efforts of both to take advantage of any opportunity to weaken the capitalist camp, however, kept the image of the socialist camp valid despite the internal split that made it no longer a bloc. The problem for the West was the containment of both China and the Soviet Union in their attempts to overturn the world order.

The brutal 1968 Soviet intervention in Czechoslovakia added a note of irreversibility to the global confrontation in the form of the Brezhnev Doctrine. This doctrine asserted the right and the intention of the Soviet Union to intervene to prevent the overthrow of any established socialist government. In practice, it also meant, in the words of Robert Manning, "that the Soviet Union maintains the right to intervene to enforce what it deems proper socialist policies if an allied Communist regime strays too far from the Kremlin line."[6] Backed by Soviet military might, the assertion that any socialist triumph was irreversible appeared to require that the non-socialist camp confront insurgency everywhere, lest failure to do so give the socialist camp an easy triumph. Thus, pressure was added in making the confrontation global.

Ideology was hence interwoven with balance-of-power considerations and opportunism to produce a global Communist revolutionary challenge to the world order. Defensively motivated balance-of-power considerations alone imply a relationship of one's actions to the actions of one's opponents that limits the need for expansion and search for allies beyond a stable balance point. The two-camps doctrine and the belief in the inevitable triumph of socialism, however, required instead a limitless struggle that would continue until the triumph of world socialism was complete.

David Holloway, in a recent *Foreign Affairs* article, notes that this conceptual basis for Soviet foreign policy continued into the 1980s. Holloway states:

> It was a central premise of Brezhnev's foreign policy that the correlation of forces in the world was moving in favor of socialism. ... This [correlation of forces] model does not regard equilibrium as either the goal of policy or as an inherent characteristic of the international system. Rather, it assumes that the world is moving toward socialism; the aim of Soviet policy is to help this transition or at least prevent the West from stopping it.[7]

The U.S. perception of the revolutionary character of the Soviet threat also extended into the 1980s and underlay the Reagan administration's response. Then-Assistant Secretary of Defense Richard L. Armitage in 1984 described the challenge in the Third World as follows:

> Unfortunately, for many . . . nations the development process itself . . . generates dislocations within societies and [applies] pressures on political systems which too often produce instability and violence, both domestically and internationally. Soviet adventurism, directly or through surrogates, exacerbates these pressures and the instability they produce and overlays the already complicated challenges of the development process with the additional complication of making them part of the East–West struggle. Moreover, the growth of Soviet military power and ability to project it, coupled with the Brezhnev Doctrine as exhibited in Afghanistan, skew the development process by injecting into it a note of irreversibility. President Kennedy once described this trait of Soviet policy as, "What's mine is mine, and what's yours is negotiable." We could amend that today to say, "What's yours is contestable by whatever means are available."[8]

The Reagan administration came into office, in part, as the result of an U.S. backlash to the events of the 1970s that had besieged U.S. interests around the globe. President Ronald Reagan's campaign promise to strengthen U.S. defenses was taken as a mandate when he won a landslide victory in the 1980 election. His ability to move quickly on that promise ironically was enhanced by programs that were already set in motion by the Carter administration's response to the Soviet support of the Vietnamese invasion of Cambodia and the Soviet invasion of Afghanistan.

The events of the early 1970s had produced a general perception of U.S. decline and Soviet resurgence. The Nixon Doctrine, Vietnamization, the demise of the Southeast Asia Treaty Organization (SEATO) and Central Treaty Organization (CENTO) all contributed to the appearance of a U.S. withdrawal from Asia. The oil crisis of 1973–1974, President Jimmy Carter's 1977 decision to withdraw troops from South Korea, and the fall of the shah of Iran and the subsequent U.S. hostage crisis all contributed to the perception of U.S. decline.

One positive development for the United States in the 1970s was the gradual improvement of relations with the PRC after the dramatic visits by then-Secretary of State Henry Kissinger and President Richard Nixon. Despite a continued Chinese determination to protect the ideological basis for domestic Communist rule, developments during the 1970s demonstrated a dramatic break from the internationalist tenets that had kept China part of the socialist camp in the two-camp global confrontation. The Chinese reassessment of foreign policy led to the termination of their support for insurgent movements in Southeast Asia, to an increased focus on the Soviet Union as their most immediate security threat, and to the gradual disuse of internationalist ideological arguments. The Sino–Soviet split had made the Chinese a security problem for both the Soviet Union and the United States. The defection of China from the socialist camp, however, made it a de facto security asset for the United States in the global balance.

The Soviet assessment of the "correlation of forces" in the late 1970s was that the achievement of strategic parity with the United States had produced a situation in which the West would have no choice but to become more accommodating as Soviet power grew. This assessment was the basis for the Soviet belief that the continued growth of Soviet military power was consistent with detente and would bring increased accommodation from Soviet rivals. It was wrong.[9]

The Soviet military buildup, in fact, produced the opposite response. The Carter administration halted plans for troop withdrawals from South Korea and increased the defense budget. The Chinese responded to the Vietnamese invasion of Cambodia with calls for a united front against the USSR and an invasion of its own into Vietnam. It was the Soviet invasion of Afghanistan in 1979, however, that produced consensus within the United States and among the Western allies that the Soviet Union remained an expansionist power and that concerted efforts were needed to improve Western security. Much to the surprise and alarm of the Soviet Union, the United States and its allies responded with determination to counterbalance the growth of Soviet military power.

By the mid-1980s, the United States had strengthened its alliances and its military forces, deployed ground-launched cruise missiles and Pershing IIs to Western Europe, provided aid to Pakistan and the mujahhedin, provided assistance to Thailand, urged the Japanese to greater efforts in self-defense, and provided limited military technology transfers to Beijing. With varying degrees of U.S. assistance, economic progress and growing political confidence had made many key countries less vulnerable to insurgency. U.S. allies in Asia had improved their military capabilities to the point that most were able to provide the bulk of their own defense against local threats, looking to the United States primarily for over-the-horizon security against threats from larger powers. Earlier doubts about U.S. capability and the will to defend U.S. interests and honor its commitments were largely overcome by the renewed U.S. confidence and strengthened presence.

After the death of Leonid Brezhnev in 1983, first Yuri Andropov and then Konstantin Chernenko proved incapable of modifying the direction of Soviet foreign policy, which was becoming increasingly dysfunctional.

Afghanistan had become a quagmire for Soviet forces just as Vietnam had been for the United States. East–West relations were at a new low. When the West strongly condemned the actions of Soviet forces in shooting down Korean Airlines flight 007, Andropov's reaction was to blame the United States for the poor state of East–West relations, presumably because the Americans had not accommodated the growth of Soviet military power. Andropov declared, "If anyone had any illusions about the possibility that the policy of the present American administration would change for the better, then the events of the recent period have finally dispelled them."[10]

In 1985, the United States and USSR were far from detente. The inevitability of global confrontation was reconfirmed. The United States exhorted its allies to help assume the continuing burden of containment. There was a significant change from the situation of a decade earlier, however. There was a new air of confidence among the Western powers and a smell of decay from the stagnating socialist economies and from the Soviet adventurism turned sour.

Gorbachev and the Soviet Reassessment

The emergence of Mikhail Gorbachev as the new Soviet leader in March 1985 was a significant generational change that brought new perspectives to the task of assessing where the Soviet Union stood and what should be done. It had been clear for some time that Brezhnev's policies were a failure. Growth of Soviet military power had not produced commensurate foreign policy gains. The Western response had made the Soviet Union less, rather than more, secure. Moreover, David Holloway notes, "The foreign policy crisis that Gorbachev faced in March 1985 was only part of a broader economic and social crisis affecting the country."[11] The difference was that Gorbachev had the courage and vision to institute dramatic changes, something that neither of his older predecessors had been able to do.

Part of the Soviet reassessment was the recognition that failure to improve the Soviet economy and technological base would mean the loss of its status as a great power. To permit greater concentration on the required domestic reforms, a stable and predictable international environment was essential. As Gorbachev told a *Time* reporter before the 1985 Geneva summit,

> I don't remember who, but somebody said that foreign policy is a continuation of domestic policy. If that is so, then I ask you to ponder one thing: If we in the Soviet Union are setting ourselves such truly grandiose plans in the domestic sphere, then what are the external

conditions that we need to be able to fulfill these domestic plans? I leave the answer to that question with you.[12]

The need for a stable international environment alone might have produced many of the Soviet actions since 1985: new arms control initiatives and attempts to improve relations with the United States, moves to normalize relations with China, overtures to Western Europe and Japan, withdrawal from Afghanistan and reevaluation of other external commitments, and requests for participation in international economic institutions. All of these actions are consistent with a Soviet desire to achieve a temporary truce in the global confrontation, a breathing space to allow time for economic recovery and preparation for renewed hostility at a later date.

Other Soviet statements and actions, however, indicate that the changes are much deeper. There is a growing consensus among Western analysts that the ongoing reassessment that began even before Gorbachev's formal rise to power involves rethinking not only the unsuccessful policies, but also the fundamental concepts on which they are based.[13] Columbia University Professor Robert Legvold, in an excellent *Foreign Affairs* analysis, notes that the basic concepts of Soviet foreign policy "have not been so thoroughly reconsidered for more than 60 years—not since the wrenching adaptations to the Treaty of Brest Litovsk, the civil war and the Rapallo accords. Literally every dimension of Soviet policy is being touched."[14]

Legvold discusses four fundamental conceptual changes. The first is the insufficiency of military power as a foundation of security and a linkage of national and mutual security. Legvold quotes Gorbachev's statement to the 27th Party Congress: "The character of contemporary weapons leaves no country with any hope of safeguarding itself solely with military and technical means." He goes on to paraphrase Gorbachev, saying that no nation's security can be achieved at the expense of another country.[15]

A second fundamental change is the assertion of the primacy of "human interests," particularly the value of peace above the value of class struggle because of the overriding need to save humanity from total destruction.[16] Holloway contends that this change is very significant in that it "implies that the goals of peace and socialism may come into conflict, and further it provides a justification for giving priority to the pursuit of cooperation with the West over the search for unilateral advantage."[17]

A third change is the Soviet view of Third World conflict. Rather than seeing Third World conflict as a heroic national liberation struggle, the Soviets now see it as a waste of resources and a source of international tension.[18]

Finally, the Brezhnev Doctrine, if not lifted, has been changed to allow far greater leeway for change within other socialist states, without the threat of Soviet military intervention. The concept of socialist internationalism, abandoned by China in the 1970s, has now apparently been abandoned by the Soviet Union as well and replaced by something closer to laissez-faire.[19] Could one possibly imagine Brezhnev permitting Solidarity to contest, much less win, an election against the Communist Party in Poland, or Hungary being permitted to disestablish its Communist Party and replace it with a democratic socialist party?

That such changes are real is no longer in doubt. In addition, they are causing other changes as well. Soviet military doctrine, for example, is striving to adjust to a new conceptual foundation with such concepts as "defensive defense" and "reasonable sufficiency." Similar changes are taking place in the ideological and doctrinal foundations of Soviet politics and economics. These changes are truly revolutionary and, like all revolutions, risky.

Gorbachev is doing no less than discarding the very ideological basis for the claim of the Communist Party to rule. This has been done with the apparent assessment that these ideological tenets have lost their legitimacy because of the ineffectiveness of the policies they produced. Although the new concepts are presented as new applications of Marxism–Leninism to modern conditions, it is a long stretch. Legitimacy for the new concepts and policies must be built the hard way—they have to work. The outcome— especially for domestic reform in the Soviet Union—is far from certain; the obstacles are formidable.

Gorbachev and Asia

Another conclusion of the Soviet reassessment under Gorbachev was that the Asian Pacific region is of increasing importance to the Soviet Union and that this region possibly will become the focus of world politics in the twenty-first century.[20] It also recognized that the Soviet preoccupation with Europe, its military buildup, and its strategy of intimidation of Asian states (for example, the invasion of Afghanistan and its support for the Vietnamese invasion of Cambodia) had produced strong resistance and resentment, rather than intimidation. The Soviet Union and its allies were increasingly isolated from the diplomatic and economic mainstream of this important region, while the position of the United States continued to grow stronger.

An inkling of the new Soviet approach to Asia appeared in Gorbachev's remarks during Rajiv Gandhi's visit to Moscow in May 1985 and in a comprehensive government statement in Tass in April 1986. The landmark statement, however, was Gorbachev's much touted and much analyzed Vladivostok speech on July 28, 1986. The Vladivostok speech, the interview with the Indonesian magazine *Merdeka* in 1987, and the speech at Krasnoyarsk in 1988 all presented and subsequently refined a broad-ranging compendium of new Soviet policies, unilateral actions, and proposals that declared the Soviet Union's intent to take its "rightful place" as an Asian Pacific nation and to act to reduce international tension and military confrontation. The Soviet policies and proposals manifest Soviet objectives that include both continuity with previous policies and new departures.

The continuity of Soviet objectives is evident in Soviet intentions to weaken the U.S. military position and its alliances in the region. This was clearly demonstrated in its arms control proposals that served as propaganda if rebuffed or produced asymmetrical reductions in U.S. forces if accepted. New departures are also apparent: Soviet efforts to improve relations with regional states, especially China; a willingness to make concessions to resolve regional conflicts, including those in Afghanistan and Cambodia; and an intention to reduce Soviet military forces in the region, beginning with forces in Mongolia. The new Soviet approach replaces the old Soviet policy of relying almost exclusively on military intimidation with a multifaceted policy that emphasizes diplomacy, economics, and the reduction of regional tension. The new Soviet policy seeks both to weaken the U.S. position in the region and to convince regional states of the Soviet commitment to a constructive and cooperative role in Asia and the Pacific.

Initially, U.S. and Asian suspicions of Soviet motives were strong. The nations of the region welcomed Soviet support for regional proposals such as the South Pacific Nuclear Free Zone (SPNFZ) and a Southeast Asia Nuclear Free Zone (SEANFZ). There was little support for most of Gorbachev's specific proposals, however. China and the United States separately noted after the Vladivostok speech that Soviet actions and those of their Vietnamese allies bore the responsibility for the security conditions that had generated the climate of distrust faced by the Soviets.

Subsequently, Soviet actions and Gorbachev's personal international popularity began to moderate those suspicions. Withdrawal from Afghanistan and Mongolia and the pressure placed on Vietnam to withdraw from Cambodia constituted sufficient progress on China's three conditions to permit a Sino–Soviet summit in Beijing in May 1989. Statements by government officials and opinion leaders throughout the region, though they remained cautious, portrayed a gradual shift from suspicion to the perception of an opportunity to reduce tension and the risk of war.

General perceptions of the Soviet Union, although still skeptical, are much more positive than before the Vladivostok speech. Meanwhile, the U.S. position in the region is again eroding as the result of U.S. trade policies and, more recently, because of regional perceptions that the United States has been too slow to respond to opportunities presented by Gorbachev's policies. Paul Kennedy's thesis that U.S. power is eroding because of a deterioration in U.S. economic power has also struck a resonant chord with

Asian scholars, who may be somewhat influenced by justifiable pride in the continued vitality of Asian economies. (Professor Samuel P. Huntington of Harvard, in a persuasive critique of Kennedy's argument, however, points out that the multidimensional nature of U.S. strength enables it to renew its power in response to perceptions of decline. He argues that "the United States is unlikely to decline so long as its public is periodically convinced that it is about to decline."[21]

The End of the Cold War?

George Kennan, author of the U.S. containment policy, put forward in a series of lectures at the U.S. National War College during the earliest days of the cold war three objectives for containment. The United States' readiness to declare the end of the cold war might be evaluated in terms of the attainment of these objectives.

> These were (a) to restore the international balance of power, thereby preventing the Soviet Union from exploiting power vacuums left by the defeats of Germany and Japan; (b) to reduce the Soviet Union's ability to project influence beyond its borders through the international communist movement; and (c) ultimately to bring about, through a combination of inducements and deterrents, a modification in the behavior of the Soviet leadership toward the outside world which would cause it to learn to live with, rather than seek to eliminate, diversity.[22]

The perception of a stable balance of power has altered with changing technologies and capabilities. Nevertheless, the establishment of NATO and the containment of Communist aggression in Korea restored the postwar balance. Strategically, the balance of power became a maintained deterrence of war between the United States and the USSR, even though Soviet military strength continued to grow, reaching strategic parity with the United States in the 1970s. The West's increasing technological capability balanced the East's greater numbers, and the balance was maintained into the 1970s. Soviet military growth in the late 1970s threatened to upset the balance, but was countered by the Reagan buildup.

The present balance appears relatively stable. Both sides appear committed to conventional arms control talks, with the aim of maintaining the stability while reducing the size of forces on each side. Gorbachev has accepted the concepts of asymmetrical reductions and intrusive verification measures. The question of naval arms control, however, remains a sensitive issue for the United States and could prove to be an obstacle to progress on conventional arms control outside the NATO–Warsaw Pact environment.

Regarding Kennan's third point—the Soviet reassessment and the resulting new concepts and policies: If the new concepts and policies last and are implemented, they promise to be the changes for which the West has been waiting for half a century. The renunciation of class struggle as the central feature of international politics, the adoption of the concept of mutual security, the change in approach to Third World conflict, and the downplaying of the Brezhnev Doctrine in relations with other socialist states all promise an end to the revolutionary character of Soviet foreign policy. One can now envision a Soviet Union that accepts a stable balance of power as the provision for its indefinite security, instead of as a temporary truce in a limitless struggle. One can envision a Soviet Union that perceives its interests to involve the reduction of tension and conflict in the Third World instead of their exacerbation in the hope of an opportunity for Soviet exploitation.

Nothing in this analysis suggests that the Soviet Union is withdrawing from international competition, however. The Soviets can be expected to continue to seek to improve their influence by increasing their standing and causing that of the United States to be lowered. The Soviets will continue to seek disproportionate U.S. cuts in arms control, to try to score propaganda points, and to look for opportunities to reduce the cohesion of U.S. alliances. There is a growing consensus that the Soviets are serious about wanting to reduce military confrontation, regional tension, and military expenditures, however. They also want better relations with the West to improve trade and bolster their economy.

The structural problems of the Soviet economy and political system are so severe that these motivations will last well into the next century, providing time for the new policy concepts to gather supporters and to build their own legitimacy. The survivability of the new concepts as presently constructed, however, is tightly entwined with the fortune of Gorbachev himself and with his domestic reforms. Their success is by no means assured. Nevertheless, if the current reform efforts fail, the old policies are probably too discredited to provide a legitimate alternative. A more likely result would be a prolonged period of instability in which the temptation would be strong to use the rallying cry of "external threat" to mobilize the Soviet population. A hostile Soviet Union is still possible; a revolutionary Soviet Union appears increasingly unlikely.

Kennan's second objective has not been fully attained, and therein lies the reason we are only at the beginning of the end of the cold war. The ability of the Soviet Union to project its influence through the international Communist movement dissipated as the movement itself crumbled. Soviet opportunism in the Third World and support for insurgency movements, however, did provide a vehicle for projecting Soviet influence. Unlike Eastern Europe, however, the remoteness of these Soviet clients or, in the case of North Korea, their ability to play off China against the Soviet Union meant that Soviet influence did not mean Soviet control.

When the concern was with Soviet expansion, disarray in the socialist camp was considered helpful to Western interests. When the Soviet Union professes commitment to the reduction of tension and Third World conflict, however, the limitations of Soviet influence become troublesome. The confrontation of the superpowers may be moderating, but local and regional confrontations spawned or exacerbated by East–West conflict have not all ended. Professing a policy to reduce Third World conflict does not mean the termination of commitments or relationships. Indeed, in his Vladivostok speech, Gorbachev stressed the need to strengthen the Soviet Union's relations with its North Korean and Vietnamese allies, even as he spoke of trying to bring about reduction of tension. Thus, there has been increased military assistance in the form of high technology weapons to North Korea at the same time the Soviets have been publicly urging progress in North–South talks and trying to improve their own relations with South Korea. Moreover, changes in the Soviet Union do not automatically mean changes in other socialist states. China and North Korea, for example, must be horrified at the developments taking place in the Soviet Union, Poland, and Hungary. Moderation in Moscow does not guarantee moderation in Pyongyang. Instead, changes in the Soviet Union may produce even greater insecurity and isolation in North Korea that could exacerbate regional tension.

For its part, the United States is also constrained by other considerations in developing new policies to deal with the Soviet Union. The U.S. military presence in Asia, for example, goes beyond simply balancing Soviet strength in the region. Many Asian nations see the U.S. presence as their ultimate guarantee against threats beyond their self-defense. These considerations must be weighed when the United States discusses arms reductions with the Soviets.

These are times of dramatic and revolutionary change that offer unprecedented opportunities to establish the foundations for a peaceful world, but there are dangers as well. The vestiges of the cold war will be present for some time, and other changes, not all for the better, are still possible in the Soviet Union. Cautious optimism is justified, but vigilance, military preparedness, and allied cooperation remain necessary as a new decade begins.

Notes

1. Molly Moore, "Steady Hand in Years of Turbulence," *Washington Post,* September 30, 1989, p. A7.

2. Robert E. Harkavy, "Soviet Conventional Power Projection and Containment," *Containment: Concept and Policy,* Vol. II, Terry Diebel and John Lewis Gaddis, eds. (Washington, D.C.: National Defense University, 1986), 322.

3. Ibid., 322–324.

4. Ibid., 343–345.

5. Marshall D. Shulman, "Overview," *East—West Tensions in the Third World,* Marshall D. Shulman, ed. (New York: W.W. Norton & Company, 1986), 7.

6. Robert A. Manning, *Asian Policy: The New Soviet Challenge in the Pacific* (New York: Priority Press Publications, 1988), 26.

7. David Holloway, "Gorbachev's New Thinking," in "America and the World," *Foreign Affairs,* 68, no. 1 (1988/89): 66–68.

8. Richard L. Armitage, Remarks at a Brookings Institution Seminar on National Defense Issues, April 10, 1984.

9. Holloway, 68.

10. Ibid., 77.

11. Ibid.

12. *Time,* September 9, 1985, p. 9.

13. See Holloway, 66–81; Robert Legvold, "The Revolution in Soviet Foreign Policy," in "America and the World," *Foreign Affairs* 68, no. 1 (1988/89): 82–98; Michael Mandelbaum, "Ending the Cold War," *Foreign Affairs* 68, no. 2 (Spring 1989): 16–36; Valery Giscard d'Estaing, Yasuhiro Nakasone, and Henry A. Kissinger, "East—West Relations," *Foreign Affairs* 68, no. 3 (Summer 1989): 1–21; Manning, 26; Robert Martin, Banning Garrett, Bonnie Glaser, and Edmund M. Ruffin, *U.S. Policy Options in Asia* (Washington, D.C.: System Planning Corporation Report 1289 [proprietary] 1989); Alexander Dallin and Gail W. Lapidus, "Reagan and the Russians: American Policy Toward the Soviet Union," *Eagle Resurgent?* Kenneth A. Oye, Robert J. Lieber, and Donald Rothchild, eds. (Boston: Little, Brown and Company, 1987), 193–254.

14. Legvold, 84.

15. Ibid., 85.

16. Ibid. See also William E. Odom, "Soviet Military Doctrine," *Foreign Affairs* 67, no. 2 (Winter 1988/89): 129.

17. Holloway, 70.

18. Legvold, 86.

19. Ibid., 89.

20. This section is based on analysis in Martin, Garrett, Glaser, and Ruffin.

21. Samuel P. Huntington, "The U.S.—Decline or Renewal?" *Foreign Affairs* 67, no. 2 (Winter 1988/89): 96.

22. John Lewis Gaddis, "Epilogue: The Future of Containment," *Containment: Concept and Policy*, Vol. 2, Terry Diebel and John Lewis Gaddis, eds. (Washington, D.C.: National Defense University Press, 1986), 722.

2

U.S. Global Strategy in the New Era of Detente

Gerrit W. Gong

Introduction

In his first major address on foreign soil after becoming president, George Bush reiterated the basic global approach of the administration he had served in for the previous eight years. Addressing the South Korea National Assembly on February 27, 1989, President Bush stated, "Peace through strength is a policy that has served the security interest of our two nations well. . . . We must complement deterrence with an active diplomacy in search of dialogue with our adversaries."[1] Thus, Bush's administration continues to focus on peace, strength, and negotiation—but with understandably more emphasis on dialogue and negotiation and less on continuing military buildup.

Many observers believe the current period of transition represents a watershed for the structure of the international system unparalleled since the end of World War II. As confrontation and tension give way to dialogue and the transformation of many socialist economies and polities, we are reminded—somewhat nostalgically—of how successful the old order has been in holding potentially high-intensity conflict in check. It has done so in a remarkably stable fashion.

Although the very speed and breadth of change offer historic opportunities to reconfigure Europe and the structure of international relations, they also present new dangers. Soviet nationality and economic tensions—and similar problems in the new East European democracies—are potentially explosive. The aftermath of the cold war would well be civil violence in the Warsaw Pact countries. In the broader world, however, the new U.S.–Soviet relationship presents opportunities for joint action in resolving regional conflict.

Positive Steps toward Resolving Regional Conflicts

George Bush entered the presidency while a concatenation of factors—Reagan administration policies, Gorbachev's "new thinking" and a more conservative Soviet role toward regional conflict, fundamental global trends, and efforts by the United Nations (UN)—contributed to positive change in regional conflicts.

- *Iran–Iraq.* After eight long and bloody years in which civilian centers were bombed, chemical weapons were used surreptitiously, and young children were brought into armed conflict, the Iran–Iraq War came to a halt, with a cease-fire, peace talks, and a UN military observer group.
- *Afghanistan.* The Soviet Union withdrew its 150,000 troops from Afghanistan after nine years of occupation. Under the April 1988 Geneva Accords, a UN good offices mission was established to supervise the troop withdrawal and implementation of the accords. The resistance (mujahhedin) remains divided and mutually suspicious. Najibullah remains better entrenched than many expected, and Soviet aid (including weapons) has been generous. An important initial step—the withdrawal of Soviet troops—has occurred, however.
- *Angola.* In Angola, after 13 years of Cuban intervention and civil war, gradual progress continues toward a diplomatic solution. Namibia is now independent.
- *Cambodia.* As part of an Indochina War that has smoldered in various forms for 40 years, Vietnam has at least publicly withdrawn its forces from Cambodia.
- *Western Sahara.* Diplomatic progress has been made in the Western Sahara.
- *Korea.* North and South Korea have each recently spoken at the UN for the first time, making the global stage of the UN General Assembly part of the ongoing effort in direct North–South dialogue.[2] South Korea's case for UN membership becomes stronger all the time.

Hopeful Global Trends

Complementing positive developments in particular regions of conflict were dominant global trends. Current U.S. global strategy is based on a positive assessment of two main trends.

"The quest for democracy," said Secretary of State James Baker in a speech given at the Center for Strategic and International Studies (CSIS), "is the most vibrant political fact of these times."[3] It is a long-term trend. It is also a powerful idea, which has led to a startling fact: Political legitimacy is now assumed to rest with the majority voice of the governed. True, democracy means different things in different places, depending on cultural and political context and on tradition. Nevertheless, today there is no country or government that does not at least pay lip service to the democratic ideal. Ironically, the Tiananmen Square demonstrations were quelled on the grounds that they constituted a "counterrevolutionary rebellion," bent on subverting China's four cardinal principles that include, "the people's democratic dictatorship." Eastern Europe is now trying to make democracy work, and it was a democratic process that brought Boris Yeltsin to power in the Russian republic.

The second global trend on which the United States has attempted to build its global strategy is the increased recognition that economic productivity and prosperity derive from private initiative, from the magic of free market economies, and from the unfettered ability to harness new information and communications technologies. These information and communications technologies have globalized markets, resource and technology flows, and capital funds. This technology has made information a form of renewable capital and, in so doing, has made global markets and investment arenas responsive to instantaneous real-time changes. The interplay of these two trends— toward democratic participation and toward market-oriented competition—has created great opportunities on a global basis for the United States and for its friends and allies.

That is the good news, but success often brings with it new challenges. Let us consider some of the security, economic, and political ramifications of the trends toward democratic participation and free market economic competition.

On the *security* side, the confluence of these two trends has contributed to a pronounced shift from confrontation to dialogue, is helping define stability at negotiated lower levels of strategic and conventional warheads and weapons, and is broadening the international agenda of shared issues. This agenda now includes such items as the environment, terrorism, and drugs. Old patterns and strategies for U.S. defense investments are being updated to reflect declining resource commitments and changing threat perceptions.

Reduced security tension and constrained resources have led to a new focus on economic competitiveness. For many, this focus on competition may intensify perceptions of a zero-sum game, symbolized by opinion polls showing that Americans now consider the military threat from the Soviet Union to be less than the economic threat from Japan. The shorthand interpretation that Japan is now the new U.S. adversary has fueled efforts to address structural impediments and other factors affecting the trade balance and long-term competitiveness.

The U.S. Congress is usually a good barometer of domestic opinion. I recall being in the U.S. embassy in Tokyo when the videotape was first shown of U.S. legislators sledgehammering Toshiba electronics products. These dramatic acts play well for local U.S. political constituencies and serve to highlight areas of friction. They reflect the deeply held frustrations many Americans feel about the need for free and fair trade. Unfortunately, such demonstrations may also politicize and emotionalize already heightened trade concerns as friction over the trade imbalance rises in saliency.

A major challenge for the United States at a time when economic factors have increased in prominence is to calibrate global macroeconomic structural measures with more bilateral microeconomic approaches. Thus, many have turned from currency exchange rates (that are clearly only one factor in the trade equation) as a means of rectifying trade imbalances, while seeking more direct bilateral measures for balancing trade (e.g., congressionally mandated "Super 301" provisions to help ensure open markets). Thus, while the Bush Administration is working to make the Uruguay General Agreement on Tariffs and Trade (GATT) Round a success, it is also double-tracking multilateral negotiations with bilateral measures.

On the *political* side, one hopes the legitimate aspirations of people everywhere for full democratic and economic expression continue to be realized. Yet, those involved in global planning recognize that the increased expression of popular impulses may in some ways complicate the ability of the United States and its allies to manage their diplomacy and national strategy.

In East Asia as elsewhere, vocal opposition parties have been given voice by the gradually less-restricted and less-inhibited media; traditionally dominant ruling parties, voluntarily and not, have increasingly come to share the political stage. Local politics have thus become even more intertwined in the formulation and implementation of already complex foreign policy concerns. Old U.S. allies are more critical of long-standing arrangements with the United States (e.g., base rights agreements, drift net fishing, and other U.S. policies).

All this underscores a general axiom of international politics: A relaxation in global tension increases the perception of security independence, and thus the potential for friction among allies and friends.

Eastern and Western Europe

The U.S. alliance with Western Europe has, beyond the perception of a common adversary, sprung from a sense of community, culture, kinship, and shared values. Although recognizing the ambivalence of some toward the prospect of a more united Europe, especially a "Fortress Europe" after 1992, the Bush administration has declared "We believe a strong, united Europe means a strong America."[4]

A united Europe represents the following: a gross domestic product roughly equal to that of the United States, a population that exceeds that of the United States, a magnet pulling countries of Eastern Europe closer, a framework based on flexible responsibilities for defense cooperation in a revitalized Western European Union (WEU), growing Franco–German military cooperation, and British and French programs to modernize their deterrence capability.

The U.S. commitment will be expressed in its support for the success of freedom in East Europe, as measured in human rights and economic pluralism. This relationship will broaden and deepen as democracy takes hold.[5]

The Middle East and Southwest Asia

The economic health of the United States and its allies continues to depend on the security of the Middle East and Southwest Asia. Two recent positive developments include the end of the Iran–Iraq War and the transition to what is hoped will be a more moderate leadership in Iran. The Bush administration has focused attention on limiting the spread of chemical and biological weapons and the proliferation of ballistic missiles not only in the region, but globally as well.

Additionally, the Bush administration places a continued priority on establishing a stable framework for defusing the Arab–Israeli conflict, including progress on the Palestinian question. In this regard, Secretary Baker has indicated the United States' willingness to help mediate in the ongoing quest for Middle East peace, a quest made more elusive by recent terrorist outbreaks and the ascendancy of a more conservative regime in Tel Aviv.

Africa

The Bush administration has three policy priorities in Africa. First, it wants to consolidate the new-found independence of Namibia. Second, it will pursue human rights and economic reform in all African nations. Last, it will work with all parties (Ethiopia, Somalia, and the Sudan) to resolve conflict in the Horn of Africa.

Latin America

In some ways, the countries of Latin America symbolize the trend toward free government and free enterprise. Mexico recently joined the GATT, and Costa Rica, Brazil, and Venezuela are broadening their export possibilities and economic base. The United States has made efforts to work with international financial institutions, debtor countries, and commercial banks to make the debt burden more manageable as Latin American countries restructure their economies.

As indicated by the "drug summits" that President Bush has attended, drugs pose a problem of increasing importance. Public opinion polls consistently identify drugs as the number one concern in the United States. Efforts to fight drug trafficking may even result in new missions for some U.S. military forces, including current speculation that U.S. naval forces may help to disrupt the drug flow from Colombia and other Latin American countries.

The current U.S. priority is to reinforce democracy in Nicaragua, Panama, and El Salvador and to strengthen the crucial relationship with Mexico.

Soviet Union

The stated U.S. objective in regard to the Soviet Union is to move beyond containment to welcome the Soviet Union back into the world order. Specifically, President Bush has called on the Soviets to reduce their forces; to support self-determination for the Baltic states; to work with the West toward practical, diplomatic solutions to regional disputes; to achieve lasting political pluralism and respect for human rights; and to increase cooperation to address global problems such as drugs and pollution.[6]

The United States will continue to press for a reduced risk of nuclear war through talks aimed at achieving strategic arms reductions, stable deterrence, and lower levels of arms and risk, while maintaining its options and flexibility on more advanced defense. It will also pursue a verifiable ban on chemical weapons. The major challenge for U.S. policy in the coming years will be to seize any opportunities to work constructively with an economically beleaguered Soviet Union while pursuing arms reduction.

As might be expected, there is no single interpretation within the Bush administration or among experts generally regarding the full U.S. policy ramifications of changes within the Soviet Union. Secretary Baker is now perceived by some to be among those most convinced that a historic opportunity in U.S.–Soviet relations requires responding positively, in a manner supportive of President Gorbachev.

In East Asia, Soviet rhetoric has softened considerably. Yet, rhetoric aside, objective analysis leaves unanswered the question of whether Gorbachev's planned restructuring is aimed at modernization or disarmament in the Asian theater. Accounts suggest that SS–25 missiles (an advanced form of the SS–20) are replacing destroyed SS–20s. The 19 ships retired from the Soviet Pacific Fleet were more than 30 years old and replaced by new construction, leaving the Soviet navy more capable than two years ago. Likewise, less-capable Soviet aircraft are being replaced by MiG 27s, 29s, and 31s—some not only upgraded, but now having twice the range of the aircraft they replace.

Consolidation is occurring among the 57 divisions and 520,000 Soviet troops headquartered in the Far East to produce fewer, but more fleshed-out, units. Thus, across the board, on air, land, and sea, Soviet capabilities seem enhanced by recent changes, even though the numerical magnitude of the Soviet presence has been reduced.

And, as South Koreans know best, Soviet military assistance to North Korea expanded during the 1984–1989 period. After 12 years without significant change in the weapons supplied, Moscow and Pyongyang began military exercises, port visits, and overflights for reasons that remain unclear. Since 1985, the Soviets have been supplying MiG L9s, SA–55s, and C–25s to North Korea. How these trends will be affected in the new 1990s atmosphere remains unclear.

East Asia

The situation in Indochina is now more fluid than it has been for the past decade. The persistent Chinese insistence on an ensured role for the Khmer Rouge in any future Cambodian government must be considered in terms of the efforts to produce a comprehensive political settlement, possibly including UN-supervised elections and a leadership coalition under a Supreme National Council (SNC).

Vietnam is determined not to be left behind in the wave of reform sweeping the Soviet Union and Eastern Europe. Yet, Vietnam's leaders were sobered by China's inability to resolve the imbalance between economic liberalization and political stability, as symbolized by Tiananmen, without resorting to armed force. Vietnam's interior ministry has reportedly been ordered to be especially vigilant against potential domestic political instability.

Vietnamese observers recently noted that their dilemma is to find a way to spur economic "renovation" *(doi moi),* while maintaining political stability. The problem is heightened by the dynamism and economic potential around Ho Chi Minh City—precisely the area, despite an infusion of northern cadres into key administrative and oversight positions, that remains somewhat politically suspect.

"We may restore walls, even mend the roof of this socialist house," one analyst said, "but we are not afraid it will collapse." "You cannot go against the law of development," the Vietnamese say. They blame not only the prolonged wars and tensions with the French, Americans, and Chinese, but also themselves for mistakes that have resulted in their current backward economic situation.

At the same time, Vietnamese officials point to several economic achievements. First, they say, because of the one-price system, inflation dropped from 400 percent in 1986–1987 to 100 percent in 1988 to 25 percent in 1989. Second, Vietnam exported more than 1 million tons of rice in 1989. Third, with a new liberalized investment law in place, 96 investment projects worth US$800 million have been started in the past two to three years, including 26 projects worth US$150 million in mid-1989. Vietnam hopes that the Republic of Korea, Taiwan, Japan, and some European consortia will be important sources of investment funds and future trading partners. Vietnam has also noted its desire to reorient its domestic and foreign policy to IMF teams that visited recently.

Vietnam is taking a more flexible, faster-paced approach, based on the following calculations:

- the likelihood that Hun Sen has sufficient military strength and political infrastructure to stand more or less independently;
- the increasingly burdensome domestic and international costs of occupying Cambodia, particularly in light of Moscow's pressure on Hanoi to put its domestic economic house in order;
- the difficulty of tapping needed financial assistance (e.g., from the International Monetary Fund) without first breaking Vietnam's international isolation.

Vietnam indicated a willingness in 1989 to move ahead in the four areas of U.S.–Vietnam bilateral humanitarian concern: Amerasian children, full accountability of prisoners of war (POWs) and those missing in action (MIAs), the orderly departure program (ODP), and reeducation camps. The United States has always denied—as has Hanoi—a specific linkage between progress on bilateral humanitarian concerns and movement toward normalized relations. Indeed, U.S. officials in Bangkok said they hoped that the Vietnamese would understand that U.S.–Vietnamese relations will be normalized only after a comprehensive political settlement is achieved in Cambodia. At such time, it will be in Vietnam's interest to have resolved any outstanding bilateral issues, including the humanitarian concerns currently being addressed.

Readings from the U.S. State Department, executive branch, and Congress also indicate that much must still occur before Washington can read the political consensus necessary to break the economic embargo and normalize relations with Hanoi. Vietnam understands this point.[7]

Australia—New Zealand

As symbolized by the Australian—U.S. ministerial talks held in Sydney in early November 1989, U.S. global thinking continues to affirm the contribution of strong relations and cooperation with Canberra under the Australia—New Zealand—United States (ANZUS) alliance. Both Australia and the United States agreed that a reduction of superpower tensions would not automatically lead to a more tranquil region, and Australia therefore attached importance to the continued active engagement of the United States in the Asia—Pacific region.

U.S. military experts continue to express regret that New Zealand's policies prevent a resumption of the full trilateral relationship; some also express concern that lost time and deterioration in morale and professionalism among New Zealand's military may hinder joint activities even if full cooperation is someday restored.

U.S. Military Bases in East Asia

As noted earlier, four main factors—the rise of nationalism, the trend toward multiparty systems with vocal opposition leaders, the gradual freeing of the media to permit open debate, and the general expectation that the public should have a say in their economic and political future—combine in a heightened sense of democratic participation in East Asia, as well as globally. The issue of U.S. bases in Asia needs to be seen in this context. Because other chapters will address the base issue in South Korea and Japan, this chapter will speak only to the Philippines situation.

Recognizing that base-related aid from the United States is $481 million a year, with an additional pledge of $200 million annually, Corazon Aquino's recent U.S. visit focused only on further U.S. trade and economic assistance. Negotiation of a new five-year agreement proceeds against a backdrop of terrorist attacks on U.S. military personnel.

Singapore Prime Minister Lee Kuan-Yew's offer to extend base rights in Singapore to the United States is consistent with the prime minister's earlier statements before a joint session of the U.S. Congress in which he stated that the U.S. military presence in Southeast Asia during the Vietnam War provided a protective security shield and needed economic stimulus for Singapore and other developing countries in the region, which made their current prosperity possible. Singapore's offer to expand the United States' use of naval and air defense facilities could enhance security, as well as provide U.S. negotiators some additional leverage with Manila.

Specific negotiations of base rights agreements in various East Asian countries have yet to be played out. Long-term pressures against base maintenance—constrained U.S. budgets, nationalism in the countries concerned, and a lessened need for forward-deployed forces in an era of diminished threat—appear to be mounting, however.

Sino–American Relations

In the fall of 1989, Alexander Haig, Richard Nixon, and Henry Kissinger each visited Beijing, in part to see how Sino–American relations might be normalized. Even before Tiananmen, however, strategic analysts in Beijing were looking for a new "motivating impetus" to advance Sino–American relations. Since Tiananmen, PRC statements have become more ideological, blaming "international reactionary forces" for shifting policy away from a "peaceful transformation" by resorting to political, economic, and cultural means to subvert socialist countries."

PRC Foreign Minister Qian Quichen recently asserted these points: differences between the PRC and other nations should be recognized and respected, while common interests are pursued and promoted; normalization of relations should not be conditioned on internal affairs; mutual trust should be cultivated; the Taiwan question should be dealt with carefully.

Although U.S. public opinion has cooled somewhat since the period when Tiananmen dominated the news, three factors have kept U.S. public interest in China high. First, the earlier media coverage has formed a psychological frame of reference for Americans regarding China, which has become as deeply embedded in the U.S. consciousness as President John Kennedy's assassination or the explosion of the space shuttle Challenger. Second, various citizen and lobbying organizations have kept the humanitarian concerns of the 43,000 PRC students caught in the vagaries of U.S. immigration law before the U.S. Congress. Third, the organizations of various PRC dissidents in exile have maintained a high profile.

For all these reasons, U.S. reactions to Tiananmen have continued, sometimes awkwardly, to strike a balance between anger and sorrow. Thus, on November 15–16, 1989, in separate actions, both the U.S. House and Senate approved the State Department authorization bill that contained provisions specifying economic sanctions against the PRC. Sanctions adopted include suspension of arms sales, postponement of U.S. satellites being launched on PRC rockets, postponement of police equipment sales and of nuclear sales or cooperation, a ban on further liberalization of export controls, and suspension of U.S. overseas investment credits.

The president preemptively imposed many of these measures under executive order to accommodate U.S. domestic opinion, while preserving long-term U.S. flexibility. In a reported compromise with the administration, the Congress adopted Senate language that permits the president to lift the sanctions if he deems such "in the national interest." This contrasts with the more restrictive House requirement that the president lift the sanctions only for reasons of "national security interest."

In return for this concession, congressional sources reported, National Security Adviser Brent Scowcroft promised the White House would not veto the bill because of its provisions on China. Further, on November 19–20, 1989, the House and Senate passed a measure allowing Chinese exchange students on J-visas to waive the two-year home country stay requirement before changing status. President Bush vetoed the bill, but extended the period that Chinese students can remain in the United States.

Deng Xiaoping's statements since June 9, 1989, the 5th plenum, and the elevation of General Secretary Jiang Zemin to head the PRC's central military commission (balanced by Yang Baibing's joining the commission as secretary general) all indicate the difficulties Beijing faces in determining a leadership succession at the same time it is setting its future economic course. In general, the U.S. president and the executive branch remain convinced that the framework for U.S.–PRC cooperation and competition built during the past 15 years and five administrations should remain intact at a time of fluidity in the global strategic situation, despite the aftermath of Tiananmen.

Regarding Taiwan, the United States is aware of the potential dilemma posed by the current trends toward flexible diplomacy and Taiwanese independence.

Taipei's determination to seek relations with countries that recognize Beijing is a policy change, but Taiwan also says its fundamental one-China approach has been preserved. According to Taiwanese officials, whether countries choose to maintain ties with Beijing after reestablishing relations with Taipei is their own decision.

Particularly striking today is the prevalence of "local Taiwan consciousness" in Taipei and Kaohsiung. Taiwanese is much more prevalent; even KMT candidates appeal to their constituencies in local dialect. The press and media are open. Movies like "City of Sorrows," which depicts the time period when mainland soldiers forcibly quelled the Taiwanese uprising, are being made and shown—something not possible before.

Beijing and Taipei appear committed to strengthening indirect trade and people-to-people contacts across the Taiwan Straits. This trend, beginning in

Beijing and Taipei appear committed to strengthening indirect trade and people-to-people contacts across the Taiwan Straits. This trend, beginning in November 1987, augurs well for Chinese on both sides of the straits working out their own modus vivendi—a key point of U.S. policy since the 1972 Shanghai Communique. In short, although Taiwan—either on its own or because the PRC chooses again to make it a bilateral issue—could again become an irritant in relations between Beijing and Washington, there is no obvious reason that it should.

Japan

Japan plays an increasingly key role in U.S. global thinking. Secretary of State Baker has added "creative responsibility sharing" to the basic concept of "global partnership" in viewing Japan's role. "Global partnership" with Japan revolves around five areas: security relations, cooperation in foreign policy, economic assistance to the developing world, bilateral economic relations, and common adherence to democratic values and human rights.[8]

With Japan's emergence as the world's second largest economy and greatest creditor nation, managing the U.S.–Japanese bilateral economic relationship has understandably become both an economic and political priority for Washington and Tokyo. The structural impediments initiative and technological cooperative efforts (e.g., FSX agreement) together form the current framework for dealing with real-time developments, which frequently outpace the negotiations established to deal with them.

As is evident from the recent spate of articles about cultural differences and a Japan that can say "no," U.S.–Japanese relations threaten to become increasingly embroiled in the domestic politics of the two countries. Liberal Democratic Party (LDP) insiders blame the party's loss of its upper house majority on a tactical error involving women and a tax issue, but nevertheless admit that it will be harder for the LDP to pass legislation, especially because more than a single election cycle will be required to regain a majority.

Internationally, the Northern Territories issue and the continued threat of Soviet deployments leave Japan hesitant to improve relations with Moscow too quickly. For this reason, some Japanese analysts feel Soviet President Mikhail Gorbachev could favorably influence Japanese public opinion if he were to offer a major initiative to reduce Soviet forces. Needless to say, interest in Gorbachev's 1991 visit to Tokyo will build as the specifics surrounding it become more clear.

Conclusion

As of mid-1990, the accelerating improvement in U.S.–Soviet relations provides an unprecedented environment for joint—or at least concerted—action to address new challenges in Europe and elsewhere. These opportunities should be seized because they could be fleeting. Disunity in the Soviet Union itself may soon become part of the problem. There is plenty to address—from the future role of a united Germany to adjustments along the entire Eurasian perimeter.

But we must recognize that the Soviet Union remains a military superpower, however, and one rendered less predictable by its internal political, economic, and ethnic difficulties. The spectrum of possible outcomes is still broad. The transition to accommodate global trends toward political pluralism and market-oriented economies is continuing. Everywhere, including in the industrial democracies, adjustments and restructuring are occurring. Thus, the challenge for relatively closed societies like North Korea is heightened, especially given the latest rapprochement between Moscow and Seoul.

For U.S. and Western policymakers, the message conveyed by both the promise and uncertainties of contemporary history seems clear. Consonant with global trends and the free expression of indigenous desires everywhere, our long-term strength and steadiness helped trigger the new dynamics of change; we will need to weather the turbulence of those changes. Let us, by all means, plan ahead for a more peaceful world, but let us not put that vision at risk by a premature lowering of our guard. Although the future will be full of twists and turns, the current international situation could provide us and other global thinkers some historic opportunities in the months ahead.

Notes

1. President George Bush, "Continuity and Change in U.S.–Korean Relations," Current Policy No. 1155, Seoul, Republic of Korea, February 27, 1989.

2. See National Security Adviser Colin Powell, "U.S. Foreign Policy in a Time of Transition," Current Policy No. 1127, Washington, D.C., October 27, 1988.

3. Secretary of State James Baker, "The Challenge of Change in U.S.–Soviet Relations," Current Policy No. 1170, Washington, D.C., May 4, 1989.

4. President George Bush, "The Future of Europe," Current Policy No. 1177, Boston, Mass., May 21, 1989.

5. President George Bush, "Proposals for a Free and Peaceful Europe," Current Policy No. 1179, Mainz, Federal Republic of Germany, May 31, 1989.

6. President George Bush, "Change is the Soviet Union," Current Policy No. 1175, College Station, Texas, May 12, 1989.

7. Frederick Brown, *Second Chance: The U.S. and Indochina in the 1990s* (New York: Council on Foreign Relations Press, 1989) is an interesting current account of the Indochina situation.

8. Under Secretary Robert M. Kimmitt, "The U.S. and Japan: Defining Our Global Partnership," Current Policy No. 1221, Tokyo, Japan, October 9, 1989.

3

Global Detente and North Korea's Strategic Relations

Norman D. Levin

The pace of recent change has been so rapid as to call into question the ability of analysts to anticipate future developments and of statesmen to manage the transition process. In the case of the Soviet Union, the speed and breadth of change has been so great as to challenge the framework within which the United States has viewed Soviet policies and to call into question the basic assumptions on which the United States has predicated its expectations of future Soviet behavior.

To emphasize the theme of change is not to deny important elements of continuity. In the case of the Soviet Union, for example, radical changes domestically and toward arms control and Eastern Europe have not been matched by comparable changes in Soviet policy toward radical Third World regimes. Aside from the special case of China, Soviet policy departures in Northeast Asia range from modest to propagandistic.

Neither is the emphasis on change meant to imply permanence. In many cases, both the direction and durability of recent changes remain uncertain. Whatever the ultimate outcome, there can be little doubt that uncertainty is now the tenor of the times.

In this environment, attention has naturally turned to the prospect for peace, stability, and, ultimately, reunification of the Korean Peninsula. This prospect clearly depends on many factors, not the least of which concerns the policies of the major powers. Because these policies are addressed in other chapters, this chapter will focus on a subsidiary issue: the way the continuation of the global trend toward detente might affect North Korea and its policies toward its strategic relationships. After briefly reviewing its

past relationships, the chapter will focus on the emerging—and prospective—effects of global detente and will suggest alternatives for future North
Korean relations.

North Korea's Ongoing Strategic Pattern

If "strategic" relations are defined as those a nation has with states that
have the capability to favorably or adversely affect its fundamental national
interest, particularly as it relates to national security, then North Korea can
be said to have three sets of such relations: with the Soviet Union and the
PRC, with the United States and Japan, and with South Korea.[1] The starting
point for such relations is always national interest. In the case of North
Korea, its interests have remained constant throughout the postwar period.
Ranked in order of priority its interests have been: preserving the Kim Il-
Sung regime, maintaining North Korean independence, furthering the
objective of reunification on North Korean terms, and generating support for
North Korean economic development and military modernization. Together,
these interests have fostered essentially a three-pronged approach to its
strategic relations. North Korea has sought to develop the indigenous
capability to subvert, and ultimately subjugate, South Korea; to undermine
South Korea's relations with Japan and the United States in the hope of
achieving the removal of U.S. forces from South Korea; and to maintain the
support of China and the Soviet Union without sacrificing North Korea's
national independence.

Most of the scholarly literature has tended to focus on North Korea's
relations with its two Communist neighbors. Generally, Pyongyang has been
portrayed as skillfully playing off one against the other and successfully
manipulating the Sino–Soviet rivalry to its own advantage. In fact, although
the split between the Communist rivals has prevented them from acting
jointly to dictate North Korean behavior and thus bolstered North Korea's
claim to independence, these have been difficult relations for Pyongyang. The
support it has received, although significant in economic and certain military
aspects, has remained both cautious and conditional.

North Korea has had the most difficulty with the Soviet Union, which
North Koreans see as having little genuine sympathy for Pyongyang's
definition of its national interest. The North Koreans have also had
difficulties with the Chinese, however, who have made clear the limits of
their willingness and ability to support North Korean aspirations. As a
general statement, the North Koreans feel a greater affinity for and
identification with the Chinese, and they see the PRC as an essential
counterweight to a potentially domineering Soviet Union. They have
periodically tilted toward Moscow, however, partly out of economic and

military necessity and partly as a means of expressing displeasure with China's foreign and domestic policies.

Since the Korean War, North Korea's relations with the United States and Japan have been rooted in its unwavering commitment to reunification on its own terms. Given this commitment, and Pyongyang's belief that the presence of these two capitalist powers is the major obstacle to reunification, ending U.S. and Japanese involvement in South Korea has been North Korea's principal objective in its relations with Japan and the United States. Toward this end, it has mixed hostile denunciations of the U.S. and Japanese roles with periodic attempts to engage Washington and Tokyo in expanded dealings. Although economic imperatives have contributed to these latter efforts, the central aim has been to bring about the removal of U.S. troops from South Korea and to undermine Seoul's alliance with Japan and the United States.

The central strategic issue for North Korean planners, however, has been the way to deal with the Republic of Korea. With its larger population, economic and technological sophistication, and broad international political support, Seoul represents both a challenge to Pyongyang's pretension to be the sole representative of Korean nationalism and a long-term threat to North Korea itself. North Korean efforts to deal with this situation during the past four decades have ranged from military conquest to political and economic competition to terrorism, political subversion, and military intimidation. Although there may be a number of motivations behind Pyongyang's periodic agreements to formal and informal discussions with South Korea, including a desire to improve the North's tattered international image, their tactical utility in furthering North Korea's fundamental strategic interests appears to remain the dominant consideration. To date, at least, such agreements have not been matched by demonstrable changes in North Korea's other domestic and foreign policies.

Viewed from this perspective, North Korea's basic approach to its strategic relations has remained remarkably stable during the past four decades. The question is how the ongoing international changes and improvement in relations among the major powers will affect these relations.

Detente and North Korea

Even before the dramatic recent developments in the Communist world and the related improvement in relations among the major powers, North Korea was facing a series of formidable challenges. Economically, the North confronts a serious, if not critical, situation. Agriculture is "catastrophic," according to well-informed sources, with population growth outstripping food supply and potential remedies being either exhausted or no longer viable.[2]

Long-standing North Korean acknowledgment of serious problems with light industry and repeated government appeals to "produce more with less" now bolster foreign reports of shortages and rationing in critical consumer areas. Raw material and energy resources are being exhausted, while economic management continues to be politicized and overcentralized. North Korea remains unable to service its trade debt to Japan, and Western Europe and is now running a trade deficit with the Soviet Union that is said to account for more than 45 percent of Pyongyang's total trade—rapidly approaching $1 billion.[3]

These economic difficulties coincide with indications of increasing tension and public discontent. Recent accounts of wall posters that criticize the government's economic policies mesh with earlier reports of opposition slogans painted on a Pyongyang railway station, of scattered industrial strikes, and of incidents of sabotage.[4] Criticism of the Communist Party cadre and of the perquisites of government officials are now said by frequent visitors to be both vocal and openly expressed, contributing to a more general sense of ideological struggle within the party and growing popular dissatisfaction. Such criticisms are presumably heightened by the apparent existence of a large black market in North Korea, which is said to have strengthened public awareness of the gap between official rhetoric and objective reality. All this is taking place against the backdrop of Kim Il-Sung's effort to transfer power to his son, Kim Jong-Il, in the Communist world's first hereditary succession. The totality of Kim Il-Sung's system of rule keeps these tensions under strict control, but there are indications that the North Korean leadership is aware of them.[5]

The dramatic changes in the Communist world and the global trend toward detente exacerbate Pyongyang's predicament. At the most general level, three effects are already evident. First, North Korea has become even more isolated internationally. Pyongyang's penchant for terrorist actions and unilateral violations of existing bilateral agreements have long made it a pariah in the Western world. Its domestic and foreign policy rigidity have now put North Korea at odds with the dominant trends in the Communist world as well. These trends increasingly dictate a move away from the Stalinist political and economic model and a move toward reducing international tension, neither of which the North Koreans show any inclination to even consider.

The tension between the global trends and North Korea's continued policies was evident in the World Youth Festival held in July 1989 in Pyongyang. Although some 15,000 foreign visitors—most from socialist and Third World nations—attended the festival, apparently many were as appalled by the cost and waste associated with its production as were impressed by the festivities themselves. For most Communist countries, as one source has noted, North Korea today represents everything that those Communist nations are trying to put behind them.[6]

Second, North Korea's ability to rely on allied support for its reunification proposals has been seriously weakened. In fact, this support has been shaky since the Cuban missile crisis in the early 1960s when the Soviets, from North Korea's perspective, backed down in the face of U.S. intimidation. The Sino–Soviet split in the mid-1960s, Soviet efforts to achieve detente with the United States in the early 1970s, and China's move toward the West in the late 1970s and early 1980s further called into question the likely extent of allied assistance. These actions also indicated to North Korean leaders the willingness of their Communist patrons to subordinate North Korea's reunification objectives to their own national interests. This lack of support has been a major factor behind the extraordinary North Korean military buildup throughout this period.

Nevertheless, Communist bloc support has been critical for North Korea. Diplomatically, this support helped counter North Korea's international isolation; militarily, it underpinned North Korea's aggressive efforts to undermine and subvert South Korea; politically, it helped bolster the legitimacy of the Kim Il-Sung regime. The dramatic developments in the Communist world and the trend toward detente between the superpowers, however, diminish the likelihood of such continued support for at least two reasons.

First, these developments dictate an easing of international tension. This increases the importance of stability on the Korean Peninsula as well and the likelihood that neither the Soviets nor Chinese would support adventurous North Korean actions. If the Soviets are unprepared to use force to stop the centrifugal forces in its own empire and if the central requirement for both the Soviet Union and China is a prolonged period of peace to concentrate on domestic economic difficulties, then North Korea's ability to count on its allies' active support for its own military adventures is clearly minimal.

These developments also increase the importance of economic interaction with South Korea and heighten Communist bloc incentives to move toward a de facto "two-Koreas" policy. Such a move is facilitated by the general lowering of the salience of ideology, further weakening tolerance for Pyongyang's extreme rhetoric and ideological position. Growing North Korean agitation about recent Communist bloc dealings with South Korea suggests that Pyongyang is increasingly concerned that its interests are being jeopardized in the process. As Kim Chung-Nin, the senior North Korean official responsible for reunification policies, recently stated,

[If North Korea tolerates the efforts] of splitists at home and abroad [to] turn North–South relations into an "East–West German-type" of "two Koreas" by inveigling some socialist countries with a few silver dollars, [then] the division of the country will be perpetuated; South Korea will not be able to extricate itself from the dual domination of the United States and Japan; and, after all, a way for the intervention of foreign forces in the affairs of Korea will open, thus laying a grave obstacle to the independent reunification of the country. Frustrating [these] maneuvers is an acute problem . . . .[7]

The third general effect of recent global change is to further complicate the task of political succession in North Korea. Under the best of conditions, dynastic succession in a Communist system is not easy. Both Communist dogma and historical experience argue against the success of such a feudal practice. The trend toward reform and detente has made Kim Il-Sung's effort to ensure his son's succession even more difficult in at least three ways: a precedent has been set, and a potential model for a radical move away from Stalinist practices has been created; pressure has been generated for North Korea to mesh better with Communist bloc transformations; and legitimacy is linked much more closely to domestic economic and social performance. Unless North Korea is able to insulate itself completely from these developments, better economic performance and greater political freedom will be essential for domestic legitimacy, whoever Kim Il-Sung's successor may be. This will strengthen reformist North Korean forces and complicate Kim's effort, and that of his successor, to ensure a continuation of his revolutionary tradition.

The Soviet Union and China

Beyond these three general effects, the changes in the Communist world and global trend toward detente have a number of more specific implications for North Korea and its strategic relations. In the case of North Korea's relations with the Soviet Union and China, at least four are identifiable.

The first is further diminishment of North Korea's leverage and ability to manipulate Sino–Soviet tensions to its advantage. Here, care should be taken not to exaggerate the argument. North Korea remains an important country geostrategically. Soviet and Chinese interests will continue to be involved, and both will continue to have an important stake in the success of their longtime ally. Thus, North Korea will continue to have a legitimate claim on Soviet and Chinese attention and resources.

Nevertheless, the global relaxation of tension decreases Korea's role as a fulcrum of cold war hostility, thereby lessening the centrality of North Korea in the global strategic competition. This improvement in Sino–Soviet relations also reduces their inclination to compete actively for Pyongyang's favor. Both points highlight North Korea's fundamentally weak and disadvantageous position vis-a-vis its two Communist neighbors and its diminishing leverage in bilateral interactions.

The second, and partly consequential, effect is likely to be increasing constraints on Soviet and Chinese assistance. Economically, the two Communist powers will be strapped by the exigencies of their own domestic situations. Global detente, coupled with domestic political reform, will undoubtedly heighten the salience of domestic considerations among competing priorities. In this environment, sustaining a high level of economic assistance to North Korea will become increasingly problematic.

In fact, this trend has already begun. The Chinese indicated publicly as early as 1985 that they would not extend much additional assistance to North Korea.[8] The Soviets, although undoubtedly pleased with the political and security benefits that Pyongyang's increased dependence on them during the past several years brings, show signs of increasingly chafing at the burden of continuing to subsidize the North Koreans.[9] In addition, because of North Korea's record of debt repayment and its widely acknowledged poor use of assistance already given, both Communist powers are likely to take a hard look at future aid requests from Pyongyang.

Militarily, the picture is more uncertain. On the one hand, military assistance represents a principal vehicle—particularly for the Soviets—for influence in Pyongyang and a central element in Soviet military strategy in the Far East. Given the uncertainties inherent in the process of political succession in North Korea and their calculations of the long-term trends in the balance of power on the peninsula, both the Soviets and Chinese are likely to have strong incentives to continue providing a certain level of military assistance.

On the other hand, military assistance is costly—particularly because North Korea does not pay cash for most of it. Moreover, at some level, it conflicts with other important Soviet and Chinese political objectives. This is particularly a problem for the Soviets because military assistance contradicts the image ("new thinking") they are trying to create as a means of improving relations with the non-Communist states of the region. In addition, both China and the Soviet Union must be concerned, given their growing interest in global and regional stability, about the effect their assistance has of bolstering the hard-liners in North Korea. The way this situation will work out is uncertain, but the pros and cons of high-level military assistance are clearly being debated—at least in Moscow. As one Soviet researcher recently confirmed, there are "increasingly divergent views on the necessity for continued military assistance among the politicians, who see it as not helping the case for reunification, and the military chiefs, who view the situation from a purely military perspective."[10]

Despite Hanoi's emphasis on *chuche* (self-reliance), economic and military support from Moscow and Beijing have been very important to North Korea. Any significant lessening of Soviet or Chinese assistance could have a major impact on North Korea's ability to sustain its high level of military effort, as well as on the long-term balance of power on the peninsula.

The third effect is to encourage greater involvement by both Communist powers in efforts to stabilize the situation on the Korean Peninsula. This process has obviously already started. For several years now, China has assumed a more activist posture on Korean issues, pursuing a range of unofficial contacts with South Korea and urging the United States and Japan to initiate similar contacts with North Korea to help draw it into the world community and to encourage Pyongyang both to pursue dialogue with the ROK and to undertake domestic and foreign policy reforms that would help end its international isolation. Beijing's role as the host for the newly started talks between the United States and North Korea is a further manifestation of this more active involvement.

Until the historic Roh–Gorbachev decision on June 6, 1990, to establish full diplomatic relations, the Soviet Union had been much slower to move in this direction, focusing instead on improving its ties with North Korea. Moscow's recent role in facilitating a meeting between former North Korean Foreign Minister Ho Dam and South Korean opposition leader Kim Young-Sam, however, may be a harbinger of Soviet behavior in an era of reduced international tension. A more active Soviet posture not only would give the Soviets greater policy flexibility, but also would further their long-standing desire to gain entree into the diplomatic process surrounding Korea. North Korea's response to greater Soviet involvement remains uncertain. Given Pyongyang's clear distaste for *perestroika* and its fundamental interest in retaining control over all issues pertaining to the peninsula, however, increased Soviet involvement can hardly be an altogether attractive prospect.

A fourth effect of the changes now occurring is the strengthening of North Korea's historic tendency to tilt toward China. Throughout the past five years, the Soviets have improved their ties with North Korea and their position relative to the Chinese. To some extent, this improvement was dictated by North Korean economic and military necessity; to some extent, it simply corrected the abnormally poor relationship of the preceding decade, during which the Soviets maintained a moratorium on the supply of advanced military equipment to North Korea. Fundamentally, the improved relationship reflected the increased commonality of strategic interests in the late 1970s and early 1980s and Pyongyang's growing disenchantment with the PRC because of its internal reform policies and its external opening to the United States, Japan, and South Korea.

The dramatic changes in Soviet domestic and foreign policies and Moscow's growing flirtation with South Korea, coupled with the recent domestic crackdown and reassertion of control by hard-liners in the PRC, have altered the strategic equation. North Korea now has greater ideological affinity with China than it has had in a decade, and certainly more than it now has with the Soviet Union. There is also greater symmetry with the Chinese in domestic economic policies, which once again emphasizes the importance of strong central planning after a decade of effort to make the economy more responsive to market forces. In addition, there is a commonality in dealing with domestic pressures for political reform and democratization, that places the two—along with Albania, Cuba, and one or two others—in a rapidly shrinking group of like-minded, repressive regimes.[11] Moscow's public acknowledgment that people took to the streets in Czechoslovakia "not at the instigation of the West but because their own problems had piled up in the country" conflicts directly with North Korea's ideological insistence that the events in Eastern Europe have been instigated by nefarious imperialist forces. This presumably strengthens Pyongyang's growing identification with the PRC.[12]

In this context, Kim Il-Sung's secret visit to Beijing in late 1989 is no surprise. Whatever specific items may have been on Kim's agenda, the central purpose could only have been to explore the possibility of restoring close bilateral relations. The result of this effort will depend largely on the evolution of events in Beijing. By moving so quickly to shore up relations with China, the North Koreans have demonstrated both their anxiety about their international isolation and their historic tilt toward the PRC. A continuation of present Chinese policies could bolster the hard-liners in Pyongyang and help shield North Korea from the effects of broader global change.

The United States and Japan

The effects of detente are less direct in regard to relations with the United States and Japan. For nearly 40 years, these relations have been determined by Pyongyang's unremitting effort to bring the entire peninsula under its control. In the absence of fundamental change in North Korean policy, the basic nature of the relationships is likely to continue.

At least two broad consequences of global detente, however, could affect these relationships. The first is the increased pressure in the United States for deep cuts in defense spending and drawdowns in U.S. forces deployed overseas. To some extent, of course, this pressure is related to the large U.S. budget deficit. For this reason alone, the defense budget has shrunk in the past several years by a few percentage points each year. Recent changes, however, have created a qualitatively different situation. Now, not only is the ability to pay for the continued defense buildup being challenged, but the need for the buildup itself is being called into question. As Congressman Les Aspin, head of the House Armed Services Committee, noted recently, the United States has just had the last of its "deficit-driven" defense budgets; now, "we [are] enter[ing] the era of Gorbachev-driven budgets that will need to respond to the changes taking place on the other side of the rapidly rusting Iron Curtain."[13]

Early projections suggest potential cutbacks of as much as $200 billion in the defense budget during the next four years, with the possible elimination of two aircraft carriers and 200,000 army personnel. If such projections materialize, lessening tension with the Soviets could result in large-scale pullbacks of U.S. forces, greater reliance on reserves, and reductions in both airlift and sealift capabilities.

Obviously, this pressure transcends the issue of Korea. It is hard to imagine, however, that South Korea will be spared from global cutbacks of this magnitude. Indeed, there has been increased questioning of the reason so many U.S. troops are needed in South Korea at a time when neither the Soviets nor Chinese are likely to support North Korean aggression and when South Korea itself is able to bear a larger share of its own defense. In this atmosphere, the feeling is growing rapidly, particularly in Congress, that the time has come for a change in the U.S. force posture in South Korea. This is perhaps doubly ironic: Not only does the pressure for change conflict with the almost total absence of change in the offensive threat from North Korea, but there has never been a time when the presence of U.S. forces in South Korea has been more acceptable to China and the Soviet Union, both of whom recognize (unofficially) the stabilizing role of the U.S. forces. Nevertheless, a continuation of recent trends will almost surely lead to increased pressure on the United States to reduce forces in South Korea specifically and to reevaluate the U.S.–ROK security relationship more broadly.

Should these pressures produce a perception of diminished U.S. resolve, they could feed North Korean illusions about the prospect for a North Korean military reunification of Korea. They could also precipitate a major arms race on the peninsula. Short of this, even pressures in the United States are likely to bolster North Korea's belief that a U.S. withdrawal is inevitable. At least in the short term, therefore, the trends are likely to strengthen the hard-line position in Pyongyang. Barring major leadership changes, North Korea is unlikely to make anything more than cosmetic concessions in arms control and confidence-building measures in exchange for U.S. force reductions in South Korea.

Over the long term, the effects may be more positive. Despite the increased pressures for defense cutbacks, strong support remains in the

United States for a continued commitment to the defense of South Korea and to an active—even if merely supportive—role in deterring potential North Korean aggression. The trend toward global detente weakens Soviet and Chinese support for North Korean actions far more than it diminishes U.S. support for the defense of South Korea. As long as the United States avoids any precipitate withdrawal and the United States and ROK make timely adjustments in the broader security relationship, a continuation of the recent trends could facilitate alterations in the existing armistice and security arrangements in ways that contribute to the prospect for peace on the peninsula. In the meantime, the challenge will be to maintain an adequate military deterrent in an era in which global trends are pushing toward force reductions.

The second consequence of the trend toward detente is greater fluidity in U.S. and Japanese dealings with North Korea. Clearly, neither the United States nor Japan are rushing to embrace Pyongyang. For its part, North Korea has not even begun to make the kinds of changes in its policies and orientation that are required for significantly expanded relations. Nevertheless, recent developments—including the dramatic changes in South Korea's policies toward Pyongyang—have loosened the constraints on some kinds of interaction. The United States and Japan will entertain new exchanges, in consultation with South Korea, partly to lessen the gap between Soviet and Chinese dealings with the ROK and their own dealings with Pyongyang and partly to facilitate the process of dialogue on the peninsula.

The North Koreans will also have more incentive to expand interactions, if only to counter the adverse political and economic trends and to test the prospects for a U.S. military withdrawal from South Korea. The extent to which this process is successful hinges on concrete changes in North Korean policies; however, a continuation of recent global trends will undoubtedly lead to further probes of the other side's intentions and to some informal interactions. It may also lead to an increased interest in exploring more formal, multilateral venues for reducing tension on the Korean Peninsula.

South Korea

Thus far, the effects of detente are least evident in the relations between North and South Korea. North Korea's central objective remains the same: to undermine the South Korean government and bring the entire peninsula under its control.

It is hard to see any effect as far as North Korean policies are concerned. Pyongyang continues to adhere to its four-pronged position: strong opposition to cross-recognition or other steps that, from the North's perspective, would solidify the division of the peninsula; insistence on a tripartite conference involving the United States and the two Koreas to discuss arms reduction, nonaggression, and peace agreements; a demand for the total withdrawal of U.S. military forces from South Korea; and a call for a confederation between Seoul and Pyongyang that would "respect" the existing systems. With the possible exception of North Korean willingness to allow a phased, rather than immediate, withdrawal of U.S. forces, there is little indication of North Korean flexibility on any of these points.

Finally, the effect of detente is minimal regarding North Korean methods. Although Pyongyang may have downgraded its emphasis on naked force somewhat (perhaps in deference to Soviet and Chinese interests), it continues to build up its offensive military capabilities. It also continues to emphasize approaches designed to subvert the authority of the ROK government and to foster instability in South Korea. There is little evidence of any North Korean willingness to come to terms with the existence of the Republic of Korea. If anything, the effect of detente has been the opposite: Pyongyang has been embarrassed by the expanded Communist bloc dealings with South Korea, and detente has made the North even more hostile and more willing to try to manipulate South Korean domestic political difficulties. Thus, change in North–South relations, it appears, hinges on changes first within North Korea.

Alternative Directions

This raises the ultimate question—not the way global detente affects North Korea's strategic relations, but the way all recent changes—including those in South Korea during the past several years—are likely to affect North Korea's basic orientation. Will Pyongyang move away from its emphasis on self-reliance and reunification and instead instigate domestic reforms, open up the country, and join the international community or will it close further in an effort to insulate itself from increasingly adverse trends? The answer is unknown. North Korea is a cloistered, enigmatic state. Not much is understood, frankly, about its calculations and decision-making processes.

Many people wonder if the developments in Eastern Europe might soon be replicated in North Korea. This seems unlikely. At least three key factors behind the change in Eastern Europe do not exist or are much less important in North Korea: the existence of a single, dominant superpower patron; the paucity of internal sources for regime legitimacy; and the domino or demonstration effect of events in neighboring countries. Each will be examined in turn.

The existence of a single, dominant superpower patron. The East European regimes were all dependent on Moscow politically, economically, and militarily for their survival. They had little to fall back on once Gorbachev decided that their continued intransigence was harmful to his own interests. Three factors have minimized North Korea's dependence on the Soviet Union, however: the PRC, the Sino–Soviet split, and North Korea's own historic emphasis on independence and self-reliance. Despite the importance of Soviet economic and military assistance, North Korea has had much greater independence than did the Eastern European satellites. Symbolized by the lack of stationed Soviet troops, Pyongyang has had more room to chart its own domestic and foreign policies. It is unlikely that Gorbachev will see the same stake in North Korean reform that he has come to see in Eastern Europe. Even if this were the case, however, North Korea would have greater ability to resist Soviet pressure.

The paucity of internal sources for regime legitimacy. Partly as a function of their dependence on the Soviet Union, most of the regimes that have been supplanted had serious problems with domestic legitimacy. Once Soviet support was weakened or withdrawn and the "fear factor" diminished, public resentment about internal economic and political conditions grew to uncontrollable proportions. In the case of North Korea, a combination of fact (Kim Il-Sung's long-standing commitment to reunification) and fiction (Kim's nearly mythological past and alleged role in liberating Korea from Japanese colonial rule) have enabled the North Korean regime to personify itself as the embodiment of Korean nationalism. Moreover, despite its serious economic difficulties, Kim has clearly improved the standard of living in North Korea. This has provided the North Korean leadership with a legitimacy that has been lacking in much of Eastern Europe. Although the extent of truly indigenous support is impossible to measure because of North Korea's totalitarian nature, it is probably safe to assume that popular attitudes toward the ruling North Korean regime are significantly different from those that existed in Eastern Europe.

The "domino" or "demonstration" effect of events in neighboring countries. Although developments in each of the East European countries have a logic and pattern of their own, clearly they have been influenced by preceding developments in neighboring countries. Access to television and other media across borders multiplied the impact of events in neighboring nations and helped internationalize their ramifications. Unlike Eastern Europe, the North Korean regime is able to control access to information because of its media monopoly. In addition, there are no neighboring states with whom the North Koreans can relate who are experiencing the profound change now occurring in Eastern Europe. The only exception—and this is only partial—is China; however, recent developments there have reinforced North Korean rigidity and, if anything, counteracted any impulse toward reform and liberalization.

For all these reasons, the effect of Soviet and East European reform on North Korean policies probably should not be exaggerated. The way North Korea sees the world and defines its national interests, at least in the short term, will likely preclude dramatic change. Absent important internal change (in particular, the transition to a new kind of leadership), Pyongyang will probably maintain its basic policies and seek to prevent the "East European disease" from infecting North Korea.

The long-term picture is more uncertain. Given this uncertainty, it is surprising to find something of a consensus emerging among U.S. and South Korean (and, indeed, even among many Soviet and Chinese) observers regarding North Korea's future. According to the emerging conventional wisdom, once Kim Il-Sung dies, his successor—whoever that may be—will "accommodate" the trends, both internally and externally. The seriousness of North Korea's economic difficulties, the need for Kim's successor to establish a political position and base of support, and the diminishing public tolerance for a continued high level of personal sacrifice—the latter fueled by rising educational levels and increased awareness because of mass communication—will inevitably force North Korea to join the wave of reform sweeping Communist systems. Although this may take some time, the conventional wisdom goes, it is bound to happen sooner or later.

It is hard to tell how much of this conventional wisdom is based on hard analysis and how much on wishful thinking. Often, several internal North Korean developments are cited as evidence that Pyongyang is likely to move in this direction: the emphasis in the North Korean media on light industry and better consumer products, the rapid turnover rate in the party's Politburo and Central Committee and relative decline of military officers, the appointment of a number of technocrats to important positions around Kim Jong-Il, and Kim Jong-Il's personal association with improving domestic economic performance. The problem is that much of this "evidence" is either difficult to support or subject to multiple interpretations. There are also a number of developments that flatly contradict such evidence. The escalating personality cult of Kim Jong-Il, for example, and the frenzied production campaigns for political objectives that have only marginal economic value, do not readily support the general expectation.

Although the scenario depicted in the conventional wisdom may very well turn out to be correct, it is also prudent to consider other possible outcomes. One would be for North Korea to isolate itself from global reform and the detente process. Joining other hard-line countries, Pyongyang could draw further into itself, emphasizing self-reliance. It could also continue its military buildup and offensive orientation. It could refuse to come to terms with South Korea, taking a hard line in North–South deliberations. This hard-line posture would allow North Korea to buy time in the hope that the local and international situation would change. Although North Korean rhetoric would likely be tough under this scenario, it would probably not, because of a lack of external support, be matched by adventurous actions.

Another potential outcome would be for North Korea to isolate itself from the reform process and take active steps to sabotage detente and South Korean progress. This might involve expanded military support from a conservative, isolated China, thus leading to provocative North Korean actions against South Korea. In this scenario, North Korea would become a recidivist state: prickly, unpredictable, and potentially dangerous. Such a state would be particularly dangerous during the period of reduced U.S. military representation in South Korea before the ROK established military parity with North Korea. A North Korean perception of diminished U.S. resolve during this period, perhaps coupled with an exacerbation of long-term trends, could prompt more militant measures by North Korea to seize the window of opportunity to advance Korean reunification.

A third possibility would be the collapse of North Korea and a very rapid movement toward reunification. This might occur in the aftermath of an unsuccessful succession, with a weakened North Korean leadership acceding to popular pressures for economic change, political liberalization, and concrete steps toward unification. This resembles the "conventional wisdom" scenario, but it differs in one critical respect: The North Korean state would simply cease to exist. Faced with overwhelming difficulties, such a state would essentially negotiate its absorption into South Korea. Although very few observers expect this to happen, and indeed it is hard to imagine, the materialization nearly every day now of previously "unimaginable" developments makes it at least worth considering.

None of these potential outcomes, it should be emphasized, are predicted, nor are they at this point predictable. They are simply meant to suggest the range of possibilities about which the United States should begin thinking.

Whatever one's expectation, the recent developments and trend toward global detente highlight even more starkly North Korea's central dilemma: whether to move away from the rigid Stalinist political and economic system and come to terms with South Korea—thus posing a risk to the legitimacy of the leadership, but offering the possibility of improving North Korea's economic situation—or to continue on its present course at the risk of economic stagnation and international isolation. Addressing this dilemma will be at the top of the agenda for Kim Il-Sung's successor.

Notes

1. For this definition and a more extensive treatment of the themes presented in this section, see Norman D. Levin, "North Korea's Strategic Relations," *North Korea in a Regional and Global Context,* Robert Scalapino and Hongkoo Lee, eds. (Berkeley, Calif.: University of California, 1984), 387–405.

2. The Economist Intelligence Unit, *China, North Korea——Country Report,* no. 1, 1989, p. 39.

3. The Economist Intelligence Unit, *China, North Korea——Country Report,* no. 3, 1989, p. 35.

4. *Economist,* April 15, 1989, p. 38; *North Korea News,* October 30, 1989, p. 2.

5. Recent party propaganda has stressed the need to "singularize" the party's ideology and assure that all party organizations "carry through decisions and directives of the party to the end unconditionally and promptly. If we allow the lack of discipline of disobeying the leader's orders and directives and even the slightest element of liberalism to exist in the party," said one recent article in the party's theoretical journal, "that party will not be able to function properly and will ultimately lose its vigor." See "The Singularization of the Ideology Is a Firm Guarantee for Ensuring the Uniqueness of the Leadership," *Kulloja,* January 1989, pp. 16–21.

6. *China, North Korea——Country Report,* no. 3, p. 29.

7. Kim Chung-Nin, "The Cause of the Fatherland's Reunification Which Advances Along the Road of Independence Shown by the Respected and Beloved Leader Comrade Kim Il-Sung," *Kulloja,* April 1989, pp. 30–36.

8. Foreign Broadcast Information Service (FBIS), *China,* January 16, 1985, D–5.

9. Soviet reports are both increasingly detailed in chronicling Moscow's assistance to Pyongyang—that the Soviets now claim involves 70 industrial facilities accounting for more than one-fourth of North Korea's industrial output—and increasingly critical of North Korean performance in adjusting domestic structures to effectively apply Soviet assistance in meeting the quantitative and qualitative requirements of bilateral aid agreements. See, for example, Y. Mikheyev, "The DPRK's Regional Economic Relations," *Far Eastern Affairs,* no. 2 (1989): 66–75.

10. *China, North Korea——Country Report,* no. 3, p. 32.

11. *Washington Post,* November 7, 1989.

12. If the Soviet response to Poland and Hungary was a difficult pill for Kim Il-Sung to swallow, Czechoslovakia must have made him choke. Not only did the Soviets insist that the Prague regime had lost popular support, they implied that it may have been illegitimate from the beginning. Nothing

at all was said in defense of socialism. For the Soviet public acknowledgment, originally published in *Pravda*, see the *Los Angeles Times*, November 25, 1989. The implication of illegitimacy was reported in the *Los Angeles Times*, November 26, 1989.

13. *Los Angeles Times*, November 24, 1989.

4

Neo-Detente and North Korean Relations with China and the Soviet Union

Park Pong-Shik

Neo-Detente

Neo-detente refers to the ongoing easing of relations between East and West. A term coined by Mikhail Gorbachev, it is used to distinguish the current state of relations from the detente first developed in the 1970s through a series of summit meetings between the United States and the Soviet Union. Detente was very limited in scope; neo-detente is larger in scope and, to an unprecedented degree, far-reaching in many areas of world politics.

In his article "Ending the Cold War," Michael Mandelbaum has stated that the international situation today is substantially different from that of the 1970s, when the Soviet Union had an ascendancy over the United States, which was beleaguered both domestically and internationally by the debacle of the Vietnam War. Today, however, the situation is reversed. Additionally, unlike the Brezhnev era, the Soviet Union of today is in need of detente to ensure the success of *perestroika* (restructuring).[1]

The reversal in the Soviet position originated from three factors. First, the Soviet Union is now in its greatest crisis since 1917, when Lenin founded the Communist state; second, Communist ideology and the Communist system have experienced a complete failure in Eastern Europe; and, finally, elites in both the Soviet Union and Eastern Europe recognize that fact.[2] *Perestroika* was developed for no other reason than to deal with this failure.

Gorbachev's speech delivered in February, 1986, at the 27th Party Convention, marked a change in Soviet foreign policy. In this speech,

Gorbachev altogether dropped Soviet support for Third World national liberation movements. Contrary to everyone's expectation, he noted the intended Soviet withdrawal from Afghanistan. Further development was made in December 1988, when Gorbachev addressed the UN General Assembly. He stated that the new international order demanded de-ideologizing relations among states. He also gave strong indications that the ideology of class struggle should be ruled out in international relations. Of course, it is necessary for the Soviet Union to separate security considerations from ideological preferences to change such statements into concrete policies.[3]

Attention should also be given to two statements recently made by the Soviet foreign minister and to the result of the conference of the foreign ministers of the Warsaw Pact countries. In his foreign policy address to the Soviet legislature, Eduard Shevardnadze confessed that the construction of a radar station at Krasnoyarsk was an open violation of the Anti-Ballistic Missile (ABM) Treaty of 1972 and that the deployment of Soviet troops in Afghanistan in December 1979 was "the most serious violation of our own legislation" committed by the Soviet Union. Shevardnadze also noted that the decision to send those troops was taken "behind the backs of [the] people." Clearly, this is a very grave criticism of past Soviet policy.[4]

What Shevardnaze said at the foreign ministers' conference of the Warsaw Pact countries is even more remarkable. Calling for a gradual end to the Eastern and Western alliances, he said that their long-term goal should be to transform those alliances by reducing all military elements.[5] In a final joint statement, the Soviet Union and Warsaw Pact nations declared sovereignty and noninterference in each other's affairs, thereby effectively abolishing the Brezhnev Doctrine, which had led to Soviet domination of Eastern Europe. The statement also said, "One of the essential prerequisites for the building of a secure, peaceful, and indivisible Europe is to respect the right of each nation to independently decide . . . its fate and freely choose the road of its social, political, and economic development, with no external interference."[6]

With this extraordinary change in Soviet attitudes and in the Eastern European situation, the U.S. government, which had previously been dismissive and skeptical of Gorbachev's sincerity, began to view his policy of *perestroika* as an opportunity to build a new world order. On October 23, 1989, U.S. Secretary of State James Baker noted this recent change in superpower relations. Said Baker, "The U.S. and Soviet Union have an historic opportunity to move beyond the cold war to a new world."[7]

Although it is still uncertain where the changes in the Soviet Union and Eastern Europe will ultimately lead, it also appears that Soviet *perestroika* and East European political change have reached an irreversible stage. Both the scope and the speed of the change in East–West relations were simply beyond imagination at the time of the Intermediate-Range Nuclear Force (INF) Treaty.

Change in Asia and Gorbachev's "New Thinking"

Unlike the trend in the East European countries, where political pluralism is in place and military organizations are giving way to political organizations, the situation in Asia has changed little. At the same time that the Soviet Union has been gradually disengaging from Eastern Europe, both politically and militarily, it has also been reinforcing its political and military situation in Asia. In this regard, Communist countries in Asia have largely rejected Gorbachev's *perestroika*.

Soviet policy toward Asia has been highlighted in two of Gorbachev's speeches—at Vladivostok and at Krasnoyarsk in July 1986 and September 1988, respectively. In those speeches, Gorbachev noted the Soviet intent to expand its participation in the Pacific region and to become the United States' equal in air and naval forces. As he stated at Krasnoyarsk, "If the U.S. agrees to the elimination of military bases in the Philippines, the Soviet Union will be ready, by agreement with the government of the Socialist Republic of Vietnam, to give up its fleet's materiel and technical supply station in Cam Ranh Bay."

Similarly, in regard to Soviet policy toward Asia, Georgi Arbatov, the director of the Soviet Institute of the United States and Canada, noted,

One of the most important achievements of the new political thinking has become a revision of the Soviet Pacific policy. Eurocentrism and Americacentrism which characterized our policy under the impact of historical realities doomed the Soviet Pacific policy [of] passivity for a long time. And, by the way, these factors influenced negatively the economic and social development of our Far East as well. We considered this very rich and worthwhile region as something really "far," far from our main concerns . . . . New political thinking, which has changed radically our approach to the Pacific region as well, originated in the [19]70s . . . . We realized the necessity "to turn to the Pacific region" as a result of our studies of the U.S. and its policy. It was hard not to notice the shift of American interests and attention [away] from [the] Atlantic to [the] Pacific—and we soon found . . . the solid grounds for that shift in American priorities.[8]

It is interesting to note that the shift in Soviet Asian policy is parallel with the heightened attention the United States has attached to the Asian Pacific region. Another important point Arbatov made was the growing strategic importance of Siberia. The negative attitude of Communist countries in Asia toward *perestroika* is likely to be maintained for a considerable period of time. Divided by ancient rivalries and present-day politics, Communist states in Asia are worried about—and even dread—the demise of Marxism in Eastern Europe. When Romania proposed a joint resolution against Poland's reform in August 1989, for example, North Korea promptly supported it. Although China is said to have shown reluctance about joining the criticism of Poland, it, too, was concerned about political reform in Eastern Europe. At that time, early June of 1989, the Chinese government used its troops to suppress the people's demand for democratization, which was experiencing its height in May when Gorbachev visited Beijing—the first Soviet leader to do so in 30 years. Vietnam supported the steps China had taken to deal with the democratization movement at home. Although Vietnam was an ally of the Soviet Union, this was quite natural because Vietnam had been bitterly attacking the dismantling of Communist rule in Poland all along, seeking to retrench its own political liberalization.[9] In view of such attitudes, it is expected that it will take a long time before any change corresponding to that of Eastern Europe occurs in the Communist countries of Asia.

This being the case, questions are raised about the impact of Gorbachev's "new thinking" on Asian countries. The first fruit of Gorbachev's new policy was the normalization of relations with China. Gorbachev's visit to China in May 1989 resulted in a joint statement with the Chinese, which provided, among other things, that Soviet troops at the border be reduced and that the two countries cooperate in as many areas as possible. Gorbachev put aside his ideological preference, respecting China's own attitude toward political reform. The turning point of this normalization was the Soviet promise to withdraw Vietnamese troops from Kampuchea. This promise has since been carried out, thus greatly improving the relationship between the Soviet Union and Asian countries. In short, this normalization has created for the Soviet Union a very favorable strategic situation in the Asian Pacific region.

A Closer Relationship between North Korea and the Soviets

North Korea has long regarded self-reliance as its diplomatic guideline. It has used manipulation and diplomacy equally in its relations with China and the Soviet Union on the one hand and its participation in the non-aligned movement to promote international revolution on the other.[10] This two-pronged approach continued until the 1980s, when it met with various difficulties.

The first difficulty was the establishment of Kim Jong-Il as the internationally recognized heir apparent at the 6th Party Congress held in

October 1980. The second difficulty was the changed policy of its allies, China and the Soviet Union, which was very worrisome indeed. China normalized diplomatic relations with the United States in late 1978 and concluded a friendship treaty with Japan in the summer of that year, opening its economic door to the West. On the one hand, the Soviet Union was compelled by President Reagan's power diplomacy to propose the reduction of international tensions in September 1981; on the other hand, the Soviet Union proposed an unconditional dialogue with China in 1982.

At that time, even China had a very worrisome situation. Chinese leaders were afraid of a possible Soviet detente with the United States, whose president might well be espousing a two-Chinas policy. The 12th Party Congress was held in September 1982 to consolidate the Deng Xiaoping–Hu Yaobang line in the post-Mao era and, consequently, to pursue new political and economic policies. Thus, China needed a more firm relationship with North Korea. It was not without reason that both Deng and Hu went to North Korea in April 1982 to congratulate Kim Il-Sung on his birthday, and Kim reciprocated by visiting Beijing in September that year.

Kim's visit to China after seven years had an additional purpose: to improve relations between the two countries. This was made clear by Hu Yaobang's welcome speech at the dinner held for Kim on September 16, 1982: "Our firm unity and cooperation under the present waveringly unstable international situation is a stabilizing element for the peace of Asia and the whole world." This desire for improved relations was also demonstrated by the fact that Deng himself showed Kim around China.[11] This particular amicability did not come into being overnight. When Kim Yong-Nam, the head of the North Korean Foreign Ministry, visited China in November 1981, then-Chairman Hu had already made a friendly gesture by proposing a toast to the health of both Chairman Kim Il-Sung and his son Jong-Il. And, it was Kim Jong-Il, the heir designate, who met both Deng and Hu at the station of Pyongyang when they visited the city in April 1982.

Since then, relations have been closer. The *People's Daily* introduced Kim Jong-Il's article "Let's March Forward Under the Banner of Marxism, Leninism, and *Chuche* Ideology" on May 21, 1983. When Kim and O Chin-U, the North Korean war minister, visited China for 12 days in June 1983, the New China News Agency reported that Comrade Kim's visit had carried the friendship of the two countries one step further.[12]

North Korea's law of "joint venture," which was made public in September 1984, was, in fact, the result of the visits of Kim Il-Sung and his son to China, where they first saw China's economic open-door policy in action. Needless to say, it was through the good offices of China that North Korea proposed the "tripartite talks" in January 1984. Launching the "joint venture" project, North Korea invited capitalist countries from the West to expand trade and economic cooperation.[13] This pro-China attitude of North Korea began to change, however, when Kim Il-Sung visited Moscow in May 1984 for the first time in 22 years.

How does one explain the North Korean welcome—the greatest ever in scale—of Hu Yaobang, the Chinese Communist Party's general secretary, who was visiting North Korea only a few days before Kim Il-Sung left Ch'ongjin for Moscow on May 16, 1984? More surprising still, the meeting between Kim and Hu reportedly ended with a complete agreement on international matters, as well as agreement on the issue of unification of the Korean Peninsula. Hu also invited Kang Song-San, the premier, to visit China that year. In Hu's address to the mass gathering in Pyongyang, he noted that when the U.S. president visited China, he would demand U.S. support for North Korea's policy of unification and the withdrawal of U.S. troops from the peninsula to ensure permanent peace. Hu emphasized that China never forgot North Korea, in spite of its pro-American policy.[14] Hu's visit and his speech made clear Chinese concern about Kim's visit to Moscow, and China tried to arrest the course of North Korea's lean toward the Soviet Union. Perhaps that is why Hu had seen Kim prior to his visit to Moscow. If so, it is apparent that North Korea's lavish welcome of Hu was intended to put Hu's mind at ease. Kang also complied with Hu's request to visit China in August 1984. Even Kim visited China in November of that year, although unofficially.

Kim, Kang, and O Chin-U arrived in Moscow on May 23, 1984, and had two official meetings with Chernenko. During these meetings, Chernenko stressed the expansion of mutual cooperation in the international arena, not only economically, but also politically. Chernenko also spoke of Soviet support for North Korea's program for unifying the Korean Peninsula. He also criticized the triangular military alliance of Washington, Tokyo, and Seoul, which was, Chernenko said, creating tension even at the borders of the Soviet Union. Chernenko failed to mention North Korea's "tripartite talks," however. Kim responded to Chernenko by saying that the Soviets had helped him with the great task of restoring Korean independence, with the war of liberation, and in rebuilding war-torn Korea, which had been invaded by American imperialism. Unlike Chernenko, however, Kim stressed the importance of the "tripartite talks."[15] Kang called the Soviets' attention to the fact that North Korea did its best to defend socialism as its oriental guard post.

Kim's visit to Moscow was followed by the visit of Mikhail Kapitsa, Soviet vice foreign minister, to Pyongyang. During his stay (November 12–17, 1984), Kapitsa signed a provisional treaty about border crossings. His official contact with Kim Jong-Il was Soviet recognition of his succession to his father. In December 1984, O Chin-U went to the Soviet Union to visit his counterpart and returned with all sorts of sophisticated weaponry. The Soviet Union, in turn, obtained the right to dock its warships at Namp'o, a North Korean port.[16]

As mentioned earlier, Kim Il-Sung visited China from November 26–28, 1984. His unofficial visit was in accordance with the invitation of the Central Committee of the Chinese Communist Party.[17] It is likely that Chinese leaders thought Kim owed them an explanation of his Moscow visit.

In regard to the events outlined above, it is surprising that Hu Yaobang visited Sinuiju for three days in May 1985. Upon Hu's arrival, both Kim and Jong-Il, as well as O Chin-U and Ho Dam, rushed to meet him. Nothing is known about the topics discussed except that the talks centered on their mutual concerns, including cooperation. In Kim Il-Sung's welcoming address, he stated, "I hope that our blood alliance will get firmer and firmer in the years ahead."[18] The purpose of this unusual contact between the leaders of the two states could be construed as a consultation about the emergence of a new Soviet leader, Gorbachev, and it is not difficult to see, lurking behind all the rhetoric, Chinese apprehension and suspicion about improved relations between North Korea and the Soviet Union.

This Chinese apprehension and suspicion were well founded. Since December 1984, Soviet reconnaissance planes have had North Korean airspace at their disposal and have carried out regular reconnaissance missions over not only South Korea, but China as well. In return for this concession, North Korea was supplied with the newest Soviet fighter planes and missiles.

On two occasions—the commemoration of the Russian victory over Germany and the twenty-fifth anniversary of the alliance between North Korea and the Soviet Union—10 MiG jet fighters from each side exchanged a visit. On the occasion of the fortieth anniversary of liberation, Soviet First Deputy Premier Aliev and his group and Soviet First Vice-Minister of Defense Petrov and his group, as well as approximately 30 additional representatives, were invited to North Korea for the first time. To commemorate the twenty-fifth anniversary of their alliance, the fleets of both countries also conducted an exchange visit. The Soviet fleet was led by Vladmir Sidorov, the commander of the Soviet Pacific Fleet, and the North Korean Fleet by Kim Il-Chol, the commander of the North Korean navy. This was an unprecedented demonstration of military friendship between the two countries. This military friendship was complemented by political friendship when Shevardnadze visited North Korea in January 1986 and recognized Kim Jong-Il's succession to his father and supported North Korea's unification formula.[19]

Gorbachev's invitation to Kim Il-Sung and Kim's consequent visit to the Soviet Union in October 1986 had a similar background. Unlike his former visit, however, Kim Il-Sung was accompanied by Kim Yong-Nam, the head of the North Korean Foreign Ministry, and Ho Dam. In his meeting with Kim Il-Sung, Gorbachev explained his view of the Asian situation and security (earlier manifested in his Vladivostok speech) and asked Kim to toe the line. Kim must have been shocked, for this approach would substantially affect his policy toward South Korea. This visit heralded new attitudes by the two countries, which were confirmed by Kim's and Gorbachev's speeches.

According to Gorbachev, the two leaders discussed the relationship of the two countries, the situation in the Far East, and the urgent international problems. They agreed on close cooperation in the areas of economics and scientific technology. Gorbachev asserted that Korean unification involves not only the Korean Peninsula, but also the whole Asian Pacific region, and he noted that the Soviet–North Korean joint struggle against imperialism is inextricably linked with the improvement and furtherance of neighborly friendship. This seems to imply that North Korea's unification policy also must conform to the Soviet Union's Asian Pacific policy. Of special interest was his remark that the reduction of tension between the United States and the Soviet Union would contribute to a reduction in tension on the Korean Peninsula and to North Korea's struggle for a nuclear-free peninsula. Here, Gorbachev is clearly referring to his summit meeting with Reagan at Reykjavik.

According to Kim Il-Sung (repeating what he had said in his talk with Chernenko about the Soviets' historical contribution to North Korea), however, the foundation of proletarian internationalism would maintain and develop the amicable relationship between the two countries. He added his support to Gorbachev's condemnation of the triangular alliance of the United States, Japan, and South Korea, as well as to his peace initiative.[20]

What can be seen from the speeches of the two men is that while Gorbachev emphasized the easing of tensions, global security, and a nuclear-free peninsula, Kim continued to parrot the obsolete term "proletarian internationalism," no longer used by Gorbachev, thus indicating how completely out of touch Kim is with the changing political and ideological situation of his closest Communist allies. In spite of the jarring note, Kim's meeting with Gorbachev was publicized in North Korea as a great success. According to the statement issued by the Pyongyang regime on October 30, 1986 (after long discussions among concerned party and administrative staff), the meeting between Kim and Gorbachev had marked yet another turning point in the friendly relations between the two countries, thus opening the possibility of a wholesale friendship. In the statement, it was also noted that Gorbachev had lauded Kim, the party chief, for having created a firm foundation for the continuance of the revolution. Noteworthy in this context is that for the first time, in October 1986, the Soviet Union and North Korea conducted a joint naval exercise, which has since become an annual event.

Whatever may be said of the talks between Gorbachev and Kim, one striking result that emerged in the course of 1987 and 1988 is the enhanced military relationship between the two countries. This was also borne out by the visit of Rushev, the first vice defense minister, to Pyongyang.[21] Shevardnadze also made a "political" visit in December 1988. A joint communique was issued at that time in which Shevardnadze confirmed that there was no fundamental change in the Soviet attitude toward South Korea and in its objection to South Korea's entry into the UN (either alone or together with the North) and that the Soviet Union would not officially recognize South Korea or establish full diplomatic ties with South Korea.[22] It appears, however, that the real reason for Shevardnadze's visit to Pyongyang was to explain the Soviet position regarding its participation in the Seoul Olympic Games and its frequent cultural exchanges with South Korea. By developing closer military ties with North Korea, it seemed by then that the Soviet Union had succeeded in inducing North Korea to toe the line regarding the Soviet approach toward international and national unification policy for the Far East and Asian Pacific region.

Sino–Soviet Reconciliation and North Korea's Equidistance Diplomacy

During the summit talks between China and the Soviet Union, the issue of Korean unification was also on the agenda, but omitted from the final joint statement. In his address at the People's Great Hall, Gorbachev mentioned, however, the necessity of eliminating tension on the Korean Peninsula and of withdrawing U.S. troops as a means of supporting North Korea's "effort" for "a peaceful, democratic reunification of Korea." To solve these questions, Gorbachev suggested that a UN-supported multilateral mechanism for consultations be formed. As to the great powers' relations with Korea, which was not included in the joint statement, it seems that the Soviets and Chinese could not reach agreement. It is easy to guess that the withdrawal of U.S. troops and the creation of a multilateral body for consultations were areas of disagreement. The creation of a multilateral body would also raise the Taiwan question and the issue of the triangular alliance of the United States, Japan, and South Korea—both very sensitive issues for China.

In spite of Sino–Soviet reconciliation, North Korea sees no reason to change its policy. Its foreign policy centers on three issues: its policy toward South Korea, its participation in the Non-Aligned Movement (NAM), and its equidistance diplomacy. Amid the contradicting Soviet statements toward North Korea's policy, Kim Il-Sung maintains his original, independent policy.

Although he was told by Gorbachev to toe the Soviet line, Kim refuses. In part this is not surprising given the Soviet endorsement of North Korean policy on various occasions. The 9th NAM Summit Talks, which were held in early September 1989, saw no change in North Korea's policy toward the movement. This movement is no longer what it used to be, however, having outgrown its anti-imperial and anticolonial position. As a result, North Korea completely failed to resolve the Korean issue in the Belgrade declaration.[23] Such being the case, the North Korean campaign against imperialism and the United States through the Non-Aligned Movement has become less and less effective. Yet, North Korea is likely to continue its membership to promote this purpose.

Despite closer ties with the Soviet Union in recent years, North Korea still maintains an equidistance diplomacy toward its two giant Communist neighbors. The Soviet first vice defense minister's visit to Pyongyang in April 1988 was followed by Kim Yong-Nam's visit to Moscow in late April 1988. To strike a balance, O Chin-U visited China in May 1988, only a month later than Hyon Chun-Guk's visit to China.[24] The frequency of North Korean visits to both China and the Soviet Union is equally balanced, but the relations between the Soviet Union and North Korea have been much closer. Nonetheless, North Korea has been very cautious not to offend China or to damage the existing ties with China because of its closer relationship with the Soviet Union.

In this connection, however, it is worth considering why Gorbachev failed to include North Korea in his travel agenda after visiting Beijing. Kim Il-Sung, when in Moscow in October 1986, had invited Gorbachev to visit Pyongyang and had obtained Gorbachev's acceptance. This is in clear contrast to Gorbachev's Cuban visit. Castro and Kim Il-Sung are reportedly the only two leaders of Communist countries who object to Gorbachev's *perestroika*. Castro did his best not to offend Gorbachev when he visited Cuba.[25] In comparing Soviet relations with Cuba and North Korea, relations between Gorbachev and Kim cannot be said to be very good. The fact that the Korean issue was not included in the joint statement of Gorbachev and Deng and the fact that Gorbachev did not visit Kim on his trip to China seem to bear out the awkward relations between the two countries.

Recent Soviet Policy toward North Korea

In the second half of 1989, a number of Soviets who are considered to be in charge of Soviet policy toward Asia went to Seoul and made statements about easing tensions on the Korean Peninsula. They spoke more or less with one voice, indicating their support for North Korea's "confederation" formula for unification and asserting the need to withdraw U.S.

troops. The only difference between the position articulated by these Soviets and that of North Korea was that, unlike North Korea, they saw the Korean Peninsula as part of the Asian Pacific region. For example, Mikhail Kapitsa, former Soviet vice foreign minister, stated that efforts could be undertaken to prevent the conflict between North and South from reaching a breaking point, that the North's offer to reduce its troop strength to 100,000 is worth considering if U.S. forces are withdrawn from the South, that the USSR is committed to supporting North Korea although it has sought to develop trade, economic, and cultural relations with the South, and that contacts between the two Koreas will bring about new prospects for peace and economic development.[26]

Pointing out that the Soviet Union has been trying to solve dangerous regional conflicts in Asia, Georgi Arbatov said, "Unfortunately, so far, these efforts have had practically no impact on the Korean peninsula." He went on to reiterate the Russian position toward the two Koreas by saying that the Soviet Union supports the Democratic People's Republic of Korea (DPRK) proposals for a peaceful settlement on the peninsula. He hastened to add that the Soviets would be ready to consider any other proposal if aimed at ensuring the peaceful unification of the country. Whenever the Soviets discuss regional security problems with the United States, he said, they put forward "the Korean issue" with increasing emphasis.[27]

It was Vladimir D. Tikhomirov, a member of the Soviet Academy of Social Science, however, who disclosed the most comprehensive Moscow view of the Korean question. He began by reminding the audience of Gorbachev's Vladivostok address and especially of Gorbachev's indication that the Korean Peninsula was a "crisis zone" that needed to be normalized without delay. He noted that without this normalization, it would be impossible to translate the ideas of Asian Pacific security into action. According to Gorbachev, the Korean problem is one of ensuring security and achieving reunification. These two things are connected, in Gorbachev's words, "dialectically and organically, since the creation of a single Korea would naturally remove the tension along with the potential possibility of a conflict (not only regional but also global, considering the high degree of the great power involvement in the Korean situation). In turn, the normalization of the situation in and around the Peninsula would noticeably speed up advancement toward national reunification." What attracts one's attention here is Gorbachev's departure from the North Korean position, which asserts reunification before anything else. He went on to say that it is important to achieve reunification, but that, because this is not yet feasible, guaranteeing security and easing tension are more important.

Having reiterated Gorbachev's position, Tikhomirov, too, stressed Soviet support for the North Korean unification formula and its demand for the withdrawal of U.S. troops. Moreover, Tikhomirov seemed to be sympathetic to North Korea's proposal of "tripartite talks," which the Soviet Union formerly was reluctant to accept. Pointing out that the starting point of any confederative system is, in fact, the coexistence of two states in a single political structure, with the sovereignty of each state belonging to it intact, Tikhomirov asserted that the North Korean confederation formula means—whether North Korea likes it or not—the recognition of two Korean states, which emerged in 1948. Drawing attention to the South's full diplomatic relations with 128 countries and the North's with 99, to the desire of both Koreas to become UN members, and to both Koreas' membership in various international organizations, Tikhomirov also asserted that both Koreas should not overlook the increasing importance of constructive efforts that unite Asian and Pacific states. In this context, relations between socialist countries and South Korea seem to be significant, he concluded. In short, according to Tikhomirov, whatever economic relations the Soviet Union has with South Korea are in accordance with Gorbachev's policy as outlined in his speech at Krasnoyarsk on September 18, 1988.

In that speech, Gorbachev stressed the importance of the economic advancement of the Soviet Far East and of expanding Soviet cooperation with all Asian and Pacific countries. He also noted that opportunities for economic ties with South Korea might become available given an overall improvement on the Korean Peninsula. According to the Soviets, Moscow–Seoul ties were being pursued because the recognition of South Korea by socialist countries will substantially improve the political climate in the region, will contribute to the materialization of the confederation formula on the Korean Peninsula (thus turning truce into peace), and will assist the ongoing North–South Korean dialogue.[28] From Tikhomirov's statements, it is clear that he in theory supports the North Korean confederation formula. In practice, however, Tikhomirov seemed to find the South Korean and UN policies more rational and much closer to the Soviet Asian Pacific security policy, although he did not said so explicitly.

Last, Vladlen A. Martynov, the director of the Institute of World Economy and International Relations, who was in Seoul for a week in October 1989 in accordance with an invitation by the Reunification Democratic Party (RDP), issued a joint statement with the RDP. This statement confirms what Tikhomirov said, that is, that relations between the ROK and the Soviet Union, which were greatly promoted by the visit, will play an important role in the eventual normalization of state-to-state relations in the near future.[29] In Tokyo, Georgy Kunadze, one of the delegates of the Soviet World Economics and International Relations Institute (IMEMO) and its Japan section chief, was reported as saying that the Soviet Union should not exercise its veto power if South Korea applies for unilateral entry to the United Nations.[30]

The statements made by the Soviet visitors tell of the dramatic change of Soviet policy toward the Korean Peninsula. Whether or not this change is the result of uncertain relations between the USSR and Japan, a more positive Soviet attitude toward the ROK is dramatic all the same.

The way that North Korea perceives these changes is interesting because North Korea has always feared the unilateral entry of the ROK—or even the bilateral entry of the two Koreas—into the UN, believing that this would perpetuate the division of Korea. North Korea refused to toe the Soviet line, although asked to do so by Gorbachev himself in talks with Kim Il-Sung. Nothing short of the withdrawal of U.S. troops could persuade Kim Il-Sung to abandon his worn-out policy toward the Korean Peninsula. It is possible, however, that the improvement of relations between the ROK and the Soviet Union could become a moderating influence on China's attitude toward South Korea's entrance to the United Nations. Yet China will never think of establishing full diplomatic relations with South Korea unless Seoul breaks relations with Taiwan. The agreement to establish diplomatic relations between South Korea and the Soviet Union, however, will very likely shift North Korean diplomacy away from the USSR toward China. The strongest variable could be a change in North Korean leadership. As long as Kim Il-Sung's leadership continues, North Korea will deplore the new Soviet diplomatic relations with the ROK.

Notes

1. Michael Mandelbaum, "Ending the Cold War," *Foreign Affairs* 68, no. 2 (Spring 1989): 16–36.

2. Zbigniew Brzezinski, "Ending the Cold War," *Washington Quarterly* 12, no. 4 (Autumn 1989): 29–34.

3. Mandelbaum, "Ending the Cold War," 22.

4. "Kremlin Assails Its Afghan Role," *International Herald Tribune,* October 24, 1989.

5. "Moscow's New Olive Branch," *International Herald Tribune,* October 27, 1989.

6. "East Bloc Countries Renounce Brezhnev Doctrine," the *Korea Herald,* October 29, 1989.

7. "World Can Move Beyond Cold War: Baker," the *Korea Herald,* October 25, 1989.

8. G. Arbatov, "New Political Thinking and the Soviet Foreign Policy in the Asian Pacific Region," Paper presented at the International Conference of the Institute of Social Sciences, Seoul, South Korea, September 11, 1989.

9. Guy Dinmore, "Asian Communists Worried by Eastern Europe," the *Korea Herald,* October 28, 1989.

10. Park Pong-Shik, "North Korea's Non-Alignment Movement," *Pukhanhakpo,* no. 7 (Journal of North Korean Studies): 171–191.

11. For more on Kim's visit to Beijing, see *Chosum Ilbo* and *Kyunghyang Shinmun,* September 18, 1982.

12. *New Chinese Yearbook for 1984* (Japanese Version), 54.

13. "North Korea's Open-Door Policy," *Sekai Suko* (World's Weekly), September 3, 1985.

14. See *Naewoet'ongshin,* no. 32 (July 1–December 31, 1985): 164–177.

15. Ibid., 190–197.

16. "The Meaning of North Korea Leaning to Russia," *Korea Hyaron* (Korea Review), September 1988.

17. *Naewoe Press,* no. 30 (July 1–December 31, 1984): 223–225.

18. *Naewoe Press,* no. 31 (January 1–June 30, 1985): 101–104.

19. *Naewoe Press,* no. 34 (July 1–December 31, 1986): 125–128.

20. Ibid., 179–188.

21. *Naewoe Press,* no. 37, pp. 129–132.

22. "The Visit of Shevardnadze to North Korea," *Naewoe Press,* no. 621 (December 30, 1988).

23. *Naewoe Press,* no. 657 (September 15, 1989).

24. Ibid.

25. "Gorbachev in Cuba: Hard Sell for Tough Customer," *International Herald Tribune,* April 3, 1989.

26. Mikhail Kapitsa, "Changing East–West Relations and the Situation in the Asian Pacific Region: A Soviet Evaluation," Paper presented at the Seoul Olympiad Anniversary Conference, Seoul, South Korea, September 12–16, 1989.

27. Arbatov, "New Political Thinking."

28. Vladimir D. Tikhomirov, "Security and the National Reunification of Korea are Vital Factors of Forming One World Beyond All Barriers: A Soviet Scholar's Point of View," Paper presented at the Seoul Olympiad Anniversary Conference held in Seoul, South Korea, September 12–16, 1989.

29. "RDP, IMEMO Blazing Trail for Seoul-Moscow Dialogue: Gist of Joint Statement," the *Korea Herald,* October 29, 1989.

30. "USSR Should Not Exercise Veto in ROK's UN Entry: Soviet Scholar Bares in an Interview," the *Korea Herald,* October 29, 1989.

PART TWO

The Context for Arms Reduction

5

The Balance of Power in the Western Pacific

Thomas H. Moorer

The stunning reverses that have rocked European communism in 1989 have yet to be reflected in most other areas of the world. Indeed, three of the four Communist states in the western Pacific—the USSR, North Korea, and the PRC—actually increased their offensive military capabilities in 1989, and the fourth (Vietnam) retains the world's fourth largest military force. There are also indications that any thoughts of political reform that may have lurked beneath the surface in Pyongyang or Hanoi, let alone in Beijing, are now in limbo following the Chinese crackdown at Tiananmen Square.

In assessing the current Communist security threat to the Pacific Basin democracies, and especially to South Korea, we have no choice but to address this situation as it currently exists. In looking further ahead—as defense planners must—it is important to speculate on how the current level of threat may evolve in the 1990s. Is Asian communism as solid politically as it is militarily? If not, can the United States prudently project a substantial retrenchment of its Pacific forces?

My answer to both of these questions is "no." This assessment is based on three crucial dynamics now at work, which are likely to prevail into the next century. These are the steady expansion of U.S. interests in the Pacific region, the technological explosion and its implications for the survival of communism as a system of government, and the total unpredictability of Soviet success in developing an alternative system.

The Dynamics of Change

U.S. Interests. The United States is at least as much a Pacific nation as it is an Atlantic nation. There are many good reasons for this. The Pacific Ocean occupies about 50 percent of the earth's surface. Many of the Pacific nations are located on islands or peninsulas and are thus heavily dependent on sea transport. Seven of the largest armies in the world exist in countries that border the Pacific and Indian Oceans. More than one-half of the world's population resides in these countries. U.S. trade in the Pacific has exceeded trade in the Atlantic for the past 17 years. This trade has increased by 50 percent in the past four years and is expected to double by the year 2000. In short, the national interests of the United States converge with those of its friends and allies—as well as those who choose not to be its friends—in the western Pacific. So, it is clear that despite what some may advocate, the United States has no intention of taking any action that would alter the balance of power that has resulted in the security and stability the United States enjoys today.

New Technologies. A second very important factor is the technological explosion that is occurring today, especially in the information and communications fields, including global access to television. Today, television is a key instrument used to form public attitudes in both democratic and authoritarian societies. Television has facilitated public access to political campaigns, entertainment, even advertising in developing countries. As a result, these citizens are now able to observe events worldwide as they happen, such as the turmoil in Tiananmen Square. They can now see, at about the same time, disasters in places as far apart as San Francisco and China. Millions of people are now able, through television, to discern their own disadvantage in terms of political freedom or a depressed standard of living and begin to clamor for the good things in life. Incoming television broadcasts via satellite, for example, have begun to create so much dissatisfaction in the outlying areas of the Soviet Union that the Soviets are attempting to jam select programs.

Aiding in the downturn of communism in the Soviet Union and Eastern Europe have been the globalization of television and the advent of *glasnost.* This should not have come as a surprise. In addition, communism has failed to provide an adequate food supply, failed to afford freedom for its people, and failed to lead in world trade. Because of the increasing flow of information, however, those people living under communism now know this and will not turn back.

The Uncertain Soviet Future

Gorbachev has been slow to take the arms reduction actions that he has promised. No movement of forces has been seen. Although he removed Soviet forces from Afghanistan, he is still delivering large quantities of materiel to his supporters in Kabul. Although agreeing to reduce inventories of the large SS–18 missile, the Soviets have nevertheless continued to develop a replacement missile with 25 percent more damage effect. In general, Soviet foreign policy under Gorbachev has not changed.

Internally, Gorbachev has witnessed demonstrations throughout the nation. He has been forced to use poison gas against some of the dissenters in Georgia, and he has 90 million Moslems to contend with in the south. Throughout all this, the Soviet economy has gotten worse.

The entire world is standing by hoping that the changes occurring under Gorbachev mean peace and stability. In my view, Gorbachev's chances of success are small and receding. No man, least of all a long-committed Marxist, can effectively convert a Communist economy into one of free enterprise. Some have likened this to a country trying to switch gradually from driving on the left hand side of the road to the right. What will be the final outcome? Some analysts say that Yegor Ligachev will take over and that Gorbachev will be thrown out. Others foresee a revolution of dissidents, led by Gorbachev himself.

Whatever the outcome in the Soviet Union, it is already clear that the dimensions of military power in Europe, the perceptions of threat in that region, and the entire postwar security structure are in a process of profound reorientation. It would be dangerously naive, however, to assume that this process will ensure peace in Europe or an enduring moderation of Soviet global strategy. There remains a lethal blend of paranoia and expansionism in Soviet leadership circles, backed up by a state-of-the-art military establishment. Like the United States, the USSR has vital security interests and the ability to pursue them militarily in both great oceans.

The Continuing Soviet Threat

It is important to discuss this uncertain future because the final outcome will have a profound effect on the balance of power in the western Pacific. It is clear that the Soviet role in the Asian Pacific during the next decade depends both on internal changes in the USSR and on the way the other powers will react to domestic Soviet change.

Within the Communist nations, political strength is based on military power. Naturally, the Soviet Union's Far Eastern forces constitute a very formidable threat. From a command and control point of view, the Soviets are organized to fight in three separate areas: central Europe, southern Eurasia, and the Far East. Although central control is maintained in Moscow, the area commanders are delegated authority to act independently. (This probably accounts for the action taken against the Korean Air Lines flight 007.) The Soviets have continued to build their forces in the Far East. Those forces are viewed by the Soviets as secondary in importance only to those in the European theater. The three regional commanders make their plans based on a single unified national military strategy, centrally developed and controlled by the general staff in Moscow. Although the Soviets claim that their forces are developed primarily for defense, the capabilities of their naval, air, and missile forces deployed in the Far Eastern theater far surpass the levels needed for defensive purposes.

Worldwide, the Soviets have given the highest priority to the maintenance and modernization of strategic forces. These include the land-based intercontinental ballistic missile (ICBM) forces, ballistic missile submarines, and strategic aviation assets, which are located throughout the Far Eastern theater. Research and development efforts continue to improve these forces. The SS–18, which is the newest ICBM and the most effective, is now being replaced by an even more effective weapon, which can strike any Asian nation. Although the details of strategic missile force modernization will not be examined in detail here, suffice it to say that the Soviets are now placing emphasis on road-mobile and rail-mobile weapons, as well as silo-based weapons.

Next, the Soviets have the world's largest submarine missile force. They have made major improvements in their submarines, as well as in the missiles they carry. Soviet efforts have been directed at making submarines much quieter and, hence, more difficult to locate. In the Pacific, these submarine-launched ballistic missiles (SLBMs) patrol the entire area, including the West Coast. Because of their range, some missiles can strike from as far as the Sea of Japan, the Sea of Okhotsk, and the Bering Sea, where protection is guaranteed by the Soviet Far Eastern air and naval forces.

Next, there is Soviet strategic aviation: The TU–95 Bear bomber is armed with air-to-surface missiles, as is the improved Bear frame, which is armed with AS–15 long-range missiles. Soviet pilots are normally trained in conducting simulated strike missions and, on occasion, have flown within 50 miles of the Alaskan coast. The Soviet air army comprises nearly 20 percent of the bombers and fighter-bombers assigned to strategic aviation, and it functions as the "deep strike" component of Soviet nuclear forces. The Backfire bomber, which is the most modern Soviet bomber, is currently replacing the TU–16. The Soviets' newest long-range bomber, the Blackjack, will soon be deployed and is capable of low-altitude penetrations with its missiles and bombs. For all practical purposes, there has been no effect on the real capabilities of the Soviet strategic forces as a result of the INF Treaty.

The Soviet Pacific fleet is headquartered at Vladivostok and constitutes the primary means of power projection throughout the Pacific Ocean. It is the largest of Moscow's four fleets and comprises 30 percent of the total Soviet navy. Included in this fleet are two of the three Soviet Kiev-class aircraft carriers. These carriers carry the Yak–38 vertical takeoff fighter aircraft, as well as antisubmarine warfare (ASW) helicopters.

Ninety-eight attack cruise missiles and auxiliary submarines are operated by the Soviet Pacific Fleet. These submarines not only have an excellent capability in both antisubmarine and antisurface warfare, but also employ state-of-the-art technology, reduced propulsion noise levels, high speeds, and advanced weaponry. The buildup of the Soviet navy's strategic and tactical nuclear-powered submarine force since the mid-1960s has been relentless. About one-third of their submarine force is in the Pacific.

Soviet naval aviation has a large number of land-based aircraft, in addition to the aircraft based on the Kiev-class carriers. Their mission is to conduct antiship strikes, although ASW maritime reconnaissance and ground attack in support of amphibious forces are also key missions.

In addition, the Pacific Fleet's contingent of Soviet naval infantry (SNI) is the largest in the navy. An SNI division with approximately 7,000 personnel is based near Vladivostok. This division is armed with PT–76 amphibious tanks, armored personnel carriers, and self-propelled howitzers. The Helix–B combat helicopter is currently entering service with the navy and could be used with naval infantry in the Pacific. It could also be deployed among several helicopter-capable combatants.

Next, Soviet ground forces have experienced improvements in both readiness and reliability for the past 20 years. Existing units have grown, and new units have been formed. The number of divisions assigned to the Far East has increased from 25 in 1968 to 57 deployed today. The majority of these divisions, including four in Mongolia, are deployed along the Sino–Soviet border, with the remainder located in coastal regions. The Soviet equipment is extensive for ground troops, with respect to the number of tanks and armored personnel carriers, as well as several thousand artillery pieces.

Soviet air forces of the military districts, which are in addition to the strategic forces already mentioned, include about 1,200 first class fighters and fighter-bombers, as well as full capability with respect to reconnaissance aircraft, electronic countermeasure aircraft, and helicopters for special missions. The fighters, of course, are used specifically for air defense and are equipped with improved air-intercept radar with look-down-shoot-down capability, as well as multiple-target tracking, infrared search and track, and laser ranging.

In total, the Soviet regional force deployed in the western Pacific is technically superior to most of the countries in the region, both in numerical strength, which is more than adequate for defensive purposes, and in force projection capability, which is well-equipped to conduct offensive operations. Viewed in relation to the other large forces deployed in central Europe, it is clear that the Soviets are ready for a sustained, two-front regional confrontation. This two-front capability may be significantly enhanced, but is nonetheless sometimes reduced by the shifting relationships of the Soviets with North Korea, Vietnam, the PRC, and Japan. Each of these relationships will be discussed in turn.

North Korea's isolation from international affairs under the leadership of Kim Il-Sung has been almost complete. This isolation could be seen in the refusal of the Soviet Union, the PRC, and the principal Warsaw Pact countries to join North Korea's boycott of the 1988 Seoul Olympics. Small wonder that North Korea has few supporters: They have mismanaged their economy, they have a history of unpaid loans, and, under Kim Il-Sung's direction, they have engaged in a single-minded pursuit of reunification by force.

North Korea has attempted to ally itself with both Beijing and Moscow, although it is now tilting toward Moscow. Following Kim Il-Sung's visits to Moscow in May 1984 and October 1986, North Korea received economic, military, and technical aid from Moscow. The Soviets have been willing to serve North Korea's economic and military needs, undoubtedly to counter the PRC's and the United States' influence in the region. The North Koreans have been receiving MiG 23 aircraft since May 1985. The SA–3 (enough to equip several battalions) arrived later. In 1987, the Soviets provided SA–5 Gammon surface-to-air missiles, together with the associated radar, and SU–25 ground attack fighters. The Soviet and North Korean navies have conducted combined exercises and port calls.

Soviet aircraft, in turn, have been granted permission to overfly the Korean Peninsula and the Yellow Sea during these missions. Soviet aircraft conduct reconnaissance of the Republic of Korea, Okinawa, and the PRC and carry out simulated missile strikes. Overflying the Korean Peninsula cuts hundreds of miles from the transit distance between the Soviet Union and Soviet bases at Cam Ranh Bay in Vietnam. Beijing and Moscow are clearly willing to sidestep North Korea and pursue their own economic interests in Seoul, and this may offer opportunities for further discussion between North and South Korea. This, however, will probably be more easily done after Kim Il-Sung departs the scene.

Moscow's other Asian supporter, Vietnam, is proving to be an expensive liability and has become increasingly hostile toward Gorbachev's reform efforts. Vietnam, Laos, and Kampuchea remain solvent only through the infusion of more than $1 billion annually in economic assistance from the Soviet Union and the Warsaw Pact. The withdrawal of Vietnamese forces from Kampuchea should cause some reduction in this obligation, but it is nevertheless a burden. The major benefit of this relationship flows from Soviet access to Cam Ranh Bay—one of the finest ports in the southwestern Pacific. Use of this facility enables the Soviets to extend their oversight to the strategic Malacca Straits area, as well as to the Indian Ocean, where the Soviets have base rights in some eight additional countries. The Soviets are fully mindful of the dependence of many in the western Pacific on the constant flow of oil through the Malacca Straits. Because of the Soviets' initial access to Cam Ranh Bay, which the United States spent more than $1 billion developing, the Soviets now have the largest naval base outside the USSR. Here, they operate reconnaissance aircraft, air defense fighters, ASW patrol aircraft, and ships of all types—all aimed at providing reconnaissance and, if need be, control of this vital Southeast Asian area. Gorbachev has suggested that he would be willing to give up this base if the United States would leave the Philippines, but that appears unlikely.

Japan and the Soviet Union have had a running battle in public relations. Last year, a Japanese poll indicated that the Soviet Union is the most hated nation in the Pacific area. Recently, a number of factors have added to the sensitivity of Soviet–Japanese relations. These include the Toshiba scandal, the export of high technology, the Japanese exposure of Soviet espionage, and Tokyo's willingness to contribute to Strategic Defense Initiative (SDI) research and development. In turn, the Soviets have overflown the island of Okinawa, and their aircraft and weapons have threatened Japan. Perhaps the primary obstacle to improved Soviet–Japanese relations, however, is the issue of the Northern Territories—several Japanese islands occupied by the Soviet Union since World War II. These islands, in effect, guard the entrance to the Sea of Okhotsk, where the Soviets operate several of their long-range, missile-firing submarines. Thus, the Soviets must move toward solving the Northern Territories problem before relations with Japan can be normalized.

Finally, in the South Pacific, the Soviets have been diplomatically active in several islands, ostensibly to gain fishing rights. It is no coincidence that these islands lie squarely across the sea-lanes between the United States and Australia.

The emphasis here on the Soviet threat in the Western Pacific region may seem an anachronism in the current environment of blossoming East–West dialogue and incipient superpower retrenchment. That emphasis is impelled by the realities of the military power in place and the pervasive and perhaps deepening uncertainty about the future course of events in the Soviet world. Power in uncertain hands is the classic formula for violence. There are, however, other threats to peace in the region. In the context of Northeast Asia, these are presented chiefly by North Korea itself, but China and Vietnam also pose potential trouble.

Non-Soviet Threats in the Western Pacific

Before the Tiananmen Square massacre in June 1989, euphoria about the decline of communism in Europe generated optimism about similar trends in North Korea, China, and Indochina, as well as the decline of Communist insurgency elsewhere in the Pacific region. It is now acknowledged that such optimism was premature. Whatever the future may hold for the long-term survival of communism outside Europe, it seems clear that Tiananmen provided an abeyance for Communist hard-liners from the pressures of reform. Although these hard-liners may pursue more flexible economic strategies, they appear committed to political authoritarianism.

It remains to be seen, however, what impact these changes will have on external adventurism. There is indeed some evidence of new rigidity in Pyongyang toward South Korean overtures and in Beijing toward Taiwan and Hong Kong. Both Beijing and Hanoi appear resistant to a democratic solution in Kampuchea, although for opposing reasons. These more rigid Communist approaches are likely to soften over time so that more pressing economic needs may be addressed.

North Korea

North Korea's population is half the size of the ROK's 40 million, and its gross national product (GNP) is about one-fourth that of the ROK. It has about 1 million personnel in its armed forces compared with 630,000 in South Korea. The North, to maintain forces at this level, devotes 20 to 25 percent of its GNP to its military organization. In contrast, the Republic of Korea uses a little more than 5 percent of its GNP for military purposes. Seoul has opted to build a strong defensive posture, which is dependent on technology and U.S. treaty commitments rather than numbers. Its demographics and economic base, however, could support a significant expansion of the armed forces if necessary.

North Korean ground forces are well equipped and trained, and many are forward deployed. The North Korean army has a substantial numerical advantage of at least 2:1 in tanks, long-range field artillery, armored personnel carriers, multiple rocket launchers, and antiaircraft systems. The

North has the ability to introduce about 222,500 personnel by air or sea to impede South Korean mobilization or other vital defense efforts.

North Korea's numerical air advantage is partially offset by a more modern South Korean air force. The North's acquisition of MiG 23 and MiG 29 fighters and some surface-to-air missiles from the Soviet Union has enhanced the North's air defense capability, but its overall relative position compared with the ROK remains essentially unchanged because of the recent South Korean acquisition of F–16 Falcons.

North Korea's navy holds an advantage in submarines and fast attack patrol boats. Recent frigate and corvette production has enhanced South Korea's naval forces, but the North still holds an advantage in overall numbers.

Natural resolve to defend the homeland is strong on both sides. Neither shows signs of decreasing dependence on its military forces. Although North Korea has significant logistics stockpiles, these are offset somewhat by the South's superior transportation infrastructure, manufacturing capability, and ready access to the ocean for resupply.

In view of the above comparison, it is my view that the military balance on the Korean Peninsula continues to favor North Korea in terms of raw numbers. U.S. treaty commitments, the strength of the ROK defense position, the size and potential of the ROK economy, the professionalism of the ROK's armed forces and the sheer South Korean population advantage, however, would make any North Korean attack a very difficult and doubtful operation.

The People's Republic of China

The world's most populous nation—a nuclear power with more than 3 million people occupying the geographic center of the western Pacific Rim—is inevitably a major factor in the regional security equation. The PRC effectively canalizes Soviet Pacific access to a less-than-ideal northern corridor and port complex, ties down large Soviet forces on its northern and eastern frontiers, threatens the nation of Taiwan, supports the Khmer Rouge in Kampuchea, and exerts a destabilizing political influence in the rest of Southeast Asia.

It would be wrong to assume that the PRC presents an active threat to South Korea, however. Prior to Tiananmen, Chinese officials often expressed frustration about their lack of influence in Pyongyang. Following Tiananmen, they probably have more influence in Pyongyang—if only because of Soviet vacillation—but there is no evidence to suggest that the Chinese are encouraging Kim Il-Sung's reunification strategy. To Beijing, the potential role of South Korea, Japan, and the United States in China's economic modernization is far too important to risk complicity with North Korea, which has little strategic value to China.

The current U.S. strategy of seeking to neutralize China as a destabilizing factor in the region should be continued. On the other hand, renewed U.S. support of PRC force modernization should be weighed with care and be consonant with changes in the levels of Soviet threat.

Vietnam

With about 3.5 million active and reserve personnel with recent combat experience and sophisticated hardware, Vietnam's force represents a constant threat to peace and democracy in Indochina and to the sea-lanes in the Indian Ocean. In the latter context, of course, continued Soviet naval and air access to Vietnamese bases is particularly disquieting.

On the other hand, Vietnam remains one of the world's poorest countries, sustained largely by Soviet aid, which may soon disappear. Like China, Vietnam desperately needs Western aid, trade, and technology. As these dynamics take hold, a continuing accommodation with the Soviets at Cam Ranh Bay will become a liability to Hanoi, as will a massive Vietnamese military establishment. The Western strategy should be to sustain pressure on Vietnam until the Soviets depart and Vietnam is substantially demilitarized.

Allied Forces

United States

The United States is, of course, the dominant non-Communist military power in the Pacific and the only one capable of projecting force to all parts of the region. It is likely that the United States will sustain this essential capability indefinitely. Numbers, hardware, and deployment will inevitably evolve in consonance with changes in budgets, technology, and threat, but the United States will continue to defend its vital interests in the region, including its alliance commitments. As the declining military threat in Europe raises popular hopes for a peace dividend, it also frees U.S. military forces for contingencies elsewhere. South Korea is high on the U.S. contingency list and will remain so until its vulnerability is eased by the power shift on the peninsula. In the context of an agreed outcome for Korea, the number of U.S. ground troops deployed there is, in military terms, a purely tactical judgment. The commitment is backed, in effect, by U.S. forces everywhere—ground, sea, and air.

The U.S. alliance with South Korea benefits, albeit indirectly, from other U.S. alliances in the region. The U.S. alliance with Japan permits forces dedicated to the Korean contingency to be stationed in, and staged from, the Japanese islands and Okinawa. Alliances with the Philippines, Australia, and Thailand enhance the security of ROK maritime links to South Asia, Africa, the Middle East, and Europe. With the possible exception of the Philippines, there is no cause to question the integrity of the alliances. They were forged to confront commonly perceived threats, they have worked to contain those threats, and they should endure. Indeed, there is sufficient reason for these cross-alliances among the six democracies involved—perhaps to include others—to develop into a multilateral mutual security arrangement.

Japan

The U.S.–Japan Mutual Security Alliance is still very much in force. The Japanese Self-Defense Force is meeting its security goals and has increased expenditures for defense more than 5 percent every year for several years. The Japanese should do more, particularly in the fields of ASW and air defense, however. As mentioned earlier, the Soviet threat to the sea-lanes and the particular Soviet ability to interdict the flow of oil requires the maximum amount of allied antisubmarine strength all the way to the Malacca Straits. To their credit, the Japanese realize that they should do more to bear the cost of maintaining adequate air and submarine defenses in the western Pacific. It would not, however, be in the interest of stability in the western Pacific for the Japanese to develop forces for power projection.

South Korea

With a consistent steady growth in defense capabilities and a growing economy, the Republic of Korea is well on its way to becoming a regional power. Both the United States and South Korea have reaffirmed that a U.S. presence today is still required on the peninsula, although there are those in both countries who think otherwise. In any event, the Republic of Korea should assume a greater defense responsibility, and the United States should certainly remain a staunch ally.

In the interest of long-range stability, the Republic of Korea should continue its efforts to hold discussions with the North Koreans, difficult as that might be. Progress toward reunification, if it comes, will come slowly and must be managed with caution. North Korea is plagued by severe economic, social, and political failures. As has happened in the case of the Soviet Union, the state of the North Korean economy—which is a disaster—will ultimately cause the North Koreans to be more receptive to discussions.

The Philippines

Despite the opposition in the Philippines to the maintenance of U.S. bases, this access is still needed. The current arrangement runs until 1991, and further discussions are under way. The benefit in terms of cash flow to the Philippines is significant, as is the security afforded the Philippines. Not only that, the investment climate would deteriorate significantly if there were a U.S. withdrawal, thus seriously damaging the economy and the standard of living in the Philippines. There is little doubt that these friends of the United States in the Pacific area understand and support the need for continued U.S. basing rights to ensure regional stability.

In view of the Soviets' strong presence in Cam Ranh Bay, the departure of U.S. forces from the Philippines would seriously upset the balance of power in the western Pacific. Corazon Aquino has recently completed her second trip to Washington. She has stated publicly that she is keeping her options open. Many are convinced that President Aquino is predisposed toward a continued U.S. presence in the Philippines if an agreement can be reached. This is in spite of the heavy opposition she will encounter in the Philippine Senate.

Conclusion

First, despite political and economic chaos throughout the Soviet Empire, the Soviet military threat to the Pacific area has not declined. Unless and until it does, U.S. military capabilities in the region related to that threat should remain in place. In addition, the North Korean threat to the ROK has not declined, although it assuredly will before 2000. In the meantime, any change in U.S. force deployments in or near South Korea should be weighed with great caution. The U.S. stake in a secure, prosperous Pacific Basin is rising, not falling. Any degradation of U.S. Pacific forces to a level insufficient to sustain that security is unthinkable.

The military balance in East Asia will always present a complex, evolving picture that defies comparison with other regions of the world, such as Europe. East Asia lacks a clearly delineated border separating two well-defined alliances and political blocs, such as is evident between NATO and the Warsaw Pact. It is not an insular geographic area like Africa or South America. There is no central command structure that coordinates the strengths of all allies. Rather, the western Pacific features the confluence of the world's two military superpowers, the United States and the Soviet Union, at their closest point; an emerging military superpower that is now a less predictable member of the community of nations, the People's Republic of China; an international economic superpower, Japan; and a highly militarized border between North and South Korea. These conditions form the backdrop for a host of regional economic, political, and military developments that demand the close attention of all allies in the western Pacific. Any review of the military balance in East Asia should be made with an appreciation of the complex geographical, historical, cultural, and political fabric.

6

The Military Balance
on the Korean Peninsula

Oh Kwan-Chi

Peace has remained fragile on the Korean Peninsula for more than 30 years since the signing of the cease-fire and the tenuous armistice. Despite direct and indirect economic exchanges and preliminary talks between South and North Korea at various levels in several areas, North Korea has not shown any sign of abandoning its scheme to communize South Korea, either by force or by subversion. To accomplish this objective, the North has wasted no time in building up its military forces during the past two decades at the expense of economic development and the welfare of its people.

Thus, it is rather surprising to find some scholars arguing that the arms race between the North and South was triggered by South Korean actions.[1] According to this hypothesis, however, the arms race on the Korean Peninsula was started when the North responded to a military buildup by South Korea—its force improvement program of the early 1970s. This argument, however, is faulty. North Korea first devised a military strategy known as "four great military lines" in December 1962 and then began to drastically increase military expenditures in 1964. Its defense budget rose from 1.9 percent of the total North Korean budget in 1963 to 5.8 percent in 1964, while the average ratio of defense budget to the nation's budget during the period of 1967–1971 increased to 31.2 percent. This published defense budget formed only 17 percent of the nation's budget in 1974 and thereafter, but this decrease did not mean a true reduction of defense spending. Rather, it meant only that North Korea hid some of its defense spending under other categories to feint reducing military expenditures after the South–North joint communique of July 4, 1972. There can be little doubt that the North has maintained the same relative share of defense expenditure in the nation's budget throughout the 1970s and 1980s.

Confronted with an ever-increasing threat from the North, South Korea has had little choice but to build its military forces, particularly after the United States started to withdraw the Seventh Infantry Division from South Korea in 1971 and stopped providing military aid in 1974. Under the Nixon Doctrine, the United States also began offering arms transfers as a substitute for the involvement of its own troops. Consequently, South Korea began feeling vulnerable to a potential attack from the North because it felt it could no longer expect timely military support from the United States.

Today there exists a military imbalance that favors the North. This military superiority provides North Korea with a range of choices that has allowed North Korea to launch a series of terrorist attacks against the South, the latest being the bombing of KAL 858. In this chapter, the North Korean defense industry will be surveyed. Then, an assessment of the present military balance between the South and North will follow. Finally, the military balance of the 1990s will be examined.

The North Korean Defense Industry

North Korea has developed its defense industry with the aim of becoming self-sufficient. Until the early 1960s, the North had to rely on military assistance and the importation of weapons to refurbish its almost-decimated forces. After the successful completion of its first five-year economic plan (1957–1960), North Korea seemed to succeed in paving the way for the development of heavy industry. Thus, in conjunction with the "four great military lines" of 1962, the North began to accelerate development of its defense industry.

Because of heavy investment, the North Korean defense industry began to produce simple arms in the late 1960s and increasingly sophisticated ones in the 1970s and 1980s. Thus, by the end of 1970s, the North was able to produce basic arms in large quantity: 152-millimeter (mm) towed field artillery pieces; 107-mm rocket launchers; 37-mm antiaircraft guns; BM–11 multiple rocket launchers (a variant of the Soviet BM–21); M–1973 armored personnel carriers (a variant of the PRC type m351); T–54/55/62 main battle tanks; several varieties of self-propelled artillery systems, followed by more technically difficult SA–7 surface-to-air missiles; and AT–3 Sagger antitank guided missiles. With the 1980s came two more improved self-propelled artillery systems, 240-mm self-propelled rocket launchers, M–1985 light tanks, self-propelled antiaircraft weapons with onboard radar, and the fielding of Scud–B surface-to-surface missile variants, as well as naval combatants.

In short, the North Korean defense industry developed into a matured arms production facility, providing self-sufficiency in improved and modernized weaponry for ground and naval forces. Although North Korea is still inadequate in developing high-technology systems, it has compensated more than adequately by producing a range of more basic systems in high volume.[2] There is little doubt that North Korea will continue its efforts to develop advanced weapon systems in the future. Table 6.1 shows North Korea's major weapon acquisition by source.

Table 6.1 North Korean Weapons Acquisition

Late 1960s	Early 1970s	Mid-1970s	Late 1970s	Early 1980s	Mid-1980s	Late 1980s
AN-2 Colt (C)	SU-7 Fitter (S)	I28 light bomber (C)	SA-7 (S) (K)			SU-25 Frogfoot (S)
MiG 21 (S)	F-6 Farmer (MiG 19) (C)	YAK-18 (C)		F-7 (MiG 21) (C)	MiG 23 Flogger (S)	MiG 29 Fulcrun (S)
AN-24 (S)	FROG-3/5 (S)	FROG-7 (S)		SPATG 85/100-mm (K)	SA-2 MOD SAM (S)	Scud-B (K)
MI-8 (S)	BM-21 MRL (S)	AT-1 Snapper ATGM (S)	AT-3 Sagger (K)	SPATGM (K)	SA-3 SAM (S)	SA-5 SAM (S)
MiG 17	BL-11 MRL (K)	RPG-7 (S) (K)	MI-4 (S)	MI-2 (S)	Hughes 500 helicopter (U)	MI-17 helicopter (S)
122-mm M-30 HOW (K)	152-mm D-20 G/H (K)	M-1974 SP 152-mm G/H (K)	M-1977 SP 122-mm HOW (K)	M-1971 SP 122-mm FG (K)	M-1975 SP 100-mm FG (K)	
130-mm M-46 FG (K)	37-mm AAMG (K)	M-1975 SP 130-mm FG (K)	M-1978 SP 170/180-mm FG (K)	SP 37-mm AA (K)		
107-mm RL (C)	107-mm RL (K)	K-61 TRK amphibious (K)		SP 107-mm RL (K)	SP 240-mm RL (K)	

(continues)

Table 6.1 *(continued)*

Late 1960s	Early 1970s	Mid- 1970s	Late 1970s	Early 1980s	Mid- 1980s	Late 1980s
	PT-76 (S) light tank			M-1985 light tank (K)		
	T-54/55 medium tank (S)	T-54/55/ 59 medium tank (K)	T-62 medium tank (K)			
	T-59 medium tank (C)					
	Type 62 light tank (C)					
	BTR- 60/152 APC (S)					
	Type 531 APC (C)					
	M-1973 APC (K)	S-60 AAA (K)		SP 14.5- mm AA (K)	S 57-mm AAA (K)	SPAA radar (K)

Note: C=People's Republic of China; S=Soviet Union; U=United States; K=North Korea.
Source: Robert H. Coffin, Jr.

The Military Balance

Since the early 1970s, in pursuing its military strategies, North Korea has started to build its armed forces in conjunction with expanding its arms production capability. Thus, major growth in numbers of weapons and force units began to emerge in the early 1970s and more conspicuous growth occurred thereafter. Table 6.2 shows the military balance as of the end of 1988.

The North Korean military buildup is the result of incremental changes since the early 1970s. Statistics for the 1970s indicate a relatively steady growth in major units, although strength figures appear to lag behind substantially. Annual assessments for the 1980s show significant changes in the force structure of major North Korean ground units, indicating a reorientation of force tactics. The scale-down of infantry divisions, the concurrent emergence of mechanized corps with motorized brigades, and the eventual reemergence of several infantry divisions all indicate that a series of select infantry divisions were used to form the new mechanized forces. Then, as new equipment and personnel became available, the infantry division themselves were reformed.[3]

Table 6.2 The Military Balance: North and South Korea, 1988

Force/Weapon Category	North Korea	South Korea
Total Armed Forces		
Active	980,000	650,000
Reserves	7,000,000	4,500,000
Ground Forces		
Infantry Division	29	21
Mechanized Infantry Division	--	2
Armored Division	1	--
Motorized Infantry Division	1	--
Reserve Infantry Division	23	25
Subtotal	54	48
Infantry Brigade	2	NA
Mechanized Infantry Brigade	23	NA
Armored Brigade	14	NA
Special Brigade	22	NA
Subtotal	61	15
Equipment		
Main battle tank	3,500	1,500
APC	1,960	1,550
Artillery	9,000	4,000
Towed	3,700	3,760
SP	2,800	100
MRLS	2,500	140
Mortar	11,000	5,300
Helicopters	170	314
Naval Forces		
Submarines	24	--
Destroyers	--	10
Frigates	2	18
Missile Craft	30	11
Patrol Combatant	106	94
Torpedo Craft	173	--
Amphibious Craft	126	52
Fire Support Craft	66	--
Other	117	115
Subtotal	644	300

(continues)

Table 6.2 *(continued)*

Force/Weapon Category	North Korea	South Korea
Air Forces		
Bombers	83	--
Attackers	30	23
Fighters	707	457
Support Aircraft	780	690
Subtotal	1,600	1,170

Note: NA indicates that the information is not available.
Source: The Ministry of National Defense, *The Defense White Paper 1989* and TISS, *The Military Balance 1988–1989.*

Concurrent with the massive increase in regular forces in the 1980s, a major restructuring of the reserve forces also occurred. Central to this restructuring was the emergence of military district commands, one per province with possibly others in special (and highly populated) administrative districts. Although the command structure of these military districts remains nebulous, they appear to be composed of three types of reserve elements and some regular force units in a coastal defense mode. With each county and city unit responsible for raising at least a brigade-sized reserve unit, a minimum force of 227 brigades is suggested, albeit of various combat, combat support, and combat service support natures. The three types of reservist can probably be graded as first-, second-, and third-line forces with the top level being "instructional units," the second line being "worker peasant guard" militia forces, and the third line, the "red youth guard."

Instructional units would be composed of the most fit young reservists (i.e., those most recently discharged from active duty service). Reportedly, they could be mobilized in 12 to 24 hours. They may number more than 500,000 and probably represent the frequently cited 23 reserve divisions figure. The worker–peasant red guard forces are essentially territorial militia that would defend local areas in an organized manner and would include all reasonably fit personnel older than 18. They number in excess of 4.8 million and would provide not only rear-area security in staggering number, but could also play a significant role in rear service support activity for regular forces. The red youth guard represents a pool of 700,000 or more men and women with some basic military training at the elementary and middle school levels. Typically younger than 18, they would also be the personnel pool base from which would be drawn long-term draftees or augmentation for the regular draft. Initial regular force augmentation, however, would more likely come from the veteran elements in the instructional units.

As the regular army forces expanded massively in size and number with the infusion of equipment in the 1970s, so too did the reserve units in the 1980s—in great part because of the large number of older weapons phased out of the regular forces. What had been a trickle down of equipment became a small torrent by the late 1970s and early 1980s. Although no reliable figures exist to enumerate exact numbers and types of equipment passed to the reserves, an assessment of 60 percent of the 1970 army inventory would not seem excessive, taking into account the wear-and-tear factor, maintenance and cannibalization, rigorous controls, and turnover levels among regular forces. Small arms, including machine guns, likely exist for all reserve force units.

Creation of the military district commands, whose function in wartime would appear to be the defense of the homeland from attack, allowed North Korean force planners to shift regular forces forward toward the demilitarized zone (DMZ). Reportedly, 65 percent of North Korean ground forces are now within 50–75 miles of the DMZ (likely south of the Pyongyang–Wonsan Expressway). With the establishment of such substantial reserve forces, the majority of the remaining 35 percent of the regular forces could also be committed to the offensive in wartime.[4]

From Table 6.2 some of most noteworthy characteristics of the North Korean forces are immediately identifiable. First, North Korea has attained an absolute superiority over the South in mechanized and artillery force. North Korea has duly paid respect to the theory of firepower: Defensive forces can be neutralized by either destroying the units or making it impossible for them to place attacking units under accurate fire. To materialize this theory, one needs the constant ability to deliver accurate and voluminous fire on enemy positions by either artillery bombardments or air strikes or a combination of both. Because North Korea lacks air wings tactically disposed to providing close air support (CAS), the burden of generating the requisite firepower has fallen on the artillery.[5]

Artillery forces have one distinct advantage over CAS: They can provide all-weather fire support to maneuver units, while the effectiveness of CAS degrades quickly under limited visibility and inclement weather. Furthermore, air support can be very costly if the enemy deploys a well-coordinated air defense system. With regard to the air defense capability of its ground forces, North Korea seems to have deployed a more than an adequate—if not impenetrable—level.

North Korea has enhanced its artillery firepower in five ways: fielding more artillery pieces, developing long-range weapons, creating a saturation ability, limiting counterbattery effectiveness, and procuring weapons of mass destruction. North Korea fielded more than 3,000 artillery pieces by 1978, with an increase to 4,000 by 1981, some of which were indigenously produced. In addition, 1,900 multiple-launched rocket systems (MLRS) were fielded. Enlargement of the artillery force has continued throughout the 1980s as shown in Table 6.2. Total artillery pieces now number 9,000, of which more than 2,800 are self-propelled and 2,500 are MLRS. The overwhelming superiority of artillery forces in quantity and range of its artillery forces will enable the North to concentrate tremendous firepower on the attack corridor.

North Korea has deployed more than 1,000 artillery pieces forward within 5–10 kilometers of the DMZ. These pieces, which are dug into tunnels in the mountains, can fire upon defense positions without exposure to air attack or counterbattery fire. The offensive capability of the North Korean ground forces has been enormously enhanced by its self-propelled artillery. Needless to say, these self-propelled artillery forces can provide continuous fire support to maneuvering units even under direct and indirect enemy fire. This is possible because of cross-country capability, armor protection, and a quick firing response. Therefore, it is mandatory for maneuver forces, such as mechanized infantry divisions or armored brigades, to be equipped with self-propelled artillery.

North Korea's main offensive forces are mechanized forces comprising 23 mechanized infantry brigades, 14 armored brigades, and 1 armored division supported by self-propelled artillery and ground attackers. These forces, together with motorized infantry units, form four mechanized and one armored corps. Thus, these corps will be used to break through deep defense positions as the second and third echelons of attacking forces. Heightened force mobility through mechanization promises greater maneuverability and flexibility in moving rapidly through dangerous areas and exploiting advantages in depth. The creation of more, but smaller and more compact, mechanized infantry brigades and armored brigades further enhances the overall maneuverability of the ground forces, which are faced with difficult terrain.

Note also that North Korea recently acquired the advanced ground attacker to augment the already existing fleet of SU–7s. These attackers will provide deep fire support to the rapidly advancing mechanized forces. Thus, North Korea has developed very powerful combined-arms offensive forces that can launch a massive attack at a stunning speed.

Second, North Korea maintains a disproportionately large special operations forces. In developing its offensive forces, the North Korean force planners must have taken the terrain feature into consideration. Because terrain poses so many difficulties to an attacker, the planners were forced to focus on how to overcome the terrain—and possibly use it to their benefit.

The terrain, which is restrictive and canalizing under the most propitious circumstances, has become steadily more difficult to traverse: Multiple lines of defense, extensive barrier systems, hardened fortifications, and lethal "kill zones" have been created; population growth and the creeping spread of developed areas have further reduced traversability.

Consequently, several approaches have been considered, implemented, and factored again, resulting in more comprehensive plans. One approach was the already-discussed "mobility solution," that is, mechanizing main offensive ground forces in more, but smaller and more compact, combined arms brigades.

A more innovative solution, however, was forming the special operations forces comprising light infantry, ranger, or commando types of forces. They are designed to create havoc, disrupt communications, obstruct the movement of reserves, and attack air bases and other military and civilian facilities. It is estimated that North Korea has about 100,000 such special operations forces arrayed either in the special elite commando corps, as brigades subordinate to conventional corps, or within each ground force division.

North Korea has developed several means of inserting a magnitude of several thousand special operations forces into the rear of the South at the onset of hostilities. One method is though tunnels under the DMZ. A multitude of tunnels, capable of allowing the passage of thousands of light infantry troops per hour, were begun in the late 1960s. It is believed that many of these tunnels are completed, awaiting only final instructions to blow out southern terminals allowing troops to exit. Furthermore, the North, to amplify the capabilities of the huge special operations forces, opted to acquire airborne means of insertion, namely AN–23s and helicopters. In addition, the North, as a third means, has taken advantage of the waters surrounding the peninsula and developed an amphibious raid capability. Although not all special operations forces could be employed, several thousand thus inserted could create a "second front" that would disrupt command and control, interrupt the logistical flow, and create panic among the population.

Third, North Korea has developed chemical agents and is known to maintain a stock of several hundred tons of chemical agents.[6] A multitude of basic artillery systems in North Korea's inventory can deliver chemical rounds. No doubt the BM–11 MLRS is most effective when used with a chemical capacity, as would be the longer-ranged 54 FROG–3/5/7 surface-to-surface missile systems when mounted with chemical warheads. The recently fielded 15 Scud–B surface-to-surface missile systems add a new dimension to the potential for mass destruction when paired with chemical warheads.

It would be anybody's guess how the chemical weapon would be used. There are at least three possibilities: the first possibility is to use chemical weapons to intimidate South Korea and the United States into giving up tactical nuclear attack when North Korea invades, the second is to use chemical weapons quickly to neutralize the defensive forces covering the key terrain along main avenues of approach, and the final possibility is to use chemical weapons to develop a favorable situation when the initial attack reaches a deadlock.

Of the three possibilities listed above, the second seems the most likely, that is, North Korea would use chemical weapons to destroy defensive forces among main avenues of approach to speed up the advance of attacking forces. North Korea may calculate that the ROK or the United States will limit nuclear attack targets to solely military ones, particularly those featuring concentrated North Korean forces. In this case, the best tactic for the North would be to advance rapidly toward Seoul with the aid of chemical weapons. If North Korea employs this tactic, it would likely fail to offer any profitable targets for a nuclear attack.

Fourth, North Korea has built an old but very capable submarine fleet composed of 24 Romeo and Whiskey class submarines. It is considered capable of blockading the southeast sea-lanes and major ports, at least initially. There is no question of the critical importance of the southeast sea-lanes through which war materials, as well as commercial goods, are shipped. Thus, the southeast sea-lanes are strategic vulnerabilities to the South.

Finally, North Korea has built a numerically superior air force since the cease-fire. It is truly remarkable to observe how the North has reconstructed its air force from total destruction. Not only is the numerical superiority worrying, so too is the ever-improving quality of its air force. The recent introduction of MiG 19s and SU–25s seems to completely counterbalance the one-time qualitative advantage of South Korea's air force.

Some of the most noteworthy characteristics of the North Korean armed forces have been reviewed. To better assess the military balance, however, it is necessary to develop a standard unit as a method of comparison. To facilitate this conversion, ground forces were grouped into infantry, mechanized, and nondivisional artillery forces; naval forces were divided into surface and underwater combatants. Table 6.3 shows the North and South military balance thus converted.

Table 6.3 clearly indicates that there exists a military imbalance between North and South. The North attains an overwhelming advantage in both mechanized and nondivisional artillery forces: the force ratio 4.8 to 1 in the former and 4 to 1 in the latter. In air and naval forces, North Korea is also at an advantage. All this indicates that North Korea could be tempted to launch a massive surprise attack against the South if circumstances permit.

The increased mobility of maneuver units coupled with the mass destruction capability of artillery firepower seems to support the strategic perception of the ability to wage a fast-moving war of less than two weeks' duration. What North Korean military superiority implies can be better depicted by making a comparison with the force balance between Germany and the Allies just before the German attack on France in May 1940.

Table 6.3 The Military Balance (standard unit equivalent)

Force Category	Standard Unit	North Korea	South Korea	Force Ratio
Ground Forces				
Infantry	Infantry Division (ROK)	55	46	1.2
Mechanized	Mechanized Infantry Division	22	4.5	4.8
Nondivisional				
Artillery	155-mm Howitzer (T) Battalion (ROK)	160	40	4.0
Naval Forces				
Surface	Destroyer	74	57	1.3
Underwater	Submarine	24	--	--
Air Forces	F-16	345	219	1.6

Source: Korean Institute for Defense Analysis.

It is striking to note that Germany had an advantage over the Allies only in mechanized forces and air power as shown in Table 6.4. Germany made the best use of its advantage in these forces by employing better strategy than the Allies. Consequently, Germany defeated the Allies in France in 23 days, which surprised both sides. Although better leadership, tactics, quality of equipment, and achievement of surprise must be taken into consideration, the decisive factor in Germany's victory may have been its superiority in mechanized and air forces.

The present military imbalance on the Korean Peninsula is far greater than what existed in Western Europe on the eve of World War II. Germany appeared inferior in total forces, although it enjoyed an advantage in mechanized and air forces, whereas North Korea enjoys a far greater superiority not only in mechanized and air forces, but also in artillery forces, as well as total forces. If the campaigns of the Western theater in 1940 were studied carefully, many valuable lessons could be directly applied to the current situation on the Korean Peninsula.

Table 6.4 Force Comparisons: Germans vs. Allies and North Korea vs. South Korea

Force Category	Germany	Allies	Force Ratio Germany/ Allies	Force Ratio N. Korea/ S. Korea
Armed Forces	2,460,000	3,000,000	0.82	1.51
Infantry Divisions	104	140	0.74	1.20
Mechanized Divisions	19	3	6.33	4.89
Mechanized Infantry Divisions	(9)	(3)		
Armored Divisions	(10)	--		
Tanks	2,576	3,600	0.72	2.33
Artillery Pieces	7,700	12,200	0.63	2.25
Aircraft	3,500	1,700	2.05	1.58

Sources: Trever N. Dupuy, *Understanding War* (New York: Pargon House Publishers, 1987), 93–94; Barry R. Posen, *The Sources of Military Doctrine* (Ithaca, N.Y.: Cornell University Press, 1984), 83–84.

The Military Balance in the 1990s

Estimating the future military balance of South and North Korea is difficult. In this chapter, however, an estimate was developed. GNP growth rates of South Korea were assumed to be in the range of 6 to 7 percent per year for the period 1990–2005, and those of the North were assumed to be 3 percent per year. The South was estimated to be spending 4.5 percent of GNP on defense, of which military investments form 30–35 percent; the North was estimated as spending 21.5 percent of GNP on defense, of which military investments form 35–45 percent. In addition, estimations of threat and force costs were made, based on past trends and published data. Under these assumptions, an estimate of the military balance was made as shown in Table 6.5.

Suppose that the estimates in Table 6.5 indicate at least a broad range of the future developments. Then, the following observations can be made.

- The military imbalance on the peninsula will be remedied very slowly. North Korea will maintain its military superiority throughout the 1990s.

• By the year 2000, North Korea's edge will diminish to a level that renders any potential North Korean offensive less successful.
• South Korea will need to introduce high technology weapons to counter the North's advantage in numbers in the early 1990s.
• Any significant troop reduction by the United States in the first half of the 1990s will worsen the military situation unless supplemented by other measures.

Table 6.5 Prospect of the Military Balance 1990–2005*

	1989			1995			2000			2005		
	NK	SK	FR[1]	NK	SK	FR	NK	SK	FR	NK	SK	FR
Ground Forces												
Infantry												
Division	55	46.0	1.2	55	42	1.3	55	38	1.4	55	34	1.6
Mechanized												
Division	22	4.5	4.8	25	9	2.8	27	13	2.1	30	19	1.6
Nondivisional												
Artillery[2]	160	40.0	4.0	180	60	3.0	190	90	2.1	200	130	1.5
Air Forces												
(F-16)	345	219.0	1.6	400	273	1.5	420	327	1.3	450	391	1.2
Naval Forces												
Surface												
(destroyer)	74	57.0	1.3	80	67	1.2	90	77	1.2	100	87	1.2
Submarine	24	--	--	25	6	4.2	26	12	2.2	28	18	1.6

*All figures have been created by the author, based on published data from the past and their attendant trends.
NK=North Korea; SK=South Korea; FR=Force Ratio.
1. Force ratio of North Korea to South Korea.
2. Nondivisional artillery is 155-mm howitzer (T) equivalent.

Conclusion

The military balance on the Korean Peninsula has favored North Korea since the early 1970s. North Korea has never avoided making use of its edge to provoke. Thus, underlying the North Korean acts of provocation on the peninsula and abroad has been its firm belief in its military superiority. Consequently, North Korea had not felt any constraints in plotting provocations as long as they fell short of an outright attack on ROK–U.S. defense forces. Hostilities today on the peninsula are deterred by a binational defense team, the ROK–U.S. Combined Forces Command.

When it comes to the long-term military balance, there is no question that time is on the side of South Korea. South Korea, however, has to cope with

North Korea's military threats at least for another decade. Only at the end of the 1990s is the South likely to free itself from these threats. Thus, the South Korean dilemma is how to maintain the tenuous peace on the peninsula for the coming decade. In addition, there is the significant possibility of a unilateral decision of a U.S. troop reduction, while its defense expenditures must compete with exploding welfare requirements for a slowly growing GNP.

Notes

1. See, for example, See Yang Sung-Chul, "Kookmin Sibo," *Kookmin Ilbo,* February 21, 1989; Ha Yeong-Sun, *A Reappraisal of the Arms Race on the Korean Peninsula* (Seoul: Ingansarang, 1988), especially chapters 6 and 8.

2. Robert H. Coffin, Jr., *North Korea/Fortress in Flux: Implications for the Future from a Force Development Focus,* Paper presented to the Council of ROK–U.S. Security Studies Conference, Seoul, South Korea, 1989, p. 4.

3. Ibid., 9.

4. Ibid., 10.

5. Ibid., 15.

6. Ibid., 17.

7

The Future of ROK–U.S. Military Relations

Cha Young-Koo

Recent progress in the bilateral arms reduction talks between the superpowers and the tremendous changes in Eastern Europe have taken the world by surprise and have ushered in a new era. Despite these global changes, however, the situation in Asia seems to have remained unchanged, at least thus far. Will the military tension on the Korean Peninsula be continued in the 1990s, regardless of these changes? If history is any guide, current waves of peace could be delayed, but not reversed.

In this light, the future of ROK–U.S. security relations will be determined largely by the new global detente and changes in bilateral relations between the ROK and the United States in political and economic fields.

The latest debate on the U.S. forces in South Korea (USFK), which began in 1989, resulted in the Nunn–Warner amendment calling for negotiations between the two governments on the future direction of ROK–U.S. military relations based on the following premises: both governments intend to maintain a strong bilateral military alliance; changes in its terms are possible provided that the present deterrent capability against North Korea is not altered; it is desirable to transform the present role of the USFK into one of support to the South Korean armed forces; the ROK should increase its share of the common defense burden; North Korea's domestic situation and its policies toward the South have not changed; Soviet and North Korean forces continue to exert a strong influence in Northeast Asia; and although it is necessary to respond actively to worldwide changes, certain parts of the present bilateral alliance should be left unaltered. Peace and security in

Northeast Asia can be assured only if both countries accept the foregoing guidelines in mapping out the future of the bilateral relationship.

Ten years after President Carter proposed withdrawing U.S. forces from South Korea, the same issue has again been raised on Capitol Hill. It appears that the new U.S.–Soviet detente, a huge U.S. federal budget deficit, the need to reassess U.S. overseas forces, and a demand for greater burden sharing with allies all signal a fundamental, rather than temporary, change in U.S. global military strategy.

In this light, the major points of recent debates on the USFK can be aptly summarized as follows: First, earlier debate on reducing U.S. troops in South Korea was driven largely by changes in the U.S. military strategy toward the Soviet Union. In contrast, the current debate is primarily an economic one. The declining competitiveness of the U.S. economy requires a reduction in U.S. defense spending, a demand for greater burden sharing among U.S. allies, and a need to solve the friction with its trading partners, including South Korea.

Second, although the past debate was initiated by a unilateral decision made in Washington, without any major changes in Soviet military posture and strategy, the current debate is generated by fundamental changes in both U.S. and Soviet strategic doctrines. Both Washington and Moscow have a compelling interest in reducing military expenditures and the size of their respective forces overseas.

Third, the strategic environment surrounding the Korean Peninsula seems to favor a partial reduction of U.S. troops in South Korea. Whether or not North Korea has really changed is not yet certain, but given the increasing contacts among South Korea, China, and the Soviet Union, as well as the economic superiority of South Korea over the North, the present military imbalance between the two Koreas is less significant than in the past. It also seems obvious that North Korea will have to iron out both domestic and international differences in the near future. In addition, given their respective domestic problems, China and the Soviet Union would hardly welcome a crisis situation on the Korean Peninsula.

Fourth, as mentioned above, the past debate was largely unaffected by the question of anti-Americanism in South Korea. Today, however, anti-Americanism, which emerged in the early 1980s, has spread rapidly and seems to have gained a sympathetic response from many South Koreans. This trend looms large in that it underscores an implicit demand by South Koreans to readjust overall bilateral relations between South Korea and the United States.

According to a recent opinion poll conducted by *Dong-A Ilbo,* the percentage of respondents who expressed a positive attitude toward the United States dropped precipitously during the past five years: 70 percent in 1984, 37.4 percent in 1988, and 30.1 percent in 1989. Those with mixed feelings toward the United States have increased in number: 24 percent in 1984, 33 percent in 1988, and 52 percent in 1989. And those who respond-ed that they "dislike" the United States have increased significantly: 3.3 percent in 1984, 16 percent in 1988, and 12 percent in 1989.[1] At least one explanation for these shifts may be increased popular confidence in South Korea's economic and security situation. It is nevertheless a trend that cannot be ignored by alliance planners.

What does this imply for the current debate about the reduction of U.S. troops in South Korea? Four characteristics bespeak a compelling need to turn attention away from the debate on the appropriate size of the U.S. force in South Korea toward a more deliberative approach in developing a new framework for ROK–U.S. military relations.

A Framework for the ROK–U.S. Military Alliance in 2010

It is extremely difficult to chart a course for the ROK–U.S. military alliance in the year 2010, but here is a possible scenario. By then, Kim Il-Sung will be dead, and the extremely rigid, Stalinist North Korean political system is not likely to survive his passing. If the current political trends in South Korea continue, it is reasonable to expect that a stable South Korean democracy will by then be firmly established. On the military side, North Korea will no longer be deemed a threat to the security of South Korea, and Japan may have emerged as the world's third strongest military power (after the United States and the Soviet Union). The United States may no longer play a dominant leadership role in the West.

Both South and North Korea are likely to obtain cross-recognition from the four major powers in Northeast Asia and will become official members of the United Nations. By then, the level of hostility between the two Koreas will be lessened to one resembling the 1980s relationship between East and West Germany.

Under these circumstances, the ROK–U.S. military alliance will certainly undergo several fundamental changes. The U.S. ground force in South Korea will be reduced to a symbolic level (a few thousand), whereas the U.S. naval force in the Asian Pacific region might be transferred to South Korea and the U.S. Air Force in South Korea transformed into a regional strategic air force. By then, the operational control (OPCON) of the combined force will have already been transferred to South Korea. ROK–U.S. operational cooperation will take a form comparable to the present U.S.–Japanese operational cooperation. The ROK–U.S. Combined Forces Command (CFC) will no longer play the role of a war-fighting headquarters, but of a joint operational coordination headquarters. Staffing of the DMZ will be under the sole jurisdiction of South Korean forces.

The United Nations Command in South Korea will be dismantled, and the present armistice agreement will be replaced by a peace agreement between the two Koreas. At the same time, the ROK–U.S. military relationship will have changed from a tactical partnership to deter a North Korean attack to a strategic partnership to safeguard peace in Northeast Asia, and North Korea will maintain a strategic partnership with the Soviet Union. As military rivalry on the Korean Peninsula is transformed into a peaceful coexistence, military tension and direct confrontation between the two Koreas will be significantly alleviated.

There is not likely to be an ROK–U.S.–Japan military bloc. Military exchanges among them, such as the standardization of weaponry and the interoperability of resources, will likely be expanded, however. To keep U.S. forces in South Korea, South Koreans will have to pay an amount equal to the present level of Japanese defense burden sharing. In addition, inter-dependence among the ROK, the United States, and Japan will deepen in the political, economic, and military fields.

By 2010, both South Korea and the United States will have to plan for a possible crisis situation in Northeast Asia or in the Asian Pacific region. At the same time, to prevent nuclear proliferation in Northeast Asia, both countries should develop preparatory measures against North Korea's acquisition of nuclear weapons.

Also, they must discuss the role of the United States and the nature of the future ROK–U.S. military relationship with regard to the reunification process. As the U.S.–Soviet–Chinese–Japanese–South Korean–North Korean arms control structure is being formed, it will likely follow the present form of conventional arms reduction talks in Europe.

Whether the new ROK–U.S. military relations in 2010 turn out as described above is a matter of conjecture. Yet, as long as such relations are valued, it seems imperative to analyze the present strategic environment surrounding the Korean Peninsula and map out the ROK–U.S. military alliance of the next century.

Issues Affecting Future ROK–U.S. Military Relations

The following issues will effect any forward planning for the ROK–U.S. military partnership:

- If the primary function of U.S. troops in South Korea is to ensure an automatic involvement (tripwire) in the case of war, is it necessary to maintain the present level of 43,000 U.S. troops?

- Is it necessary for the purposes of deterrence to have alleged U.S. tactical nuclear weapons on the Korean Peninsula? In other words, is it not possible to deter an attack from the North with the combined conventional forces of the ROK and the United States?
- Is U.S. operational control over the South Korean armed forces still necessary?
- If the Yongsan U.S. army base located at the center of Seoul—a city of 10 million people—is relocated, which country should pay for the moving costs, and under what plan?
- The United States has played a major role in the defense of South Korea. From now on, should U.S. troops in South Korea play a supplementary role to ROK forces? If this change is inevitable, what is the required level of U.S. troops, and how should the USFK be restructured?
- Should the USFK's mission in the DMZ, including Panmunjom, be continued?
- Should the ROK–U.S. CFC continue to function as the war-fighting headquarters?
- What is the "fair" South Korean share of the defense burden? How should South Korea plan for burden sharing?
- Should the present ROK–U.S. military exercises, including "Team Spirit," be continued?
- Is the USFK an obstacle to the reunification of Korea, or to South and North Korean relations?
- Is it necessary to revise bilateral agreements between South Korea and the United States? Is so, how should they be revised?

Some of the above-mentioned issues have already been examined or negotiated between the two governments; still others are being raised by scholars, by the U.S. Congress, and by radical students in South Korea. Whatever the motives or background behind those issues, it seems necessary to look into each question. It is important to identify underlying factors as well as prospects. One of the most important issues, then, is the nature of change in U.S.–Soviet strategic thinking and its impact on the future of ROK–U.S. military relations.

The strategic meaning of Gorbachev's policy of *perestroika* can be interpreted as an effort to redefine Soviet national interests, thus breaking from the previous ideological belief that Soviet security could only be ensured by domination in the diplomatic field and in the arms race. This change seems to result from a critical self-evaluation by the Soviets, who recognize that even though the past Soviet security policy (based on military power) has achieved its primary goal in a negative sense, it has been achieved with heavy costs to the Soviets, including a spiraling arms race with the West, a further consolidation of the Western alliance, a deepening Sino–Soviet feud, and, most important, a sluggish economy and technological stagnation.[2]

This new strategic thinking by the Soviet Union has been evidenced by a series of arms reduction talks with the United States since the mid-1980s, the normalization of ties with China, and a direct involvement in questions pertaining to the Korean Peninsula. As revealed in his July 1986 Vladivostok speech and the September 1988 Krasnoyarsk speech, Gorbachev's new Asian policy is designed to improve relations with China, induce capital and technological investment by South Korea and Japan in the Soviet Siberian development project, weaken the U.S. naval force and the military alliance between the United States and its allies in the region, increase Soviet military influence on North Korea, and institutionalize a multinational system of cooperation to prevent an accidental war in the region.[3]

It seems only fair to say that Gorbachev's new Asian policy has been quite successful. The Soviet Union not only struck a heavy blow to the U.S.-led alliance system through its own unilateral arms reduction policy, it also established an image as a peacemaker. And, if China continues to suffer from domestic instability and diplomatic atrophy—reflected in the Tiananmen incident of June 1989—Soviet diplomatic influence in the Asian Pacific region is likely to increase in the near future.

On the other hand, it is worth noting that there has been new thinking in U.S. strategic doctrine in response to Soviet initiatives. In the United States, the greatest impetus for change can be found in the economic situation. The United States suffered from a net foreign debt of more than $360 billion in 1987 and is running a chronic trade and federal budget deficit of more than $100 billion annually.[4] It is widely recognized that the status of the United States as the most powerful nation in the world is being rapidly eroded, and many Americans believe that excessive military spending is the chief culprit. To overcome the present economic crisis, a consensus is emerging that the U.S. government should trim its military spending by $300 billion during the next five years and demand greater burden sharing by its allies.

The emergence of new thinking about U.S. strategy is closely connected to the changes in U.S. attitudes toward the Soviet Union. According to a recent U.S. opinion poll, 75 percent of Americans doubt that the Soviet Union would launch a nuclear attack on the United States, and 60 percent believe that an economic threat is more significant than a military threat. Related to this point, 86 percent of the U.S. population believes that excessive military spending has adversely affected the U.S. economy. Given the fact that 84 percent of Americans are opposed to an increase in defense spending, the consensus has become to curtail military spending.[5]

In sum, the majority of Americans believe that the probability of nuclear war with the Soviet Union is very low. They seem to view Gorbachev's reform policies positively, to emphasize the importance of economy and trade, and to oppose any increase in military spending.

In this context of domestic and international change, the United States is likely to opt for a more conciliatory policy vis-a-vis the Soviet Union; the more Americans emphasize economic rather than military power, the greater the role "economic security" will play in U.S. foreign policy. In line with these changes, U.S. military policy is likely to be based on the pursuit of maximizing limited military resources. At present, the United States is working on the development of high-tech weapons, while scrapping many vital programs, including the presence of U.S. overseas military personnel and bases.

In terms of U.S. strategic posture, these changes would entail a shift from the current forward base strategy to long-distance logistics, coupled with improved airborne and sea transportation capability. In practice, this means that U.S. allies will be forced to face either a weakened U.S. commitment or greater burden sharing.[6] New thinking by the United States and the Soviet Union regarding global strategy is likely to affect future ROK–U.S. military relations in several ways.

First, global detente may stir up public opinion in both South Korea and the United States, leading to an eventual withdrawal of the USFK. Indeed, Gorbachev's unilateral arms-reduction policy and his concessions in bilateral arms talks with the United States are desirable for world peace. In the ensuing period of uncertainty, however, it is not clear what the impact of the new detente will be on the Korean Peninsula. People in the Asian Pacific region will have to struggle between the Scylla of an actual military threat and the Charybdis of an expected peaceful atmosphere. Furthermore, the South Korean arms buildup, pursued in the cold war military environment and aimed at achieving a self-defense capability by the early 2000s, is likely to lose popular support in South Korea.

Second, qualitative changes in the framework of the present alliance system in Northeast Asia, following the new U.S.–Soviet detente, will place a heavy defense burden on South Korea. Particularly, the lessened role of the United States and the heightened responsibility of Japan will make South Korea more visible in the emerging regional power balance.

The Asian security system is different from that of Europe in that it is maintained by a bilateral alliance between the United States and its allies in the region. Thus, the emerging alliance system will inevitably entail the replacement of the United States by South Korea as the major power capable of deterring a war on the Korean Peninsula. At the same time, it prescribes that South Korea improve its relations with its neighbors—Japan, China, and the Soviet Union—to strike a strategic balance in Northeast Asia. The 40-

year-old Asian security system is not likely to change easily, but new external elements combined with the above-mentioned domestic factors could jeopardize the security of South Korea if it does not act to ensure a strategic balance.

Third, progress toward a new U.S.–Soviet detente may have a great impact on the future of the USFK. In fact, the USFK has never yet been a topic of discussion between the United States and the Soviet Union in their bilateral talks. Gorbachev's speeches regarding the Asian Pacific region specifically refer to U.S. bases in the Philippines and other foreign military bases in the region. Should there be strategic arms reduction talks in this region—between the Soviet forces in the Far East and U.S. Pacific Fleet, for example—the stationing of U.S. troops in South Korea would become a burning question.

Other important factors determining the future ROK–U.S. military relationship include anti-Americanism in South Korea, prospects for change in North Korea, gradual resolution of the military imbalance between North and South Korea, and South Korea's relations with its northern socialist neighbors.

According to a recent study by *Korea Research,* 94.1 percent of South Koreans believe that the USFK is needed until South Korea develops its own self-defense capability, while a mere 5.9 percent believe that the USFK should leave South Korea immediately. In addition, 80.6 percent believe that conditions will be ripe within the next 10 years for the withdrawal of the USFK. Only 34 percent believe that North Korea would attack the South if the USFK pulls out within the next two or three years, while 51 percent worry about an attack from the North if the USFK pulls out. These data seem to indicate a fundamental change in South Korean attitudes about the deterrent role of the USFK.[7] If the current gap in national power between North and South Korea widens and if South Korea improves its relations with China and the Soviet Union, the number of South Koreans demanding change in the military relationship with the United States is likely to increase.

In addition, political democratization in South Korea is likely to enhance national consciousness among South Koreans. The USFK will no longer aid South Korea in overcoming political instability; rather, it will serve as a deterrent force in a purely military sense. When South Korean military power becomes superior to that of North Korea, the USFK will lose its raison d'etre on the Korean Peninsula. Critical reviews of the role of the USFK are likely to increase as political democratization increases. Accordingly, a readjustment of ROK–U.S. military relations, including the transfer of OPCON and the relocation of Yongsan base, will be greatly affected by the process of political democratization in South Korea.

In regard to the prospect for change in North Korea, there appear to be too many uncertainties to expect a significant change in North Korean behavior in the near future. As is well known, North Korea recently resumed a dialogue with the South and invited several U.S. scholars as a conciliatory gesture. Nevertheless, according to the *Military Balance, 1988—1989* published by the International Institute for Strategic Studies (IISS), in recent years, North Korea increased the number of its ground forces to 1 million and imported state-of-the-art weapons from the Soviet Union, including 14 MiG 29s, 28 Su–25s, and 18 SAM–4 surface-to-air missiles.[8]

North Korea has not ceased its clandestine operations, which induce antigovernment leaders in South Korea to visit Pyongyang. When the South and North Korean talks resumed, for example, there was a North Korean denunciation of the arrest of a South Korean congressman and a female university student named Lim Su-Kyung who visited Pyongyang without South Korean government authorization.

Because change in North Korean policy toward the South is the most important factor shaping ROK–U.S. military relations, it seems only prudent that any change in the present relations between the two countries should take into account the future actions of North Korea.

The Future of U.S. Forces in South Korea

Any discussion about the future of the USFK must include a critical evaluation of both the positive and negative roles of the USFK, as well as possible losses and gains accruing from USFK withdrawal. From a military perspective, the most important function of the USFK is to deter an attack from the North. As long as there is a U.S. tripwire, an invasion from North Korea would, in the end, lead to military intervention by the United States. The USFK's second function is to compensate for the relatively weak combat capability of the South vis-a-vis North Korea. The third role is to prevent nuclear proliferation in the region and reduce the chance that a small-scale conflict between North and South Korea will escalate into a full-scale war.

Under Washington's Northeast Asian military strategy, the USFK has played the role of a balancer, preventing military intervention by China or the Soviet Union in case of a crisis situation on the Korean Peninsula. The presence of the USFK has a political, economic, and psychological aspect as well: It provides psychological comfort by securing social stability and assists in the continued economic growth of South Korea by allowing it to maintain a proper level of defense spending.

Notwithstanding the above-mentioned positive roles of the USFK, one cannot discount its negative effects: providing ample ammunition for North Korean political propaganda, striking a severe blow at South Korean national pride, increasing the chance of military threat from China or the Soviet Union, and pushing North Korea into closer military relationships with China and the Soviet Union.[9]

What problems can be expected as a result of the reduction of the USFK? Probably the most important issue is filling the deterrence gap. It would take 10 years for South Korea to develop its own deterrence capability according to the ROK government. Japan may not be willing to assume the responsibility of filling the power vacuum on the Korean Peninsula, and South Korea's rapprochement with China and the Soviet Union may not be translated into enhanced deterrence.

Another problem is South Korea's inability to pay for the increased defense spending incurred by the USFK reduction. Also, the USFK's contribution to the stability of Korean society cannot be overlooked. Are there any possible gains arising from the reduction of the USFK? Perhaps anti-Americanism in South Korea and North Korean propaganda will lose much of its usefulness, perhaps debate between South Korea and the United States on the USFK will diminish, and perhaps its reduction will enhance South Korea's diplomatic position in dealing with China and the Soviet Union.

Given the pros and cons of withdrawal listed above, it seems imperative that any reduction plan take into account the difference between possibility and reality, as well as the urgency of policy changes in ROK–U.S. relations. The present debate in the United States on the USFK does not center on a complete withdrawal; rather, it focuses on a partial reduction—from 3,000 to 10,000 troops. The underlying factor in the withdrawal debate is mostly the result of U.S. economic difficulties, which demand greater burden sharing by U.S. allies and a reduced U.S. role overseas. In this light, the long-term policy planning and coordination between South Korea and the United States, which are intended to redefine the role of the USFK and to readjust its size, are the appropriate steps toward developing a sound military relationship between the two countries.

The following issues should be considered in this regard:

- the reduction of the USFK must be linked with the relocation of Yongsan military base, burden sharing, a change in the USFK's role, and the transfer of OPCON, so that both countries can develop a long-term, comprehensive military policy;
- the reduction policy must be used as a bargaining chip in political and military talks between North and South Korea or as an inducement for change in North Korean policy;

- the reduction policy must take into account not only the impact on the military, but also the impact on political, diplomatic, economic, and social conditions on the Korean Peninsula;
- the reduction must proceed in a cautious, gradual way so as not to disrupt the precarious military balance on the peninsula; and
- political leaders of both countries should seize the opportune moment for implementation so that the issue is not politicized in the congresses of both capitals.

In view of the foregoing discussion, 1990 seems to be a good year to begin mutual consultations on the future of the USFK. Three policy options appear to lie ahead.

The first option is to develop a 10-year (1991–2000) reduction plan. During this period, the USFK would be gradually reduced without demanding a corresponding action from North Korea. Notwithstanding the merit of this option, that is, the resolution of the reduction issue in a relatively short period of time, it does not utilize the reduction issue as a bargaining chip in future arms reduction talks between the two Koreas. Also, during the transition period, North Korean leaders may initiate an attack on the South while the military balance is still in their favor.

The second option is for both South Korea and the United States to work on the reduction plan and its means of implementation until 1995. Then, a certain portion of the USFK could be reduced between 1996 and 2000. This option delays the resolution of the reduction issue, thus avoiding a dramatic solution. Yet, avoiding the reduction issue would continue to be a source of irritation in both Seoul and Washington, and South Korea would have to bear a greater share of the defense burden during this period.

The third option is to develop two consecutive reduction plans: a first five-year plan (1992–1996) and a second five-year plan (1997–2001). During the first five-year plan, a gradual reduction of the USFK would be carried out bilaterally by the United States and South Korea, while the implementation of the second plan would hinge upon changes in North Korea as a result of arms reduction talks. This third option is a compromise of the first two options. The third option recognizes the eventual resolution of the reduction issue, given the present domestic situations of both countries. Assuming rapid progress in relations between North and South Korea, ROK–U.S. military relations in 2010 are likely to resemble those of U.S.–Japan at present.

Defense Burden Sharing

Recent debates on the readjustment of ROK–U.S. military relations seem to revolve around the questions of which country will pay to what degree for the security of South Korea, and how the defense responsibilities will be shared between South Korea and the United States. From the U.S. perspective, South Korea does not bear a fair share of the defense burden, and it is no secret that many U.S. policymakers equate South Korea with Japan. In the case of Japan, about one-half of total expenditures on U.S. forces in Japan come directly from the government budget, which is largely directed toward the construction of U.S. military facilities and the wages of workers at the U.S. bases.

In 1988, direct costs constituted $2 billion out of a $2.6 billion share by South Korea; indirect costs (facilities, KATUSA, real estate, etc.) comprise as much as 87.5 percent, and the remaining 12.5 percent are direct costs. This claim seems to overlook the differences in each country's budget structure and per capita GNP. For example, although Japanese workers at the U.S. bases get lower salaries compared with their counterparts in the industrial sector, South Korean workers at U.S. bases earn salaries at least two to three times more than ordinary workers. In addition, Japan spends only 1 percent of its GNP for defense annually, while South Korea spends 5 percent.

During President Roh Tae-Woo's recent visit to Washington, he promised to increase South Korea's share of the defense burden. What are the practical problems related to burden sharing that will arise between the two countries? First, with the exception of the Combined Defense Improvement Plan (CDIP)—under which South Korea pays for the costs of stationing the USFK—the status-of-forces agreement (SOFA) does not provide a legal basis for burden sharing. Satisfying an increasing demand for a greater share of the defense burden requires more than temporary, case-by-case solutions. Second, the United States must present clear evidence and make demands that correspond to the current level of South Korean economic development. Piecemeal approaches, such as those made in the past, can be construed as "unfair" by South Koreans. Third, both South Korea and the United States must agree upon the criteria for, and the amount of, burden sharing and take into consideration the future of the USFK and the evolving combined ROK–U.S. defense system.

Conclusion

The 1990s will be an important era of qualitative change in ROK–U.S. military relations. In particular, the well-known Nunn–Warner amendment requires that the Bush administration report to Congress by April 1, 1990, on the results of the ROK–U.S. negotiation on the USFK and burden sharing issues. As a result, the Department of Defense must report to Congress on the following issues: the military balance in Northeast Asia, the force structure of the USFK, role adjustment, South Korea's additional share of the burden, and confidence-building measures in Northeast Asia.

In fact, no easy solution is available for any of the issues outlined above. In the complex geopolitical environment of Northeast Asia, where the diverse interests of the United States, Japan, China, and the Soviet Union are deeply intertwined, a reduced role by the United States may invite increased Soviet influence in the region and a greater security responsibility for Japan. In that case, not only the military balance, but also the peace and stability of the region, will be in jeopardy. As long as North Korea fails to alter its revolutionary attitude toward the South, the symbolic importance of the U.S. ground force in South Korea (as the only combat division of U.S. troops stationed in Asia) should not be underestimated. If the USFK withdraws, the United States must devise a regional deterrence strategy toward the Soviet Union. The United States should also consider that it will be very difficult for Japan to expand its military role in the region because memories of a Japanese military threat are still too vivid for its neighbors—including China, the ASEAN countries, North and South Korea—to allow Japan to assume major military power.

As Gorbachev's active peace offensive and arms reduction policies become sources of dispute among NATO members, so too will Soviet arms reduction policy in the Asian Pacific region have a constraining effect on the ROK–U.S. and U.S.–Japanese alliance systems, especially when it is coupled with Sino–Soviet rapprochement. Because the USFK has been the cornerstone of peace on the Korean Peninsula and is directly related to U.S. national interests in Northeast Asia, both South Korea and the United States must proceed to alter the present ROK–U.S. military relations in a cautious yet steady manner.

Notes

1. *Dong-A Ilbo,* April 1, 1989.
2. Mikhail Gorbachev, *Perestroika: New Thinking for Our Country and the World* (New York: Harper & Row, 1987); Rajan Meron, "New Thinking and Northeast Asian Security," *Problems of Communism* (March–June 1989): 4–5.
3. See Mikhail Gorbachev's speeches in Vladivostok and Krasnoyarsk.
4. *White Paper on the World Economy* (Tokyo: Japanese Economic Planning Board, 1988), 101.
5. D. Yankelovich and R. Smoke, "America's New Thinking," *Foreign Affairs* 67, no. 1 (Fall 1988): 1–18.
6. Fred C. Ikle et al.
7. *Chosun Weekly,* September 17-24, 1989, pp. 40–43.

8. International Institute for Strategic Studies, *Military Balance, 1989–1990* (London: IISS, 1989).

9. Cha Young-Koo, "The ROK–U.S. Military Alliance in the Year 2000." Paper presented at the First ROK/U.S. Defense Forum, Korean Institute for Defense Analysis, Seoul, South Korea, December 13–14, 1988.

8

The Future of ROK–U.S. Security Ties

William J. Taylor, Jr., and Michael J. Mazarr

A Scenario to 1994

It is January 1994. South Korea's president has arrived in Washington to meet with the U.S. president. The two exchange friendly greetings and retire to a private conference to plan the final stages of a radical restructuring of the ROK–U.S. security relationship, a restructuring that has been under way for four years. There are no recriminations on either side; the atmosphere is friendly and cooperative. Both leaders agree on a future vision of the Korean Peninsula, one that is united and free from all foreign military presence. As little as five years ago, that vision would have appeared foolish, but today it is considered only slightly optimistic.

Most of the major barriers to some form of eventual North–South reunification have been overcome. Perhaps recognizing that the continuation of reform in China (more slowly after Tiananmen) and the Soviet Union rendered complete North Korea's alienation from the world, ailing North Korean leader Kim Il-Sung in 1991 finally began to show signs of a true desire for progress on reunification by making two important, successive moves. First, Kim took a step long awaited by Washington: At Panmunjom, he returned the remains of five remaining U.S. MIAs from the Korean War. Second, Kim proposed a daring compromise between the South's strategy of recognizing both Koreas and Pyongyang's preference for immediate unification through confederation. North and South Korea signed a peace treaty in August 1991 and were jointly admitted to the United Nations the same month, but under the status of "divided territories seeking reunification." Both sides have abandoned political propaganda.

Serious negotiations are under way on the potential character of a unified Korea. It is clear that the North's leaders are not willing to surrender power; South Korea's president, however, seems willing to negotiate anyway, and many South Korean analysts express the opinion that, under any unified system the bureaucracy of the North would wither away eventually. Of course, questions of economic and political dominance are proving sticky, but it appears that both sides are at least willing to declare themselves "unified" in the near future while reserving regional authority for existing governments. Proposals under discussion would call for foreign economic, political, and joint sports teams—something from which only the North can benefit and that the South feels would allow it to "moderate" the feelings of many midlevel North Korean officials.

Pyongyang's willingness to talk constructively about reunification is also believed to be a product of its recognition that neither Beijing nor Moscow is likely to finance any assault on the South. The flower of reform, planted gingerly in Moscow in 1985 and in Beijing some years earlier, has now broken into full bloom. After some initial dislocations, the Soviet economy has begun to show signs of a slow, steady upswing, financed in part by newfound foreign investment. China continues to face problems of food distribution, lack of a strong central banking institution, and local politicization, but it has once again begun to grow and attract foreign capital after nearly a five-year hiatus of stagnation after the political crisis of 1989. It is just exiting the first of its three planned stages of development, the "out-from-poverty" stage, and is now entering the drive for "relative prosperity."

Neither China nor the Soviet Union would have anything to gain, and both would have a great deal to lose, in a war on the Korean Peninsula. And if a war did occur, the importance of economic ties between both those Communist giants and South Korea suggests that they might actually be more amenable to a peninsula unified under Seoul's leadership than under the aged, unpredictable, stubborn, and costly (in both arms and regional affection) Kim Il-Sung or his controversial son, Kim Jong-Il.

North Korea's economy has acquired modest but ever-increasing ties with the South since about 1990. Tourist hotels, manufacturing plants, and other joint ventures have slowly been opened throughout the North. Once Pyongyang and Seoul adopted a more encouraging attitude toward such plans, South Korean business executives quickly put together a series of deals. The North has benefited from the convertible currency and improved relations with the United States, Japan, and other regional non-Communist powers. Agreement on the first phase of an arms reduction treaty with the South has helped mute criticisms from Pyongyang's hard-liners, of which many remain. Seoul is achieving one key goal with its near-open-door policy, however: It is opening North Korea, exposing both its citizens and its middle-

and low-level government officials to the freedoms and amenities of life in a capitalist Asian tiger. It has done so during the twilight of Kim Il-Sung's regime, placing his imprimatur on the process as partial insurance against an anti-detente revivalism upon his death.

In some ways, the 1988 Olympics presented an unrealistic picture of politics within South Korea. Nearly every segment of Korean society seemed to band together to ensure that the portrait of their nation painted before the world was a favorable one. Whatever the success of that effort—and it was only a partial success—the post-Olympic competition between government and opposition in Korea proved lively. Most prominent in the opposition are the radical students, who are as ready for concerted political action as ever. Their anti-Americanism is fueled by a revisionist history that blames the United States for the division of the peninsula and by continuing U.S. trade pressures to open Korean markets. In the wake of political reform and new elections, the focus of student protest has shifted from government repression to questions of nationalism and reunification.

The more formal opposition, centered mainly in the National Assembly, became increasingly active after 1988. The lessons of the 1988 presidential election—which left the opposition divided and the Roh government with a majority—were well learned. An ongoing investigation of Chun-era corruption and repression undercut support for the Roh government, although respect remains for Roh personally and many former members of his government. The mere existence of an opposition legislature massively complicates decision making in a country unfamiliar with negotiation and compromise.

Labor unrest still simmers just below the surface of Korean economic life. The average Korean worker has not profited as much as expected from the economic miracle: Many workers still toil in sweatshops—as earlier revealed by the National Broadcasting Company (NBC), whose coverage of the Olympics was deeply resented by many Koreans. In addition, the phenomenon of "rising expectations" became more tangible as economic growth continued. Already unions are demanding pay raises of as much as 30 percent. Union support was critical to the victory of the ROK's president in the 1991 elections.

The U.S. military presence in Korea became more controversial than ever in the wake of 1989 votes in the U.S. Congress to reconsider U.S. military deployments in South Korea. Radical students charged that U.S. units stood literally and figuratively in the way of reunification and called for their removal. Soviet peace offensives in the Far East, beginning with a February 1990 call by Soviet leader Mikhail Gorbachev for a "denuclearized Asia" and the removal of all superpower troops on foreign soil, placed further pressure on the U.S. military presence.

Faced with the inevitability of cuts, the U.S. Department of Defense (DOD) finally responded. In April and August 1990, the DOD, under the terms of the Nunn–Warner amendment to the fiscal year (FY) 1990 Defense Authorization Bill, provided reports to the Congress on the status of U.S. forces in Korea. The reports called for a gradual reduction of U.S. troops—10,000 to be withdrawn by 1992, and all but a tripwire force on the DMZ removed during the following three years. A guarded announcement was also made that stated by January 1, 1992, South Korea would be free of any and all U.S. nuclear weapons, although the DOD would neither confirm nor deny that any had been there to begin with.

To soften the impact of the report, the DOD recommended a series of steps the United States could take to reaffirm its commitment to the security of the South, including provision of advanced weapon systems and the continuation of reconfigured annual exercises. It also consulted with South Korea, China, the Soviet Union, and Japan and managed to secure expressions of support from all four for the phased reduction plan. Today (1994), only a token U.S. tripwire force remains on the DMZ.

The DOD's report was released along with a statement by the U.S. president indicating that the ultimate U.S. and South Korean goal was the reduction of tension on the peninsula, with the long-term goal of reunification and the removal of all foreign troops from Korea's soil. Washington challenged the North to respond to the first of those goals. Anxious to keep the unification talks alive, and perhaps genuinely impressed at U.S. flexibility, in February 1991, North Korea entered serious tripartite negotiations with the South and the United States (the latter in an observer status) on arms reductions on the peninsula. A little more than a year later, in April 1992, an agreement on the reduction of conventional forces in Korea was reached.

Incorporating many lessons from the successful talks on Conventional Armed Forces in Europe (CFE) and some elements of Pyongyang's November 1988 arms control proposal, the agreement contained a number of stipulations. The entire process was to be supervised by a UN inspection team, which would deploy dozens of inspectors to both sides of the border to ensure compliance and the lack of offensive preparations. From May to August 1992, North Korea would withdraw 75 percent of the forces it had deployed within 25 miles of the border and would reduce by 50 percent its slight remaining numerical superiority over the South. From August to December 1992, both sides would reduce from their existing force levels (roughly 800,000 troops each) to 500,000 troops, 1,000 tanks, and 1,500 other armored fighting vehicles. Artillery and aircraft were similarly constrained. By the end of 1993, both sides were to be down to 300,000 troops and 800 tanks; by 1994, to a final level of 250,000 troops and 500 tanks. A wide variety of confidence-building measures were included in the agreement.

Today, in 1994, both sides continue to move active-duty soldiers, sailors, and airmen out of their militaries and into their ever-growing reserves. Each side deploys about 360,000 troops and 850 tanks—numbers that are constantly declining. UN inspection team members report occasional problems in the North—such as World War II-vintage T–34 tanks having only their guns removed and being reclassified as "tractors"—but, when caught, Pyongyang seems willing to compromise.

Japan has emerged as a significant economic, political, and military partner of the United States in Asia. After a series of government scandals beginning in the late 1980s, its ruling party reflects a considerable mix of perspectives. As a result, it has become at once more forthcoming on trade disputes with the United States and less willing to shoulder increased defense expenditures. Indeed, with the announcement of a Soviet–Japanese agreement on the withdrawal of Soviet military units from the Northern Territories, a true appreciation of the magnitude of Gorbachev's reforms appear to be realized in Tokyo, and the Japanese defense budget has grown little if at all since 1991. Precisely because Japan's leadership has become more liberal and restrained its defense spending, Tokyo has managed to increase Japan's pledge to the defense of other regional states, such as South Korea, and yet avoid the expected regional censure.

The U.S. and South Korean presidents emerge from a fruitful, three-hour discussion to announce several new initiatives—most dealing with trade disputes. The new U.S. president, proving to be no prisoner of interest groups, has loosened protectionist measures created by earlier administrations, and U.S. popularity among farmers and the middle class in Korea has been growing significantly as a result. South Korea's leader takes the opportunity to restate the central theme of his December 1992 speech to the Korean National Assembly: a bold challenge to the North to arrive at an acceptable first step toward unification by 1995. The U.S. president announces complete support for the notion and pledges that all U.S. troops would be withdrawn upon completion of such an agreement if so requested by Seoul. The U.S. president also reconfirms the U.S. commitment to Northeast Asian and ROK security, however, and warns any parties intent on "disturbing the path" toward peaceful reunification that U.S. retaliation for such action would be "swift and sure."

Making the Scenario Real

The foregoing portrait of ROK–U.S. security relations—indeed, of the future of the Korean Peninsula—admittedly is quite sanguine. Some would term it unrealistic. The primary contention of this chapter, however, is that such a result is achievable *if* the United States pursues a more flexible policy toward the ROK, *if* the government in Seoul moderates its stance toward the North, and *if* Pyongyang recognizes what is obviously the most promising course for it to follow.

For the United States, bringing about a promising future for ROK–U.S. security relations and U.S. Asian policy more generally requires innovative thinking. In an era of *glasnost* and *perestroika*, it is more apparent than ever that "national security" encompasses far more than military considerations; if it were not so, Beijing and Moscow would have seen far less need for reform. Yet U.S. Asian policy continues to place strongest emphasis on deterring Communist aggression and, apparently, infuriating foreign governments with a continuing stream of demands and threats on trade issues. Something must change.

Washington could take a bold first step toward such change by creating a microcosm for a new Asian policy on the Korean Peninsula. Initiatives are required on at least three issues: U.S. troops and nuclear weapons, trade disputes, and inter-Korean relations.

With regard to U.S. troops, the Defense Department should take advantage of the requirement created by the Nunn–Warner amendment to the Defense Authorization Act for two 1990 reports on the status of U.S. troops in Korea to recommend reductions in troop levels. The reductions need not and should not occur immediately—in fact, they should be implemented over a period of years—but the immediate *announcement* of such a step would help restrain anti-Americanism in South Korea, would respond to Moscow's suddenly subtle Asian diplomacy, and, it is hoped, would impel Seoul to seek arms reductions on the peninsula. Perhaps more to the point, sentiment is growing within the U.S. Congress to reduce the size of U.S. forward deployments worldwide, especially in South Korea. Unless the administration establishes a well-thought-out plan to accomplish that end, it is probable that Congress, under ever-more severe pressures for reduced defense spending, will mandate it in a hasty and counterproductive fashion.

Obviously, the United States must take a number of corresponding steps to ensure that such action is not misinterpreted by North Korea. Objectively, there appears little chance that a reduction of, say, 10,000 U.S. ground troops over two years would be a source of danger. South Korea would almost have matched the military strength of the North by the time U.S. troops leave, Pyongyang has certainly been made aware that neither China nor the Soviet Union would fully support them in a war, and reductions in U.S. troop levels have been accomplished in the past (most recently under the Nixon administration, when the North held a much more sizable military advantage than it does today) without risk of conflict.[1] A critical aspect of deterrence on the Korean Peninsula, however, has been the firm U.S. pledge to come to the defense of the South, and Washington must make clear that a partial troop reduction does not signal a flagging of the U.S. commitment to prevent DPRK subjugation of the South.

When the plan for a partial troop reduction is announced, Washington should declare in the strongest possible terms that South Korea's security is essential to that of Northeast Asia, whose safety is in turn a vital national interest of the United States. Modified annual exercises with South Korea should continue. The Department of Defense should make a detailed review of its reinforcement capacity and, if necessary, acquire additional sealift or airlift to bolster the credibility of a rapid U.S. response. Washington should also attempt to secure pledges of commitment to South Korea's security from other regional powers (i.e., Japan), although this is bound to be controversial.

The case for a partial reduction of U.S. troops in South Korea and possible steps to reaffirm the U.S. commitment to South Korea's security have been discussed in more detail elsewhere. Thus, it is necessary here only to reiterate that the danger lies not in the fact of troop reductions, which are inevitable, but in the manner in which they are accomplished. Careful planning is required to avoid the dangers and fully realize the opportunities of this process.

The second issue the United States must come to terms with in its relationship with Seoul is trade. Although commonly thought of as an "economic" rather than a "security" issue, trade disputes today threaten to undermine several U.S. security alliances in Asia, and a resolution of those disagreements may well be a precondition for continued security ties in several cases. One such case is South Korea: The fires of already growing South Korean nationalism and anti-Americanism are being stoked by U.S. bullying on trade issues. As long as anti-American protests in Korea are confined to students, there may be little danger to the alliance, but trade friction is exactly the spark that could draw the Korean middle-class into the fray. It would be unwise to underestimate the power of student-based protests that draw in segments of Korea's agricultural, labor, and urban business groups; such a coalition brought down the government of Chun Doo-Hwan in the early 1980s.

Washington has a fundamental decision to make. Unfair trade practices by South Korea—and there is no denying that there are many—do not threaten the health of the U.S. economy. Rapidly spreading anti-Americanism in South Korea (and Japan) might, in the long term; it might also serve to undermine U.S. interests in Northeast Asia—the United States' largest regional trading partner—by turning key Asian states against the United States. When the relative advantages and disadvantages of very public, very noisy trade pressure on Seoul are weighed, it appears obvious that the United States ought to adopt a quieter approach. Negotiations on such issues should be done tactfully, behind closed doors, in the interests of both the

United States and the ROK. Such a moderated approach also assumes that, in the long term, the ROK–U.S. trade imbalance will probably work itself out: Demands of the Korean public at large for cheaper food might well lead to diluted agricultural protectionism, and, as South Korea's trade becomes more diversified (especially in terms of exports to Communist nations), its need to export heavily to the United States will also decline.

The third and final issue to be addressed in the ROK–U.S. security relationship involves U.S. policy toward inter-Korean relations. Slowly, subtly, the prospects for some form of long-term reunification are growing. Never since the division of the peninsula have the interests in unification by all parties been so great. Washington must respond to this trend and should make every effort to encourage the reality or appearance of a unified Korea; to do otherwise, or to appear to do otherwise, would at once risk condemnation in Korea and undermine an opportunity of historic proportions.

In July 1988, South Korean President Roh Tae-Woo offered the North perhaps the most ambitious reunification proposals ever, proposals he echoed in October 1988 speeches to the South Korean National Assembly and to the United Nations. Roh announced a six-point "policy on reunification" to encourage trade, cultural, and scientific exchanges, as well as other contacts between the two Koreas. He also pledged to help the North develop its relations with the United States and Japan. In September 1989, Roh called for a much more specific step, one he called the "Korean national community unification formula": a commonwealth governing all of Korea through a Council of Presidents, Council of Ministers, and Council of Representatives.

At first glance, Roh's proposals, similar in form to those of the early 1970s, hardly seem unique. This time around, however, the convergence of a number of factors makes it clear that the current reunification talks between the two Koreas are a significant break with the past. First, economic and political developments in the Republic of Korea have opened South Korean minds to the possibility of rejoining the peninsula. South Korea's dynamic economy has provided the self-confidence to pursue reunification boldly and an inducement to tempt citizens and officials of the North into an accord. Politically, presidential and legislative elections have also bolstered South Korean confidence, and the climate of openness, coupled with rapidly emerging Korean nationalism, has provided a forum for calls for reunification by students, religious groups, and others.

Second, North Korea's economy remains in poor health. Pyongyang desperately needs to improve its economic and diplomatic relations with the outside world, especially in light of South Korea's recent rapprochement with Communist states that culminated in the Roh–Gorbachev agreement of June 6, 1990. Third, as noted above, North Korea's two principal allies, the Soviet Union and China, have dynamic new objectives, and neither wants to pay the economic and political costs of supporting the North in a conflict on the peninsula. Fourth, South Korea has made impressive new business and diplomatic advances to the Communist world, including Eastern Europe, China, and the Soviet Union. These developments are a symptom of the decline of the cold war in Northeast Asia, and they allow Seoul to consider better relations with the North.

The actual form that reunification might take is far from decided. Both sides have proposed solutions modeled roughly on a confederated system, but the timing and details of these ideas differ markedly between Seoul and Pyongyang. Nevertheless, the commitment to peaceful unification of the Korean Peninsula is real—and apparently genuine—on both sides.

These developments create both great opportunities and real dangers for U.S. interests and policy. A significant further improvement of relations on the peninsula, cross-recognition, and North–South rapprochement would have obvious benefits for all parties concerned, benefits mirroring on a smaller scale those of total reunification. Such steps would virtually eliminate regional tension and the role of Korea as a flashpoint for clashes between major powers and would open prospects for significant arms control. Better relations would also create trade opportunities involving both Koreas and outside powers and would reduce the long-term requirement for a large foreign military presence and military or economic aid. Perhaps most important, better relations would answer demands by both Koreas, especially the South, for real progress toward unification.

An overly cautious U.S. approach to reunification could prove disastrous. South Korean students desire progress toward national unification and distrust the United States, and U.S. foot-dragging would further embolden their protests, with detrimental results for South Korean stability as well as U.S.–ROK relations. There are a number of steps Washington could take to demonstrate its flexibility and to promote the reunification process. The gradual reduction of U.S. ground forces in South Korea is one such means. U.S. officials must recognize South Korea as a regional power with its own unique interests, priorities, and policies and one with which it will differ despite its ally status. Most of all, the United States, which is already portrayed by Korean revisionist historians as an interloper in the North–South situation, must not in any way be perceived to oppose the first stirrings of reunification. The reaction among restless South Korean student and labor groups could be ever more violent.

If the requirements to guarantee ROK–U.S. security relations appear daunting to the United States, they are even more so for Seoul. Although Washington sometimes appears pedantic in taking the diplomatic initiative, it has been—and remains—much more flexible on many issues confronting the two Koreas than have been North or South Korea. In part, this is an inevitable product of the luxury afforded by distance and the fact that the immediate territorial integrity of the United States does not hang in the balance. Still, the stated goals of the United States and North and South Korea are the same: regional stability, peace on the Korean Peninsula, and reunification without conflict. The two Koreas have thus far chosen to pursue those goals very cautiously, but geopolitical caution is rapidly becoming an anachronism. Seoul must become bolder and more mutable.

South Korea today stands at the tender junction of development between dependence and independence. It demands treatment as an equal in economic and political meetings with U.S. officials, yet in the same breath insists on trade concessions based on its "developing" status and the continued presence of U.S. military forces to offset its vulnerability. As might be expected, the U.S. government, especially the Congress, has grown frustrated with this stance. If Seoul is not careful, it might end up with the worst position of all: fractured economic and security relations, growing anti-Americanism in South Korea, and anti-Koreanism in the United States.

As is the case with Washington, there are three overriding issues to which Seoul can turn for opportunities to seize the peninsular initiative. None would appreciably threaten its security in the short run, and all would assuredly bolster security in the long run.

Seoul, in consultation with the Department of Defense and other regional actors, should declare its willingness to have 10,000 U.S. ground troops removed gradually between 1990–1991 and 1993. Several South Korean defense officials have already suggested that, by 1991, South Korea will possess 70 percent of the military strength of the North, enough to success-fully defend against an assault. Although roughly 5 percent of that figure is attributable to U.S. forces, by 1991, the way will be opened for the gradual reduction of U.S. ground forces; the increasingly large and competent South Korean ground forces, combined with continued U.S. air and naval support, would remain at or above the 70 percent figure even with the U.S. with-drawal. By the mid-1990s, the South is expected to have sufficient military power to defend and counterattack. Therefore, U.S. troop reductions would not imperil South Korea's security in purely numerical terms.

Second, South Korea should take North Korea's November 1988 arms control proposal as a basis for discussion and establish a truly workable plan for arms reductions on the Korean Peninsula. Pyongyang has repeatedly declared its willingness to engage in such reductions; Seoul could add confidence-building measures of the sort drafted at the Stockholm negoti-ations. A truly realistic arms reduction proposal would undoubtedly garner the approval of all major regional actors and would force the North, in a sense, to show its true hand.

Third and finally, South Korea must take a more flexible approach to relations with the North. Disappointingly, the efforts inaugurated by President Roh Tae-Woo's July 1988 reunification speech have proven less radical in practice than at first promised, if recent actions are any indication. The South Korean government has so thoroughly cracked down on those of its citizens attempting a dialogue with the North that it has not only soured bilateral relations with Pyongyang, it has also garnered a significant dose of international censure for human rights violations as well. Admittedly, the North is proving as intractable as usual in these talks, and it would be wrong to lay much of the blame for the slowed talks on Seoul. Precisely because of the North's historic intransigence, however, the South should take the initiative in pursuing reunification with unprecedented vigor and flexibility.

Seoul has many nonmilitary avenues available. The two capitals remain at odds about the route to reunification: South Korea favors interim steps such as mutual cross-recognition and sponsorship for entry into the United Nations, while the North claims those measures would only institutionalize the division of Korea and favors more elaborate and immediate unification plans. Still, both sides are leaning toward a similar idea—a confederated system in which, for the time being, a "unified" Korea would be governed in two "states," the same sort of general framework proposed by China. There is certainly room for compromise solutions to be proposed, and Seoul ought to do so. It should also gradually repeal those sections of the National Security Law dealing with individual exchanges with the North, instead truly encouraging cultural, sports, and economic exchanges between the two Koreas.

A large part of the motivation underlying Roh Tae-Woo's *nordpolitik* was apparently the desire to expose North Korean middle- and low-level officials and others to the burgeoning, prosperous capitalist societies that surround the North. Indeed, that policy is a sound one, but its goals will never be achieved as long as Seoul, reacting to a perhaps overly enthusiastic interpretation of *nordpolitik* among its citizens, continues to clamp down on anything giving the appearance of sympathy for the North—for example, arresting an artist merely because his antigovernment painting was reproduced in the North. President Roh had it absolutely right in July of 1988: South Korea does want to draw the North out of its geopolitical insularity in the hope that its tangled bureaucracy will wither, but South Korea cannot exempt itself from that process.

Few observers would claim to be able to predict with any accuracy the behavior of North Korea. What could one possibly say about a regime whose greatest recent accomplishment was the construction of a massive hydroelectric dam at enormous cost that produces far more electricity than can be used within the country? Obviously, North Korea remains subject to the apparently arbitrary whims of its leader, Kim Il-Sung, and perhaps increasingly those of his son, Kim Jong-Il, as well.

Unfortunately, all of the ambitious initiatives outlined above could be laid waste by North Korean intransigence. The only hope, ironically, is that North Korea will somehow decide to do exactly what would serve its domestic and international interests best: honestly participate in reducing tensions on the Korean Peninsula (including arms control negotiations) and establish more cordial relations with capitalist powers worldwide. The trouble is that those steps require a tighter integration of North Korea into the community of nations, an outcome Pyongyang has fought for four decades.

It would seem, for example, that an arms reduction treaty calling for ceilings of perhaps 250,000 troops and 1,000 tanks on either side would appear tempting to Kim Il-Sung and his lieutenants. It would save North Korea large sums of money, which could be used to jump-start the country's economy. Moreover, by creating an equal balance, it would also eliminate the feared "crossover point" in the late 1990s when South Korea is expected to overtake the North in military capability. (For that latter reason, of course, arms control is also in Seoul's interest because many analysts have suggested that Pyongyang's fear of the crossover point is so great that they might attack before it occurs.) Northeast Asian history since 1950, however, has demonstrated that it is wrong to assume Pyongyang will do something merely because it appears logical.

Given a relatively equal military balance on the Korean Peninsula, as noted by Korean scholar Ha Young-Sun,

> The crucial question is whether the leadership on either side has such a strong perception of superiority or vulnerability or such an unshakable commitment to the reunification of Korea on its own terms that it is prepared to risk war against a militarily equal foe.[2]

It is today unclear whether Pyongyang is subject to any of those conditions. If it is, all U.S. and South Korean efforts to improve the security of the Korean Peninsula may be for naught; North Korea may neither rationally follow its best interests nor be subject to traditional deterrence. In that case, however, there is nothing Seoul and Washington could do to preserve peace: Both strength and weakness would risk war, and walking the thin line between them may prove neither possible nor desirable. The United States must therefore operate as if Pyongyang calculates its decisions rationally and be prepared if it does not.

In this chapter, the desirable policies that Washington and Seoul must follow to bring about the scenario described at the outset of this chapter have been outlined. It is only fair, then, to do the same for Pyongyang. North

Korea should follow through on its pledge to wind down the foolish propaganda war on the Korean Peninsula; several of its fellow Communists are doing just that in other regional contexts. North Korea should also begin to demonstrate flexibility, honesty, and commitment to reducing tensions with the South and working toward reunification.

Most important, however, North Korea must, like the Soviet Union, combine deeds with words. It could declare an immediate, unilateral removal of a significant proportion of its forces from the DMZ. The DPRK need not fear an attack from the South, which is the ostensible reason for the maintenance of a huge army of 850,000 (one of the most militarized societies in the world). The United States would not support South Korean aggression. Indeed, the United States would use all the nonmilitary resources in its possession to prevent such aggression—even if Seoul desired such a course, a contention for which there is little or no evidence. If a partial withdrawal of U.S. forces becomes necessary, the North could declare unilateral military reductions to match the U.S. cuts. Finally, the North could expand upon its November 8, 1988, arms control proposal (that has gone largely unnoticed in the West), declaring that it would be willing to allow on-site inspections and to subject itself to various forms of confidence-building measures. These steps would provide both South Korea and the United States with real reasons to trust Pyongyang. Trust will remain a precious commodity on the Korean Peninsula until one of the parties involved breaks the deadlock with bold, honest diplomacy.

The general conclusion of this chapter, then, may appear hardly surprising and not terribly reassuring. It is that to establish a lasting and robust peace on the Korean Peninsula, to move toward reunification and toward an end to foreign military presence on Korean soil, all three of the major actors involved must display an unprecedented amount of courage, creativity, and flexibility—courage to overcome past fears, creativity to uncover innovative solutions to decades-old problems, and flexibility to compromise on heretofore absolutist principles and priorities. This is what has always been required, a skeptic might reply; there is no more reason to expect it today than in the past.

Although we would agree with the first part of the argument, our quarrel is with the second. The current period of international relations is the most exciting and promising since 1945. Massive reforms are taking place in Communist societies throughout the world, reforms that have created real doubts whether the traditional authoritarian/bureaucratic Communist state will ever recur. Regional conflicts are being settled everywhere—except, to date, in Korea. Precisely because they are reforming, however, neither the Soviet Union nor China wants to support North Korean adventurism, a fact that creates at least some hope that, as the remaining wild card in Northeast

Asian security, Pyongyang will choose accommodation (if not internal reform) over bellicosity and war.

The U.S. and South Korean goal in the short-term must not be Gorbachev-style reform in the DPRK, for this will simply not be forthcoming anytime soon. Rather, Seoul and Washington must seek—and declare publicly that they seek—actions on the part of the North that prove as conclusively as possible that Pyongyang has abandoned the military option on the peninsula. They must also alert Pyongyang that they are willing to offer diplomatic and trade concessions, along with troop cuts mandated in arms reductions, for such steps. Limited progress on issues such as troop reductions, confidence-building measures, and other military questions is all that can be expected from Pyongyang, but, to a large degree, they are all that is required. In the longer term, the passing of Kim Il-Sung and progress toward reunification will take care of the broader social issues at stake.

Critically, too, one of our major arguments has been that South Korea and the United States do exert influence on the future of regional security. A thoughtful new set of overtures to the North—including reasonable arms reduction proposals, the offer of U.S. troop reductions, and a more malleable policy by Seoul toward supporters of reunification below the DMZ—could provide a critical impetus toward peace. North Korean scholars and diplomats have repeatedly emphasized their desire for South Korea and the United States to take the symbolic "first step." However much that request accommodates the nationalistic pride so often characteristic of Kim Il-Sung's regime, there is no good reason, given the stakes, not to do so, providing that the measures would not endanger South Korea's security.

Washington and Seoul thus possess a unique opportunity to recapture the strategic initiative in Asia and truly put North Korea's intentions to the test. Kim Il-Sung may possess strong reasons to continue a confrontational posture on the Korean Peninsula and to avoid serious discussion on peace and reunification. North Korea may respond badly, or not at all, to more ambitious overtures; however, finding out if Pyongyang is willing to be flexible is the whole object of the attempt. Seoul must recognize that a negative North Korean answer to requests for legitimate steps toward peace would be the best argument possible against any cuts in U.S. military deployments in South Korea.

Notes

1. Several South Korean defense officials have already suggested that by about 1991, South Korea will possess 70 percent of the military strength of the North and that this would be sufficient for "defensive operations." See former Defense Minister Lee Ki-Baek, *Present and Future Security Problems*

of Korea (Washington, D.C.: Center for Strategic and International Studies, 1987) and the statement by former Deputy CINCCFC Sang Hoon-Lee in *Wolkan Choson* 9, no. 8 (August 1988): 251–252, as quoted in Ha Young-Sun, "The Korean Military Balance: Myth and Reality," *ROK–U.S. Security Relations,* William J. Taylor, Jr., Young Koo Cha, John Q. Blodgett, and Michael Mazarr, eds. (Boulder, Colo.: Westview Press, 1989).

   2. Ha Young-Sun, "The Korean Military Balance."

9

Soviet Foreign Policy and Its Implications for Peace and Security in Northeast Asia

Kim Yu-Nam

The Road to Gorbachev

Watching the course of events taking place in the Soviet Union today, one cannot ignore the undeniably important role of ideas in bringing about *izmenemie* (change or alteration). This concept acknowledges that such ideas are brought to bear through the agency of specific persons and groups in society. In terms of social change, the Soviet Union is unique in its successful transformation to an industrialized, urbanized, and educated society; it is one of even fewer large-scale societies to have made such a transformation. The process of that evolution in social change can be simplified into three periods: the pre-industrial period of change, the period of great transformation, and the period of advanced development.[1]

The first period—the pre-industrial phase—extended from the formation of the Muscovite state in the fifteenth century to the third quarter of the nineteenth century. By the end of this period, Russia had acquired many attributes essential to its attainment of rapid development later. Modern knowledge readily entered the country through the *Academiya nauk* (Academy of Sciences) and a system of universities and was disseminated among the elite through a unified language, which was capable of expressing the full range of modern ideas. The government proved able to defend its territory by means of a relatively modern army and to impose its will on its principal neighbors by force when necessary.

The second and most dynamic phase in Russia's social change took place between the late nineteenth century and the early 1950s. During that era, the state changed—first through reform and then through the violent Bolshevik revolution—into an instrument dedicated, above all, to the economic and social transformation of society. The old elite was either absorbed into the new system or eliminated, and a much larger new elite was created in the 1930s through the mobilization of heretofore marginal social groups. Using quasimilitary means, the Communist government, like that of the tsars, shaped the application of new technologies. Thanks to state control, literacy and education were made available through the overall process of development. During this period, sharp differences emerged among political institutions, which in turn fostered rapid change in the Soviet Union, and there was suppression of liberal economic institutions in the country.

The third period was characterized by the post-Stalinist era, especially in the easing of repression and opening of channels of expression. The patterns of forced modernization that contributed to effective change between the late nineteenth century and the mid-twentieth century continued throughout the Brezhnev era and became the chief impediment to further development.[2]

These periods of social change help explain the problems of socio-economic and political change today in the Soviet Union. The challenge facing Gorbachev's policy of *perestroika* is not merely "to get the country moving again." Rather, it is to renew the country so as to assure its ultimate survival—a process that requires fundamental innovations that should have been introduced a generation ago.

With the rise of a new party general secretary in Mikhail Gorbachev, the Soviet Union has shown a greater flexibility and energy in its foreign policy than at any other time in its history. The present Soviet leadership has proven itself more resilient, wise, and macroscopic than its predecessors in the conduct of international affairs.

Perestroika refers to a restructuring of the Soviet Union. In the name of *perestroika,* the Soviet Union is attempting to seize the political initiative within and beyond the socialist commonwealth. Although it appears that the underlying objectives of Soviet foreign policy have changed little, improving the image of the Soviet Union has become an important new aspect of foreign affairs.

Actual change in Soviet foreign policy has been slow to emerge, and its policy processes and objectives remain resistant to major reform. The only change evident to the West has been the foreign policy rhetoric of the Soviet leadership. Most of the recent changes witnessed in Soviet foreign policy (including the June 1990 Roh–Gorbachev rapprochement) have been made in the name of Gorbachev himself or in the name of his new foreign minister, Eduard Shevardnadze, who replaced Andrei Gromyko in July 1985.

Gorbachev has already demonstrated a tenacious bargaining style, which was evident at the the November 1985 Geneva Summit, the Reykjavik Summit of November 1986, the Washington Summit of December 1987, and the Moscow Summit of May–June 1988. At these summit meetings and more recently at Malta (1989) and in Washington (1990), Gorbachev demonstrated his ability to go head-to-head with Presidents Reagan and Bush. Remarks made before the foreign press at these summits portray an openness not seen in past Soviet leadership.

Gorbachev's first four years in office seem to indicate that he has at least minimum control in both domestic and foreign policy areas, which has allowed him to be much more flexible than his predecessors. Gorbachev has been able to replace 9 of 11 (reduced from an original 12) Politburo members with his own men, thus ensuring his control of the powerful political machine in the Kremlin.

Within a month after his rise to the supreme position of power in April 1985, Gorbachev had replaced six Politburo members with his political allies—Secretary Vadim A. Medvedev, Secretary Leksandr N. Yakovlev, Secretary Viktor P. Nikonov, Foreign Minister Eduard A. Shevardnadze, Secretary Nikolai N. Slyun'kov, and Moscow City First Secretary Lev N. Zaikov.

At the 1989 September Plenary Meeting of the Central Committee of the Communist Party of the Soviet Union (CPSU), Gorbachev again reshuffled the Politburo by ousting three members—Secretary Viktor M. Chebrikov, formerly head of the KGB; Ukrainian First Secretary Vladimir V. Shcherbitskiy; and Secretary Viktor P. Nikonov. Two new Politburo members were appointed in their place: Vladimir A. Kryuchkov as head of the KGB and Central Committee member Yuriy D. Maslyukov as head of economic affairs and the Military Industrial Commission. As a result, Premier of the Russian Soviet Federated Socialist Republic (RSFSR) Vitaliy I. Vorotnikov was, until June 1990, the sole survival of the Brezhnev elites, who showed neither a resistance to the Gorbachev reform nor a desire to harm Gorbachev's power base.[3]

As early as the April 1985 Plenary Meeting of the CPSU, Gorbachev asked for a program of radical reform and was given sanction to initiate *perestroika*. Gorbachev formally announced his reform policy at the 27th Party Congress of the CPSU on February 25, 1986. The 27th Party Congress, taking place almost a year after Gorbachev's rise to power, placed the authority of the party's forum behind Gorbachev's policies and leadership.

Three key themes emerged from the Congress as the party's political slogans for the reform policy: *uskorenie* (acceleration), *energiya* (energy), and realizm (realism). The adoption of these three symbols at the Congress clearly distanced the new Soviet leadership from previous policies.

Although the focus of the 27th Congress was primarily on domestic issues, Gorbachev's speech also touched on the question of competition between capitalist and Communist systems and on Soviet relations with the United States. Gorbachev's consistent call for flexibility leads one to sense the transition from an "accelerating, energetic, and realistic" domestic policy to a similar posture in the foreign policy arena. Gorbachev specifically proposed the following overall examination of the international security environment:

The USSR is giving considerable attention to a joint examination, at an international forum as well as within the framework of the Helsinki process, of the world economy's problems and prospects, the interdependence between disarmament and development, and the expansion of trade and scientific and technological cooperation. We feel that in the future it would be important to convene a "World Congress on Problems of Economic Security" at which it would be possible to discuss as a package everything that encumbers world economic relations.[4]

What is strikingly different in this comment is Gorbachev's emphasis on linking international security with economics. In a break with previous Soviet leaders, Gorbachev has explicitly articulated the need to link the USSR's international agenda with its domestic economic condition.

In general, Soviet foreign policy goals and directions—reflected both in the 27th Party Congress of 1986 and two years later in the 19th Party Conference of 1988—have underscored the need for peaceful coexistence, cooperation, and interdependence, based on mutual respect for territorial and political realities, that is, the recognition of the post-World War II status quo in Europe and Asia. The specific foreign policy approach as reported at the 19th Party Conference is as follows:

The foreign policy for *perestroika* relies on a new mode of thinking, one that is consistent and based on research and free from historically hackneyed stereotypes. The new mode of thinking reflects the [practical] realities of the modern world, versatile and controversial as it is, a world that questions the very survival of humanity and yet contains a formidable potential for coexistence, cooperation, and quest for political solutions to urgent issues.[5]

Many in the West question whether such shifts in Soviet thinking are mere tactical maneuvers or more fundamental strategic moves. A study by the U.S. Army Combined Arms Center, notes, however, that there is sufficient reason to believe that "the overall conception of the East–West struggle has not changed the minds of the Soviet leadership."[6] Those who take such an approach, however, do foresee a greater Soviet appreciation of the necessity and opportunity for a flexible shift in shaping subsequent operations.

If, on the other hand, the Soviet Union is taken at face value, then the response by the United States to Soviet flexibility has not been sufficient. The Soviets have complained of this lack of response by the United States to a number of Soviet peace proposals. Among others, Gorbachev's regional collective security proposal for an *Aziatsko-Tikhookeanskiy-Mirnyy S'ezd* (Asian Pacific Peace Conference) made in his July 1986 Vladivostok speech has been ignored.[7] The "seven-point peace proposal" made in Gorbachev's September 1988 Krasnoyarsk speech is another that has failed to elicit a U.S. response.[8]

Point three of the seven-point peace program contained in the 1988 Krasnoyarsk statement, for example, appears to have been aimed at strengthening Soviet security measures in the Asian Pacific region. For the first time, the Soviets specifically suggested that the USSR, China, Japan, North Korea, and South Korea agree to joint security talks with the goal of easing military confrontation in the region and limiting military air and naval activities.

Is *perestroika* merely a respite or *peredyshka* (breathing space)? If it is a state of *peredyshka* to shape subsequent operations, the Soviet "new thinking" is but one manifestation of a deeper crisis within the USSR. Singularly absent in Gorbachev's speeches, however, were the strict requirements for loyalty to Marxist–Leninist teachings, for strict observance of Leninist norms, and for ties based on "socialist internationalism"—all previously acknowledged key factors for the advancement of world socialism.

Today, in 1990, Gorbachev faces daunting new challenges to his leadership—a decline in his personal popularity due to economic distress, violence, and incipient defection in some Soviet republics, and a populist rival in Boris Yeltsin.

Against this confusing background, this chapter will attempt to address Gorbachev's policy of *perestroika* in reference to peace and security in Northeast Asia. It will examine the meaning of *perestroika* and its implications for Northeast Asia, particularly for North and South Korea. Throughout this chapter, however, a constant assumption is made—that is, Gorbachev's Asian initiatives and the Soviet interactions with other major powers in the region hold important implications for the peaceful settlement of a divided Korea.

New Political Thinking and Soviet Military Strategy

At the 27th Party Congress of the CPSU, in March 1986, Gorbachev announced that, henceforth, Soviet military posture would be defensively oriented, and forces would be determined by the principle of "reasonable sufficiency." Although there is no concrete basis for determining the level of sufficiency, trying to set a minimum ceiling on the Soviet force structure is certainly new thinking in the Soviet Union.

According to Gorbachev, Soviet foreign and security policy aspects of *perestroika* are reflections of *novoe politicheskoe myshlenie* (new political thinking). Gorbachev notes that the concepts of "reasonable sufficiency" and a defensive orientation are the result of *novoe politicheskoe myshlenie* and a reorientation of the Soviet approach to international relations.[9] In other words, *novoe politicheskoe myshlenie* is the foreign policy counterpart of the domestic concepts of *perestroika* and *glasnost.*

In Seoul, in 1989, a young Soviet scholar from the Institute of the U.S.A. and Canada noted that the *novoe politicheskoe myshlenie* of Gorbachev is a new approach for solving the problems of mankind:

> It [*novoe politicheskoe myshlenie*] is usually referred to as a concept. I would like to say that it is premature to call it a concept. Up to now it [has been] . . . an approach. [A] concept is usually rather rigid, it has its own mythology, it is unlikely to change soon. [An] approach is flexible, it can be applied creatively—and that's the source of its power . . . . So the main features of new political thinking as an approach to my mind are:
> - the priority of mankind's global human interests over class and national interests;
> - the priority of national interests over class interests and class solidarity concept;
> - pragmatic approaches to all issues;
>   the end of self-isolation from the world community.[10]

The military concept of "reasonable sufficiency" articulated by Gorbachev seems to have gained currency both inside and outside of the Soviet Union. The Kremlin now argues that the rational approach to military security requires a reasonable sufficiency, not a superiority. In the years of the cold war, the Soviet Union engaged in the arms race, using the concept of counterforce strategy to maintain its military parity with the United States.

The 19th Conference of the CPSU in June–July 1988 adopted a resolution that efforts in the military sphere should correspond to economic priorities, not quantitative parameters.[11] This decision was followed by a June

1989 decision by the newly elected Supreme Soviet to cut the defense budget of 77 billion rubles (about US$48 billion) by 50 percent by the end of 1995.

According to the Soviet doctrine of reasonable sufficiency, the Soviet defensive military doctrine postulates that the goal of its military forces is not to win a nuclear war, but to prevent it. This means that military procurement, construction, R&D, structure, and training of military forces should have defensive and not offensive purposes. Thus, reasonable sufficiency means sufficiency for defensive—not offensive—purposes. Military superiority or even numerical equality in all components of strategic force is not necessary for keeping the strategic equilibrium.

Theoretically, there could be three schools of thinking in the West about the Soviet foreign policy of *perestroika*. The first is a positive view about Soviet change in international attitudes. The second is a negative view of the Soviet foreign policy of *perestroika*. The third is a mixed view.

The positive approach to the new Soviet political thinking reflects concern about the very survival of humanity in the nuclear age. Those who view the Soviet foreign policy of *perestroika* positively tend to accept the Soviet proposals for peace, including Gorbachev's plan for a nuclear-free world by the year 2000. A Canadian scholar, reflecting such a view, said that Soviet political thinking calls for a "sudden access of planetary consciousness" to ensure human survival on Earth.[12] Gorbachev, too, notes in his 1987 book, *Perestroika,*

> Our new thinking goes further. The world is living in an atmosphere not only of nuclear threat, but also of unsolved major social problems .... Mankind today faces unprecedented problems and the future will hang in the balance, if joint solutions are not found. All countries are now more interdependent than ever before, and the stockpiling of weapons, especially nuclear missiles, makes the outbreak of a world war, even if unsanctioned or accidental, increasingly more probable, due simply to a technical failure or human fallibility. Yet all living things on Earth would suffer .... We are all passengers aboard one ship, the Earth, and we must not allow it to be wrecked. There will be no second Noah's Ark.[13]

The negative view of *perestroika*, on the other hand, questions Gorbachev's pronouncements, asking instead for real change. This has been the approach taken by a number of political leaders in the United States. Many in the West have questioned the validity of Soviet pronouncements since the 27th Party Congress in 1986. The term "reasonable sufficiency" is now being used by the Soviets to describe their deployment of force levels as sufficient only to defend themselves, not to attack others. Gorbachev even went to the

UN General Assembly in December 1988 to announce that Moscow would unilaterally reduce conventional forces in Europe by 500,000.[14]

Despite an extensive purge of the Soviet Union's top military hierarchy, there is no hard evidence to suggest that Gorbachev has been able to curb military spending to finance his economic reforms, critics in the West have noted. The U.S. intelligence community believes that the Soviet Union continues to spend between 15 and 17 percent of its GNP on defense, in contrast with about 6 percent in the United States and considerably less in Western Europe and Japan. Indeed, intelligence sources indicate that Soviet military spending, rather than declining, grew by about 3 percent in both 1986 and 1987, almost double the rate of growth in the 1981–1986 period.[15]

Although there has been considerable rhetoric about military *perestroika* and an emphasis on the Soviet defensive posture, critics argue that there has been no discernible change in Soviet military posture, tactics, procurement practices, equipment, deployment of weapon systems, or training procedures that can be attributed to Gorbachev's initiatives.[16]

Last, those who approach the Soviet new political thinking with a mixed view contend that Gorbachev's foreign policy of *perestroika* is a task to be pursued in cooperation with the United States. Although this approach questions the validity of Gorbachev's call for change, it also tends to be critical of the United States' lack of cooperation. In reality, however, if the West is going to develop any sound options for responding to Soviet military policy, it must have a better understanding of policy concerns in Moscow.

Moscow's global strategy involves two separate elements of leadership: a party apparatus, less concerned with the specifics of warfare and more interested in the political purposes of military power, and professional soldiers, whose preoccupation is the preparation for war. Although Soviet history reflects long periods of cohesion between these two spheres, there have also been periods of extreme turbulence.[17]

The transition from the Brezhnev era to the Gorbachev era is precisely such a period. Gorbachev's desire to link politics and economics under a military *perestroika* is confronted by the old thinking of the Soviet military. Certainly, Gorbachev is concerned with the security of his country, but he seeks to "ensure security not through the arms race but through political and economic means, by fostering a climate that removes hostility, suspicion, and mistrust." Yet there have been signs of resistance from the Soviet military.

While closely watching China's development of the special economic zones and open cities long the coastline of the Yellow Sea, the Soviet Union has attempted to lured the West by stating that its own Far Eastern maritime coastal areas could become special economic zones.[18] Gorbachev seems to have convinced the professional military to open Vladivostok, the home port of the Soviet Pacific Fleet, to Western visitors for foreign trade.[19]

Gorbachev now describes his program as "disarmament for development" and clearly states that his domestic economic agenda necessitates an overall decrease in Soviet military spending. If other countries in the West cooperate in the creation of a global security system, Gorbachev will then be able to apply Soviet economic and human resources more thoroughly to economic restructuring. Furthermore, engaging other nations in mutual security efforts would undermine criticism from more orthodox Soviet policymakers concerned with the military defense of the nation.

Although it may be difficult to draw a balance sheet for the past four years of Gorbachev's military *perestroika,* it is not difficult to see that the dynamics of *perestroika* in the name of new political thinking can make things different. For example, the INF treaty and the withdrawal of Soviet troops from Afghanistan within the planned time frame are the two most significant results of Gorbachev's military *perestroika.* The INF treaty of December 1987 was only possible because of two unilateral concessions by Gorbachev: the discarding of a linkage between the treaty and SDI and the destruction of all medium-range missiles in the Asian part of the Soviet Union.[20]

Gorbachev clearly tries to make use of international issues, such as nuclear war, both to promote domestic *perestroika* and to challenge the West. The use of "global problems" as a Soviet political weapon against the West is reflected in Gorbachev's repeated statement that "the class conflict extends directly to the sphere of interstate relations." Clearly, it is not basic Soviet doctrine that Gorbachev has opened to reconsideration and discussion; rather, it is the practical choices that are to be made on the basis of that doctrine.

Such a reading of Gorbachev's statement appears to be confirmed by Gorbachev himself, who defines new political thinking as a methodology of action.[21] In other words, he sees new thinking as a new way of applying fixed principles. He extends this innovation only to methods, not to substance. A German scholar on Soviet affairs once stated that the Soviet Union is two dimensional in its foreign policy:

> In Soviet theory and practice, foreign policy is a two-tier affair. Traditional diplomacy at the "interstate" level is complemented by efforts to mobilize political forces in Western societies in support of Soviet policies. Previously, this process was seen as an "ideological struggle" waged at the "societal" level under class auspices. Today, Gorbachev appears to be pursuing an approach designed to link the two aspects of foreign policy more closely.[22]

In the final analysis, if this is the context in which Gorbachev views the East–West conflict over security, the West may be forced to view *perestroika* as an instrument of class struggle against capitalism. The Soviets themselves see the concept of security in a multidimensional way. In fact, they differentiate the security concept in relations between East and West, in the context of contradictions within NATO, and in the debates among West European countries.[23]

Perestroika and Northeast Asian Security

In its superpower rivalry with the United States, the Soviet Union tends to view as inseparable its global posture and that of its regional and subregional interests. After achieving global parity with the United States in the 1970s, the Soviet Union began to consider the Far East in a new light. If its primary task during the 1960s was to repel the enemy from attack, the early 1970s saw a drastic change in the Soviet perception of threat and its global strategy. Its new approach to this regional theater was twofold: global strategic rivalry with the United States and the possibility of a war with China. Hence, the Soviet Union spared no effort to create a blue-water navy with strategic nuclear capability. It also moved to establish a strong army on the border with China, particularly during the Cultural Revolution.

It soon became clear that the Soviet military potential in the Far East had turned out to be politically and diplomatically counterproductive for the Soviet Union. It allowed the United States to inspire fear of a Soviet threat in Asian countries. The most serious blow to the Soviet military buildup was the economic drain on the Soviet Union by the end of the 1970s. Its use of resources in the Soviet Pacific maritime region overwhelmed the civilian sector. With limited financial and labor potential, the Soviet Union spent resources mainly on military programs: building new weaponry, maintaining and expanding the army and navy, and providing heavy military aid to its regional allies—Vietnam, North Korea, and Afghanistan.

With the advent of the Gorbachev government, the Soviet Union now hopes to reverse the trend. In 1985, the Soviet challenge was laid out when the concept of new political thinking was advanced by Gorbachev. Now it is clear that Gorbachev intends to regionalize the deadlocks by calling on Asian neighbors for help.

Asia and the Pacific region have been increasingly visible in Moscow's foreign policy rhetoric. Addressing the 27th Party Congress of the CPSU on February 25, 1986, Gorbachev revealed the heightened Soviet interest in Asia and the Pacific. Gorbachev described the Asian Pacific region as one of growing importance to the Soviet Union and called for solutions to the area's "tangled knots" and unstable political situations.

The significance of the Asian and Pacific direction is growing. In that vast region, there are many tangled knots of contradictions and, besides, the political situation in some places is unstable. Here it is necessary, without postponement, to search for the relevant solutions and paths. Evidently, it is expedient to begin with the coordination and then the pooling of efforts in the interests of a political settlement of painful problems so as, in parallel, on that basis to at least take the edge off the military confrontation in various parts of Asia and stabilize the situation there.[24]

On April 23, 1986, two months after the party congress, Moscow officially stated that it would actively pursue policies of cooperation with all countries in the Asian Pacific region and would do so "irrespective of differences in their social systems" and on the basis of equality and mutual benefit.[25] Foreign Minister Shevardnadze's visit to Tokyo in January 1986, the first by a Soviet foreign minister in some 10 years, dramatically emphasizes the increased Soviet interest in the Pacific.[26]

The Soviet Union, under Gorbachev's leadership, has articulated its powerful strategic, political, and economic reasons for seeking friends in Asia and the Pacific region. Although economic interests have become increasingly important as Gorbachev attempts to revive the ailing Soviet economy, security concerns remain paramount. Moscow wants to secure free passage in the Pacific for its commercial and naval vessels and for its air force. To secure these strategic objectives, the Soviet Union in its dealings with Asian nations tends to emphasize economic and cultural cooperation, while minimizing political and ideological differences.[27] China has also increased its interest in economic opportunities within Asia and the Pacific region because of the recent Soviet emphasis on developing the Soviet Far East following the completion of the Baikal-Amur Mainline (BAM). China thinks it can supply the "northeast continental bridge," a continuous land route, that would give the Soviet Union a warm water port and access to the Asian Pacific market through Dalian (or Dairen) and provide Japan with a land route and access to Europe.

The Soviet Union's major overtures toward Asia appear to be oriented mainly toward China and Japan. This should not overshadow Moscow's recent increase of interest toward South Korea following its successful participation in the 1988 Seoul Olympics. In fact, Gorbachev mentioned South Korea twice in his Krasnoyarsk speech in September 1988. Soviet scholars interested in Northeast Asian affairs admitted that this mention of South Korea was especially noteworthy because it appeared on the eve of 1988 Seoul Olympic Games and "could be considered as a token of an entirely new political line." Gorbachev's June 1990 meeting with Roh Tae-Woo, of course, carried this process a giant step further.

With China, Moscow needs peace and stability because of its long border. With Japan, Moscow hopes to secure valuable sources of technological know-how and investment capital. Both China and Japan are also important to the Soviet Union strategically. China's common border with the Soviet Union and Japan's security treaty with the United States make the importance of a possible Beijing–Moscow–Tokyo triangle crucial to Soviet national interests. Reduced tension in the region and improved relations with China and Japan would allow the Soviet Union to redirect defense costs in the region toward economic development projects in Siberia and the Far Eastern maritime district.

The Soviet interest in China and Japan and, to a less extent, in South Korea can be seen in reference to "primary" and "secondary" levels of relationships. The Soviet Union's security concern belongs to the primary level of relationship, with the secondary being Moscow's economically related interactions with these neighbors.[28] To achieve the primary interest of stable security in the Asian Pacific region, Gorbachev has actively been promoting his own version of an Asian collective security scheme, based on Soviet experiences in the Helsinki process of 1975.[29] The idea was first tested with Indian Prime Minister Rajiv Gandhi during his visit to Moscow in May 1985. On the other hand, Gorbachev promulgated the Soviet National Committee for Asia-Pacific Economic Cooperation (SOVNAPEC) on March 25, 1988, to achieve the secondary interest of economically related interaction with China and Japan.[30]

The most conspicuous Soviet offer for collective peace in the Asian Pacific region is no doubt Gorbachev's July 28, 1986, speech delivered in Vladivostok. In this speech, Gorbachev made several proposals of direct interest to China, Japan, and South Korea. In regard to China, the Soviet Union offered joint efforts to exploit the Amur River Basin, hinted at concessions on the Sino–Soviet border disputes, promised cooperation in constructing a railway link from northeastern China to Soviet Central Asia, and offered Soviet cooperation in space science, which included the training of Chinese cosmonauts.

Gorbachev's Vladivostok speech repeated the Soviet desire to improve relations with the Chinese "anywhere, on any subject." He also announced the withdrawal of Soviet troops from Afghanistan and implied a possible reduction of Soviet forces from Mongolia and along the Sino–Soviet border. Normalization talks between Gorbachev and Deng Xiaoping have been relatively successful. The communique on the latest round of talks in Beijing in October 1987 said that each side had given an account of its ideas on solving the Kampuchean question. A second round of talks was held in June

1988 in Moscow, with satisfying results for both sides. A final agreement for a Sino–Soviet summit came recently at the end of Shevardnadze's four-day visit to Beijing in February 1989. With the successful Sino–Soviet summit in May 1989, Gorbachev's *perestroika* seems to be working.[31]

As for Japan, Gorbachev proposed progressive forms of economic links, including production cooperation, joint enterprises, and the creation of specialized export zones and production bases for Japanese businesses in the Soviet Far Eastern maritime provinces. Japan is keenly interested in the Soviet development of Siberia and the Soviet Far Eastern maritime district. As a resource-deficient country, Japan continues to seek ways to ensure access to raw materials and to diversify its suppliers.[32]

Public consensus in Japan indicates that the Northern Territories issue (about the four islands of Etorofu, Kunashiri, Shikotan, and Habomai) poses the single most significant obstacle to present-day Soviet–Japanese relations. The Soviet Union, however, continues to maintain its stance on the issue of Japan's Northern Territories in a far more intractable manner than it has with China over three major obstacles—the withdrawal of Vietnamese troops from Kampuchea, the withdrawal of Soviet troops from Afghanistan, and Soviet troop reduction in Mongolia and along Chinese borders.

Two major developments occurred in 1986, in Soviet–Japanese relations. First, in January 1986, Soviet Foreign Minister Shevardnadze visited Tokyo, the first such visit by a Soviet foreign minister in 10 years. The second major shock to Moscow–Tokyo relations occurred during Gorbachev's July 28, 1986, Vladivostok speech in which he made unprecedented conciliatory gestures toward China, but failed to mention or offer any concession on the Northern Territories issue.[33]

Prospects for Soviet–Japanese relations on the economic front appear promising, although Japan appears reluctant to commit itself to long-term economic agreements. In early 1986, a trade and payments agreement for 1986–1990 was signed, and the two countries agreed to continue the annual exchange of visits between foreign ministers. Gorbachev has been winning on the Chinese front, although he has gained little on the Japanese front. The consensus in Japan is that although little change has occurred in the substance of Soviet foreign policy, a distinct change in tone and appearance has occurred.

Japan knows that the Soviet Union regards Japan as "a power of first ranking significance," but Japan appears reluctant to actively cooperate with the Soviet Union as long as Moscow remains intransigent on the Northern Territories issue. Japan hopes that Gorbachev's assertion in his Vladivostok speech that Moscow "places importance on an improvement of its relations with Japan" is more than mere lip service. In short, Gorbachev wants the Soviet Union's "secondary" interests from Japan (Japanese participation in the Soviet economic *perestroika*). Japan, however, wants to see Gorbachev release Soviet "primary" interests (Gorbachev's security *perestroika* regarding the Northern Territories) in exchange for Japanese help for Soviet economic development.[34]

Perestroika and the Two Koreas

Thus, are we to believe that the Soviet new thinking means the Soviet Union views the world, not as a balance of power (or balance of forces), but rather as a balance of interest? Are we also convinced that the notion of national security will be replaced by the notion of universal security? If *perestroika* is characterized by the balance of interest and universal security, what effect will *perestroika* have on Soviet foreign policy toward the Korean Peninsula in general and Gorbachev's two-Korea policy specifically?

Those in South Korea hear that the Soviet Union is willing to eliminate its intermediate- and short-range missiles—436 in all. Moscow has also voiced its willingness to freeze or radically reduce other nuclear missiles and naval forces, as well as conventional weapons and troop concentrations in the region, if the United States will undertake similar steps. Moreover, in Krasnoyarsk, Gorbachev unilaterally imposed a freeze on Soviet nuclear and other forces, which is, in itself, an invitation for other countries to participate in further dialogue.

Early in 1989, Gorbachev proposed cutting 500,000 Soviet troops stationed east of the Urals in 1989–1990. In Beijing, in May 1989, Gorbachev again announced the Soviet dissolution of 12 army divisions, 11 air force regiments, and 16 navy battleships of the Pacific Fleet. What do all those elements mean in regard to peace and security on the Korea Peninsula?

Perestroika may not yet have direct bearing on the two Koreas. Yet, there are signs that indicate Gorbachev is willing to approach the situation on the Korean Peninsula in a new way from that of the cold war era. When he was interviewed by a German newsweekly, *Der Spiegel,* in October 1989, on the occasion of Chancellor Helmut Kohl's Moscow visit, Gorbachev was asked what effect *perestroika* has had on Soviet foreign policy. He replied,

> When we began *perestroika* and looked at the world around us with a magnifying glass, we saw a strange situation. The world had changed, other realities had arisen, yet international conditions continued to be molded by the principles of the period just after the war . . . . The same cliches prevailed. So, the need for restructuring here, too, became apparent. We now have a new notion of international conditions, what we call "new thinking."[35]

Gorbachev publicly acknowledged that conditions on the Korean Peninsula today are drastically different from those that existed in the 1950s. Gorbachev's Krasnoyarsk speech on September 16, 1988, was his first public statement that acknowledged Soviet "new thinking" on this issue:

> The situation on the Korean Peninsula remains complicated, even though the outlines of progress to dialogue between North and South have begun to show there, as well . . . . The USSR suggests that the question of lowering military confrontation in the areas where the coasts of the USSR, the People's Republic of China, Japan, the Democratic People's Republic of Korea, and South Korea converge be discussed on a multilateral basis, with a view to freezing and commensurately lowering the levels of naval and air forces and limiting their activity . . . . I think that in the context of general improvement of the situation on the Korean Peninsula possibilities could open up for forming economic relations with South Korea as well.[36]

Many in Seoul think such a direct response by Gorbachev was made possible because of Soviet participation at the Seoul Olympic Games and Seoul's *nordpolitik*, which seeks to reach out to the Soviet Union, the People's Republic of China, and other socialist countries to establish better relations.[37]

In principle, the Soviet Union supports a peaceful settlement of the Korean issue. In his Krasnoyarsk statement, Gorbachev suggested that the question of diminishing military confrontation in Northeast Asia—where the coasts of the Soviet Union, China, Japan, South Korea, and North Korea converge—be discussed on a multilateral basis with a view to freezing and commensurately lowering the levels of naval and air forces, as well as limiting their activity.[38]

It appears that Gorbachev's approach to international relations toward the Korean Peninsula is not a simple development of previous trends, but a rather radical departure from previous positions. He has been seeking to build two political bridges with two parts of Korea, at the same time keeping the allied relationship with North Korea intact. The Soviet Union has begun to see its national interests tightly intertwined with the peace and stability of the Korean Peninsula and closely related to the economically prosperous South Korea.

The Korean issue in the Krasnoyarsk statement did not affect South Korea as much as other issues, such as the proposal for dismantling Soviet and U.S. naval bases in the western Pacific (the Soviets at Cam Ranh Bay in Vietnam and U.S. bases at Subic Bay and Clark Air Base in the Philippines) and the proposal for an early Soviet–Chinese summit.

Gorbachev's call for the establishment of a South Korean–Soviet trade and economic relationship and multilateral arms control discussion including the two Koreas falls within the realm of new thinking. Because of successful Seoul Olympic diplomacy, the two sides quickly agreed to establish trade offices in Seoul and Moscow by March 1989.[39] Although there was no discussion of Gorbachev's proposal for multilateral talks in the western Pacific, the trade and economic cooperation issues between South Korea and the Soviet Union have developed quickly.

The development in trade and economic contacts between South Korea and the Soviet Union become all the more important to Gorbachev's foreign policy *perestroika* when these phenomena are placed in context with other proposals revealed in the Krasnoyarsk speech. Gorbachev's proposals include the creation of special economic zones in the Soviet Far Eastern maritime district with reduced customs tolls and favorable terms for foreign investment, a favorable response to recent Chinese calls for the launching of joint Chinese–Japanese–Soviet economic projects, and a suggestion for joint agricultural and forestry ventures along the sensitive Sino–Soviet border, where major military clashes occurred in 1969. In other words, the Soviet Union has recently become increasingly interested in luring South Korean business executives into joint ventures in the Soviet Far East with Chinese and/or North Koreans.[40]

The sudden Soviet change of attitude toward South Korea poses a number of questions as to what prompted Gorbachev to initiate this new thinking. No sooner had Soviet thinking changed, than North Korea became suddenly interested in forming a joint venture with South Korea to develop the Mt. Kumkang area's resort facilities, located northeast of the DMZ facing Korea's Eastern Sea. In January 1989, North Korea invited one of Seoul's successful business veterans to Pyongyang and suggested that South Korea join in a joint venture with the North in establishing Siberian development projects and other joint ventures in the Soviet Far East. At the same time, North Korea (contrary to the idea of dialogue) unilaterally postponed scheduled meetings of North–South talks on the pretext of Seoul's "Team Spirit" exercise, thus contradicting Pyongyang's overture for economic contacts.[41]

Gorbachev's perception of South Korea in reference to his new thinking is centered on the rapid expansion of economic and military power by Seoul—a major factor in the political calculations of both North Korea and the Soviet Union. Structural rigidity, together with poor management, obsolete technology, and huge military investment created a backward economy in North Korea.[42] Moreover, despite the larger size of the North Korean army, air, and naval forces—even allowing for the addition of Soviet

MiG 29s to the air force—the North has clearly lost much of its very costly military superiority over South Korea.

The weaker the North, the more it depends on the Soviet Union. Despite its history of instability with North Korea, Soviet interests increasingly match those of North Korea. Like Moscow, Pyongyang watched with growing concern the expanding Chinese relationship with the United States and Japan in the late 1970s. North Korea frequently indicated an interest in improved relations with Moscow, a policy consistent with Pyongyang's wish to avoid dependence on Beijing. By 1985, there were more official North Korean visitors going to the Soviet Union than to China. From 1986 to the present, goodwill visits, joint celebrations, and joint naval exercises have continued at an impressive pace.[43]

The Soviet Union's military aid in the form of MiG 23s and other advanced weapons, such as SA–3 and SA–5 missiles, SU–25 aircraft, and, since July 1989, MiG 29 fighters, went to Pyongyang accompanied by economic, scientific, and technological agreements. The transfer of MiG 23s was matched with Soviet overflight rights and the use of North Korean port facilities. With successful results from the Seoul Olympic *perestroika* in hand, the Soviet Union again busied itself helping Pyongyang with its Youth Festival in July 1989 for another gain from an international sports venue.[44]

Thus far, Soviet policy has concentrated on rebuilding ties and influence in the North, while closely watching the rapid changes in South Korea, and doing so with an impressive sophistication of observation, analysis, and approach whenever Moscow finds an opportunity. Like the Chinese, the Soviets find that there is no need for an intermediary, such as the United States or China, to develop a new relationship. Indeed, the Soviet Union competes with China for closer cooperation with economically useful South Korea.

Conclusion

The military *perestroika* of the Soviet Union in the Far East is a two-front tactic. Its first component is the maintenance of Moscow's correlation of forces in the region, while its foreign policy *perestroika* is at work both in the area of the INF treaty and a force reduction plan in Europe at the strategic level. In the meantime, token forces from various areas can be reduced or withdrawn in the name of Soviet security.[45] The reality is not convincing, however. The Soviets are still building their forces in Asia. A U.S. authority noted the reality: Moscow has increased its Far Eastern force from 53 to 57 divisions; 40 vessels have been added to the Soviet Pacific Fleet since 1984, for a total of 860 vessels; and it has been supplying North Korea with SA–3 and SA–5 missiles and MiG 23, SU–25, and MiG 29 fighters.[46]

For the Korean Peninsula, the Soviets have also initiated overflights by strategic bombers from the Soviet Union, across the Korean Peninsula, and over the Yellow Sea. During these missions, Soviet aircraft conduct reconnaissance of South Korea, Okinawa, and China and simulate missile strikes against South Korea and Okinawa.[47]

Unprecedented Soviet–North Korean naval exercises were conducted off the eastern coast of North Korea in October 1986. During the same month, Soviet bombers returning to Cam Ranh Bay overflew the Korean Peninsula instead of flying around Japan. After 1986, the Soviet–North Korean naval exercise became an annual event.

The Soviet Union's other tactics for security include nongovernmental trade and other economic activities to help solve its economic problems in the region. SOVNAPEC is one organization designed to extend Soviet economic contacts with rich capitalist countries in the region.[48] The committee, because of the composition and variety of its personnel, focuses on a comprehensive analysis of the state of Soviet economic relations with the countries of Asia and the Pacific, as well as on an evaluation of the export potential of Soviet Pacific areas. The Soviet Union's activities through nongovernmental contacts in economic circles of the region, however, have always been carried out in the name of economic security.

The economic security of the Soviet Union is just another face of security *perestroika,* which states that the economic conditions required to build an "all-embracing system of international security" include

- excluding all forms of discrimination from international practice;
- renouncing the policies of economic blockades and sanctions;
- jointly developing a just settlement of the debt problem;
- establishing a new world economic order that guarantees equal economic security to all countries;
- elaborating principles for using some of the funds released as a result of a reduction of military budgets for the good of the developing nations;
- pooling efforts to explore outer space and developing a peaceful use of space to resolve global problems on which the destiny of civilization depends.[49]

As Soviet foreign policy interest in the region grows, improvements in Soviet–North Korean relations will accelerate both quantitatively and qualitatively, and Moscow's military assistance to Pyongyang will continue to grow. As Soviet military assistance to North Korea grows, military *perestroika* on the Korean Peninsula will remain in the hands of Moscow. This could, if it persists, force South Korea to feel the need for a *nordpolitik* toward Moscow, while it continues its system of joint security with the United States.

Seoul should not entertain any naive assumptions or hopes for an immediate or fundamental change in North Korean attitudes or perspectives. In the past, in contrast to Seoul's attempts at constructive dialogue, Pyongyang has consistently used bilateral forums for propaganda purposes. Nonetheless, South Korea has little to lose by getting Moscow and Pyongyang to sit down and discuss regional security issues in a forum in which Moscow's security *perestroika* can be used to temper Pyongyang's often inconsistent negotiating behavior.

Perhaps it is the right time for South Korea to respond to Gorbachev's Krasnoyarsk proposal. South Korea should applaud Gorbachev's foreign policy *perestroika*, but refuse to finance it until the Soviet Union helps to bring about a meaningful dialogue between North and South. Until mid-1990, the Soviet Union had sought only to improve its economic interest vis-a-vis South Korea, while leaving political dialogue between the two countries undone.[50] Now, with full diplomatic relations, the security dimension can be no longer evaded.

Notes

1. This period follows that of Cyril E. Black et al., *The Modernization of Japan and Russia* (New York: Free Press, 1975), 10–11.

2. On the question of the patterns of forced mobilization, see S. Frederick Starr, "The Changing Nature of Change in the USSR," *Gorbachev's Russia and American Foreign Policy,* Seweryn Bialer and Michael Mandelbaum, eds. (Boulder, Colo.: Westview Press, 1988), 6–9.

3. There remains Secretary Yegor K. Ligachev, who is known as the chief opponent to the Gorbachev reform policy, who has been removed from the party's number two post and has been demoted to a post supervising agricultural affairs. Premier Nikolai I. Ryzhkov, who began his advancement in the party under Yuri Andropov, seems to have adopted Gorbachev's leadership to his liking. For more on personnel changes, see Jerry E. Hough, "Gorbachev Consolidating Power," *Problems of Communism* (July–August 1987): 21–43.

4. Mikhail Gorbachev, *Political Report of the CPSU Central Committee to the 27th Party Congress* (Moscow: Novosti Press Agency Publishing House, 1986), 96.

5. *Theses of the CPSU Central Committee for the 19th All-Union Party Conference* (Moscow: Novosti Press Agency Publishing House, May 1988), 27.

6. Jacob W. Kipp et al., *Gorbachev and the Struggle for the Future* (Fort Leavenworth, Kansas: Soviet Army Studies Office, U.S. Army Combined Arms Center, 1988), 2–6.

7. For a full text, see "Gorbachev's 28 July Speech in Vladivostok," FBIS–Soviet Union, *Daily Report,* July 29, 1986, p. R7.

8. For details, see "Gorbachev (Krasnoyarsk) Speech—Foreign Section," *News Release—Communique,* (Ottawa, Ontario: Press Office of the USSR Embassy in Canada, September 19, 1988).

9. "Vneshpolitika—Vneshenpoliticheskiy razcel zechi Mikhaila Gorbacheva v Krasnoryarske," Tass, September 17, 1988, p. 8.

10. Constantin V. Pleshakov, "Soviet Foreign Policy and Its Implication for the Peace of Northeast Asia," Paper presented at the Conference on Northeast Asian Security and World Peace in the 1990s, Kung Hee University, Seoul, South Korea, September 19, 1989, p. 10.

11. *Materialu XIX Vsesoyuznoy Konferentsii Kommunisticheskoy Partii Sovetskogo Soyuza* (Moskva: Politizdat, 1988), 120.

12. Gloria Duffy and Jennifer Lee, "The Soviet Debate on 'Reasonable Sufficiency,' " *Arms Control Today,* October 1988, p. 19.

13. Mikhail Gorbachev, *Perestroika: New Thinking for Our Country and the World* (New York: Harper & Row, 1987), 11.

14. The Soviet leader seems to have impressed the United Nations with his new thinking. For a related comment, see "Moscow on the Hudson," *Newsweek,* December 12, 1988, pp. 12–15.

15. "Gorbachev, the Army and *Perestroika,*" *Washington Times,* October 26, 1988, p. F3.

16. For remarks on the Soviet reform by Robert M. Gates, deputy director of the U.S. Central Intelligence Agency, see "For the Record," *The Washington Post,* November 2, 1988, p. 20.

17. See, among others, Morris Borstein, "Soviet Economic Growth and Foreign Policy," *The Domestic Context of Soviet Foreign Policy,* Seweryn Bialer, ed. (Boulder, Colo.: Westview Press, 1981), 227–255.

18. For details, see Gorbachev, *Political Report of the CPSU Central Committee to the 27th Party Congress,* 136.

19. For details, see Gorbachev's implications made in his speech at the ceremony of the exchange of the INF treaty ratification documents in *USSR–USA Summit: Documents and Materials, Moscow, May 29–June 2, 1988* (Moscow: Novosti Press Agency Publishing House, 1988), 75–76; *Matelrially Plenuma Tsentral'nogo Komiteta KPSS, 17–18 Fevralya 1988 goda* (Moskva: Politizdat, 1988); Richard C. Holbrooke, "The 'Fortress' Opens—A New Soviet Policy in the Pacific," *Newsweek,* October 17, 1988, pp. 27–28.

20. For more on the issue, see "Gorbachev Interviewed by Indonesian Paper, Merdeka," *Pravda*, July 23, 1987, pp. 1–2.

21. Gorbachev Address to the International Peace Forum in Moscow on February 17, 1987, as published in *Pravda*, February 18, 1987.

22. Gerhard Wettig, "New Thinking on Security and East–West Relations" *Problems of Communism* (March–April 1988): 14.

23. For a full text, see *Disarmament and Security, 1988 IMEMO Yearbook* (Moscow: Institute of World Economy and International Relations, USSR Academy of Sciences, 1988), especially chapter 17.

24. It is believed that the Soviet Union has been deploying about 25 percent of its military forces east of the Urals and about 700,000 troops along the border with China. For details on the Soviet Pacific Fleet and the two-front war-fighting capability, see *Soviet Capabilities in the Pacific* (Washington, D.C.: Technical Service Division, Intelligence Center Pacific, 1989), 15–17.

25. "Basic Aims and Directions of the Party's Foreign Policy Strategy," *Political Report of the CPSU*, 88–89.

26. For a full text of the Soviet statement, see "Soviet Government Statement on Asia-Pacific Region," FBIS–Soviet Union, *Daily Report*, April 23, 1986, p. R5.

27. For the renewed relations between Japan and the Soviet Union and for a Japanese viewpoint, see Hiroshi Kimura, "Japan's Relations with the Soviet Union," *Harvard International Review* 10, no. 4 (April 1988): 30–33.

28. See Edward A. Hewett and H.S. Levine, "The Soviet Union's Economic Relations in Asia," *Soviet Policy in East Asia*, Donald S. Zagoria, ed. (New Haven, Conn.: Yale University Press, 1982), 226.

29. For differences of the Soviet level of interests, see Joseph M. Ha, "Soviet Policy in the Asian-Pacific Region: Primary and Secondary Relationships," *Acta Slavica Iaponica*, Tomus V (The Slavic Research Center, Hokkaido University, Japan, 1987), 93–110.

30. John Borawski et al., "The Stockholm Agreement of September 1987," *Orbis* 30, no. 4 (Winter 1987): 643–645.

31. The SOVNAPEC consists of more than 68 representatives of scientific, economic, and public organizations, ministries, and departments from the government and Communist Party. At present, the office of SOVNAPEC is located in the Pacific Studies Department of the Institute of World Economy and International Relations (IMEMO), USSR Academy of Sciences.

32. "A Green-Light for Sino–Soviet Talks," *Dong-A Ilbo*, February 7, 1989, p. 4.

33. For a related analysis on the subject, see John P. Hardt, *Perestroika and Interdependence: Toward Modernization and Competitiveness*, Paper

presented at the international conference on the Soviet Union, China, and Northeast Asia, cosponsored by the Korean Association for Communist Studies and the Institute for Sino–Soviet Studies, George Washington University, Seoul, South Korea, July 25–27, 1988, pp. 2–4.

34. See, among others, Gaye Christoffersen, "The Economic Reforms in Northeast China: Domestic Determinants of the Region's Open Door Policy," Paper presented at the Slavic Research Center, Hokkaido University, Japan, September 1988.

35. For more on the subject, see Herbert J. Ellison, "Recent Soviet Policy in Northeast Asia," Paper presented at the international conference on the Soviet Union, China, and Northeast Asia, cosponsored by the Korean Association for Communist Studies and the Institute for Sino–Soviet Studies, George Washington University, Seoul, South Korea, July 25–27, 1988.

36. "Mikhail Gorbachev's Address to the Chinese Intellectuals," *Pravda*, May 18, 1989; "Joint Sino–Soviet Communique," *Pravda*, May 19, 1989, p. 1.

37. "Gorbachev: *Perestroika* Seeks New Era of Democratization," as quoted in *Current News* (Special Edition), no. 1795, December 14, 1988, p. 46.

38. "Vneshpolitika—Vneshenpoliticheskiy razdel rechi Mikhaila Gorbacheva v Krasnoyarske," Tass, September 17, 1988, pp. 5, 8, and 13.

39. The deputy chairman of the Soviet Chamber of Commerce and Industry, Vladimir Kolanov reportedly has visited Seoul to deliver a memorandum to establish trade offices in Seoul and Moscow on October 15, 1988. For details, see *Hankook Ilbo,* October 16, 1988, p. 7.

40. "Gorbachev's Krasnoyarsk Speech—Foreign Section," *News Release-Communique* (Ottawa, Ontario: Press Office of the USSR Embassy in Canada, September 19, 1989), 4.

41. For the background of Korea's *nordpolitik* in the early 1980s, see Kim Yu-Nam, "Changing Relations Between Moscow and Pyongyang: Odd Man Out," *North Korea in a Regional and Global Context,* Robert A. Scalapino and H. Lee, eds. (Berkeley, Calif: Institute of East Asian Studies, University of California, 1986), 152–176.

42. During Kim Il-Sung's recent stopover in Khabarovsk in July 1988, he discussed establishing North Korean collective farms in the province of Khabarovsk with the Soviets to produce rice, soybeans, and early vegetables. It is also reported that the Soviet Union would like to have South Koreans join in this agricultural venture. See Sophie Judge, "Pacific Growth Depends on Asian Enterprises," *Far Eastern Economic Review,* August 4, 1988, p. 26.

43. "Mt. Kumgang and Mt. Sorak to be Developed for a Joint Tourist Complex between North and South Korea," *Segye Ilbo,* February 8, 1989, p. 1.

44. By the mid-1980s, the GNP of South Korea was more than twice that of North Korea, and the combination of a substantial margin of technological superiority and a higher growth rate in the South indicated that the disparity would continue to grow. See IISS, *Military Balance,* May 2, 1986, p. 13.

45. Kim Il-Sung added to the new view of the Soviet role in Korea's liberation when, in August 1986, he referred to "defeating Japanese imperialism jointly with the Soviet Army." See Herbert J. Ellison, "The Soviet Union and Korea," Paper presented at the Sixth Korea–U.S. Conference on Northeast Asian Security, cosponsored by the Institute of Foreign Affairs and National Security and the School of Advanced International Studies, The Johns Hopkins University, Seoul, South Korea, December 14–15, 1987, pp. 6–12.

46. "The Doctrine of Minimal Defense Unfolded Slowly," *Far Eastern Economic Review,* August 4, 1988, p. 28.

47. For cases in which the new Soviet security *perestroika* can be seen, see documents and materials in *Security in the Asia-Pacific Region——The Soviet Approach* (Moscow: Novosti Press Agency Publishing House, 1988).

48. U.S. Assistant Secretary for Defense Richard Armitage in a speech before the World Affairs Council in Washington, D.C., July 1988.

49. For details, see *Pacific Threat Digest,* August 1987, pp. 10–12.

50. See "Soviet Union in Asia-Pacific Region: Economic Development and Cooperation of the Soviet National Committee for Asia-Pacific Economic Cooperation," *SOVNAPEC Newsletter* 1, no. 1 (May 1988).

10

Sino-Soviet Rivalry in Korea

Parris Chang

The Democratic People's Republic of Korea (DPRK), or North Korea, is a creature of the Soviet Union. Not unlike Frankenstein's monster, however, the DPRK has evolved over the past three decades into a highly assertive and independent international actor, much to the distress of its creator. There has been much instability in Soviet–DPRK relations, which have also been affected by the Sino–Soviet conflict since the late 1950s. Mikhail Gorbachev's visit to Beijing in May 1989 and the normalization of Beijing–Moscow relations notwithstanding, the Sino–Soviet competition and rivalry on the Korean Peninsula has persisted.

This chapter will briefly review the historical legacy of the rivalry, examine the changes and continuities in Chinese and Soviet policies toward the DPRK and Republic of Korea, and assess the impact of the continued rivalry on peace and stability in Korea and East Asia.

The DPRK under Moscow's Tutelage

On August 8, 1945, after the United States dropped atomic bombs on Japan and one week before Japan surrendered, the Soviet Red Army invaded Manchuria and the Korean Peninsula. The Soviets, who trained two Korean Communist divisions in Siberia to facilitate the Soviet occupation of Korea, quickly installed Kim Il-Sung as the leader of North Korea. Kim was reported to have said that "loving the Soviet Union and the socialist bloc is just to love Korea."[1]

Soviet General T.K. Shtikov clearly stated Soviet strategic interests in Korea. At the opening session on March 20, 1946, of the U.S.–Soviet Joint

Commission to establish a provisional government in Korea, Shtikov said: "The Soviet Union has a keen interest in Korea being a true democratic and independent country, friendly to the Soviet Union, so that in the future it will not become a base for an attack on the Soviet Union."[2] Shtikov also told his U.S. counterpart, Lieutenant General John R. Hodge, that the Soviets wanted a "loyal" Korean government.[3]

In 1948, the Soviets refused to allow election monitors from the United Nations into Soviet–occupied Korea. Thus, in May 1948, only in the South was an election held, and on August 15, 1948, the Republic of Korea was officially proclaimed with Dr. Syngman Rhee as its first president. Less than one month later, on September 9, 1948, Kim Il-Sung became the first leader of the Democratic People's Republic of Korea. Both governments claimed sovereignty over all of Korea.

According to Nikita Khrushchev, Stalin approved of Kim Il-Sung's planned invasion of South Korea when the latter visited Moscow in late 1949.[4] Kim assured Stalin that the United States would not intervene and that an uprising among the South Koreans would occur once North Korea had invaded the South. Events in early 1950 bolstered Kim's confidence. In January 1950, Secretary of State Dean Acheson defined the U.S. "defense perimeter" in the Far East, and it excluded Korea—a position that apparently had the backing of the Joint Chiefs of Staff. A week later, the U.S. Congress defeated an administration-sponsored bill for economic aid to South Korea.

Soviet policy toward Korea was extremely cautious, one of "maximizing gains to its security interests in East Asia without risking a direct confrontation with the U.S."[5] Before the Korean War began on June 25, 1950, the Soviets withdrew their advisers and technicians from North Korea. During the war, the Soviets supplied North Korea with arms, but did not send troops to fight the Americans. In November 1950, it was the Chinese—not the Soviets—who intervened to save the North Koreans from total defeat. A cease-fire was signed in July 1953, four months after Stalin died.

The Korean War left both the Soviet Union and North Korea with a bitter aftertaste. Moscow saw Kim Il-Sung as a reckless and dangerous client, almost dragging the USSR into direct armed conflict with the United States. To his chagrin, Kim Il-Sung discovered that when push came to shove, the Soviet Union was not a trustworthy and dependable ally.

Soviet–North Korean Relations and the Sino–Soviet Conflict

Over time, the DPRK has failed to measure up to Moscow's expectations as a worthy and loyal ally. Indeed, Kim Il-Sung instead has been a liability and irritation for Moscow. The Sino–Soviet conflict that originated in the

1950s and intensified in the 1960s has had an enormous impact on Soviet relations with North Korea. With the advent of the Sino–Soviet dispute, Moscow had to contend with China—in addition to the United States and Japan—as a rival power in Asia. Kim Il-Sung steered a neutral course in the dispute between the two leaders of the socialist bloc, but showed a tendency toward China. The conflict allowed Kim to assert his independence, playing one Communist power against the other in seeking favors for his regime.

Soviet–North Korean relations were very much a function of Sino–Soviet relations and Chinese–North Korean relations. The triangular relationship was quite evident in the 1960s. This period was the lowest point in Soviet–North Korean relations. Mutual resentment, which had been building on each side for several years, came out into the open. Moscow criticized Kim Il-Sung's policies, his growing personality cult, and his *chuche* ideology. Kim accused the Soviets of meddling in North Korea's domestic affairs and of economically exploiting North Korea, and he criticized Khrushchev's handling of the Cuban missile crisis. The Sino–Soviet conflict was at its height in the mid-1960s, and Pyongyang openly sided with Beijing. In 1963, Khrushchev brusquely cut off military and most economic aid to punish Pyongyang.

The ousting of Khrushchev in October 1964 allowed Moscow and Pyongyang to mend relations somewhat. The new Soviet premier, Alexei Kosygin, visited Pyongyang in February 1965 and, in the following years, economic, technical, and military aid again flowed. Meanwhile, Chinese–North Korean relations deteriorated during the Cultural Revolution as Chinese Red Guards attacked Kim Il-Sung personally, labeling him a "fat revisionist" in 1967–1968. Subsequently, it took the considerable efforts of Premier Zhou Enlai, including the master diplomat's personal visit to Pyongyang in April 1970, to repair the damage to PRC–DPRK relations caused by the Red Guards and their radical sponsors in the Beijing leadership. Especially in the wake of large-scale armed clashes on the Sino–Soviet border in Manchuria in March 1969, it became even more imperative for the PRC to maintain good relations with North Korea as Beijing perceived an attempt by the Soviets to invade or encircle China.

Even since the late 1960s, the DPRK has placed enormous emphasis on Kim's *chuche* ideology and asserted North Korea's independence in foreign affairs. Kim realizes that his country must be on good terms with both the PRC and the USSR and needs their political and material support—hence, he has tried to maintain equidistance in Pyongyang's relations with Beijing and Moscow. This is not to say that Pyongyang has been pleased with the two big neighbors; as a matter of fact, Pyongyang has had considerable grievances because Moscow and Beijing have not, in the eyes of the North Korean leadership, provided sufficient support for the national objectives of the DPRK.

For example, Moscow's flirtation with South Korea was quite irritating to North Korea. In the 1970s, Moscow allowed South Korean citizens and diplomats to visit the USSR and allowed Soviet officials to visit Seoul. Moscow's endorsement of the North Korean proposal for Korean reunification was lukewarm at best. Moreover, whereas Moscow periodically denounced South Korea as a dangerous U.S. puppet, it refused to provide North Korea with advanced weapons.

Likewise, North Korea was alarmed by Beijing's reconciliation with the United States and Japan in the 1970s. True, Kim Il-Sung sought to capitalize on China's opening with the United States and Japan by developing a dialogue with South Korea in July 1972 and concluding an agreement on the principle of unification. The more concrete benefits that Kim sought—improved relations with Washington and Tokyo—failed to materialize, however. Kim must have been very disappointed and bitter when he rushed to Wuhan in central China in April 1975, in the wake of the U.S. pullout from Indochina, to urge Chairman Mao on joint actions to expel the U.S. forces from the Korean Peninsula and Taiwan, but found Mao unresponsive. Kim's anger and frustration were vividly displayed over the suspension of talks with the South and the brutal axe murder of two U.S. servicemen at Panmunjom in 1976.

From the perspective of Moscow (or Beijing for that matter), the disappointment appears to have been mutual. In Soviet eyes, North Korea had not been a loyal and dependable partner because it had often sided with the PRC against the USSR. For example, Kim hosted and housed Prince Sihanouk and joined Beijing against the Soviet Union and Vietnam on the issue of Kampuchea. Moscow saw Kim's obsession with Korean unification and tendency to resort to force as dangerous, and Moscow was unwilling to provide North Korea with MiG 23 fighter-planes and SA–6 and SA–7 surface-to-air missiles, which the Soviets sold to their Arab allies, and T–72 tanks, which they sold to India.

It seems obvious that Moscow feared advanced weapons might tempt Kim Il-Sung to create another crisis on the Korean Peninsula. Moscow apparently disapproved of North Korean wanton provocations, and this was reflected in Moscow's cautious reactions following the 1968 Pueblo capture, the 1969 downing of a U.S. EC–121 plane, and the 1976 Panmunjom axe murders of two U.S. soldiers. The Soviets even offered assistance in salvaging the remnants of the EC–121. Moscow was apprehensive that these reckless North Korean provocations might draw the Soviets into an unwanted direct confrontation with the United States.

There are indications that for personal and policy reasons, the Soviets strongly disliked Kim Il-Sung. That Kim intends to make his son Kim Jong-Il his successor, thus setting up for the first time a family dynasty in a socialist state, is also an embarrassment for Pyongyang's allies. Moscow also found Pyongyang's repeated *chuche* ludicrous and repugnant because North Korea had become extremely dependent on Soviet and Chinese assistance. Although the Soviet Union would like to gain access to one of North Korea's warm-water ports for military purposes, Kim Il-Sung has been unwilling to comply. Soviet commercial ships have used the North Korean port of Najin since the late 1970s, but there is no evidence that it is a Soviet naval base.

Given Moscow's estranged relations with virtually all of the major Asian States—China, Japan, South Korea, and the United States—during the 1970s and early 1980s and given North Korea's strategic location, the Soviets still saw in North Korea an important ally and were willing to pay a modest price to retain Pyongyang's friendship. This situation, coupled with continued Sino—Soviet competition, enabled North Korea to do a balancing act to maximize assistance from both countries.

North Korea's Balancing Act

Pyongyang's relations with Moscow have improved enormously in the past five years. The dramatic rapprochement between North Korea and the Soviet Union began in May 1984 when President Kim Il-Sung returned to Moscow for a state visit after a hiatus of 23 years. Since then, military and economic cooperation between the two countries has been stepped up.

In the military sphere, the DPRK is reported by mid-1986 to have obtained 36 MiG 23 fighters, 30 SAM–3 missiles, and 47 M–2 helicopter gunships from the Soviets. More recently, Pyongyang has also received dozens of MiG 29s. Moreover, the two countries held joint military exercises in recent years in the Sea of Japan, based on their Treaty of Material Aid and Friendly Cooperation.

Likewise, the DPRK has strengthened economic ties with the Soviets. In accordance with their five-year (1986–1990) agreement for trade and economic cooperation, Moscow has provided additional economic assistance and pledged to help the DPRK modernize its production technology. Soviet aid programs include a nuclear power plant that will produce 1.76 million kilowatts, modernization of the Kimchaek ironwork complex to double present production capacity, and the construction of 19 more major industrial plants.

If a Radio Moscow broadcast in October 1986 was correct, more than 60 of North Korea's major industrial plants have been reconstructed or newly built as a result of Soviet aid.[6] Currently, Soviet—DPRK trade constitutes more than 60 percent of North Korea's total foreign trade.[7] Moreover, 5,000 or more Soviet advisers and technicians work in the DPRK. Pyongyang's emphasis on the idea of *chuche* notwithstanding, North Korea is very much dependent on Soviet largesse.

Moscow's assistance has never been cost-free, however. Since 1985, Soviet military planes have acquired the right to fly through North Korean airspace in their missions to and from Vietnam, thus changing previous routes over the Sea of Japan. Soviet warships of the Pacific Fleet have called on Wonsan and conducted joint exercises with North Korean naval forces. Also, there are unconfirmed reports that Moscow is seeking to establish naval bases inside the DPRK.

On the other hand, officials in Pyongyang have categorically denied the accuracy of such reports. One of them told the author flatly in August 1987 that "the DPRK is not a satellite of the Soviet Union or China. We value highly our independence and sovereignty, and would never permit any foreign base on our soil." Nonetheless, Soviet advances in Pyongyang are discernible and threaten to change the equidistant relations with Moscow and Beijing that Kim Il-Sung has so skillfully maintained throughout the years.

In this context, President Kim's trip to Beijing in May 1987 was significant. It was one of his clever balancing acts, designed to reassert the independence of the DPRK, reassure Chinese leaders of Pyongyang's everlasting friendship, and restore the delicate equilibrium. Kim knows only too well that the DPRK needs both China and the Soviet Union to underwrite its security, to furnish economic and military aid, and to support unification. Thus, North Korea cannot afford to cozy up to Moscow at Beijing's expense, and Kim has to maneuver adroitly between them and play one off against the other to secure support and assistance from both.

Kim's talks with Deng Xiaoping and other ranking Chinese cadres served other purposes as well. In the wake of the forced departure of Party General Secretary Hu Yaobang and the campaign against bourgeois liberalization early that year, the North Koreans wanted to know of any change in the Chinese leadership, of any shift in China's domestic and foreign policy, and the attending implications for the DPRK.

Likewise, the Chinese used the summit to clarify their policy toward the Korean Peninsula and allay Pyongyang's misgivings and grievances, which resulted from the recent port call in Qingdao by the U.S. Seventh Fleet and the ever-growing economic ties and contacts between China and South Korea. The Chinese felt compelled to display solidarity with North Korea—they reiterated China's support of Pyongyang's proposal for tripartite talks among North Korea, South Korea, and the United States, and of Pyongyang's opposition to cross-recognition of the two Koreas by the major powers and their simultaneous admission to the United Nations—proposals that have been advanced by South Korea and the United States. In private conversations, Chinese cadres blamed U.S. intransigence and efforts by Seoul and Washington to isolate North Korea as reason for Pyongyang's tilt toward Moscow.

As the DPRK launched its third seven-year economic plan in April 1987 in the hope of accelerating technological modernization of its industries and speeding up overall economic development, President Kim also sought more economic aid from China when he met with his host. Reportedly, Deng Xiaoping suggested to President Kim that he inspect the Shenzhen special economic zone that, in Deng's eyes, was the showcase of his reforms. Apparently Deng hinted to Kim that North Korea should institute similar reforms.

Throughout the years, Pyongyang has shown interest in China's reform efforts. When Kim Jong-Il, President Kim's son and political heir, visited China in June 1983, he inspected several factories, including the Baoshan Steel complex—a Sino–Japanese joint venture outside Shanghai. Vice Premier and Foreign Minister Kim Yong-Nam and other North Korean officials did visit Shenzhen to acquire a first-hand knowledge of foreign investment.

In fact, since 1984, without much fanfare, Pyongyang has pursued measures to encourage foreign investment, joint ventures, and expanded trade with the West. This outreach has included openness toward capitalist countries that have no diplomatic ties with North Korea. To justify such a major shift, Kim Jong-Il is quoted as having said: "Building an independent national economy on the principle of self-reliance does not mean building an economy in isolation. An independent economy is opposed to foreign economic domination and subjugation; but it does not rule out international economic cooperation." In September 1984, the North Korean Supreme People's Assembly enacted a joint venture law to regulate and boost foreign investments in "industry, construction, transportation, science and technology, and tourism."

North Korea will need much more than the passage of a joint venture law to attract foreign investment, however. The West's continuing mistrust of North Korea and Pyongyang's failure to service its previous foreign debts, resulting in the default recently announced by Western banks, stand out as the two major obstacles discouraging Japanese and Western investment. Moreover, cadres in North Korea seem rigid and still largely ignorant of the outside world.

Gorbachev's New Tack in Asia

Since Mikhail Gorbachev took over the Soviet leadership in 1985, the Kremlin has fashioned a new Asian Pacific strategy. To implement the new strategy, the USSR has mounted fresh initiatives to improve relations with

China and seek to avert the much-feared encirclement by a Sino–U.S.–Japanese alliance. Unlike his predecessors, who repeatedly claimed they were ready for reconciliation but blamed the Chinese for prolonging the Sino–Soviet conflict, Gorbachev seems willing to take the first step to break the deadlock. Thus, following Gorbachev's speech at Vladivostok in July 1986, in which the Soviet leader proposed a series of measures to ease tensions and enhance economic and technical cooperation, the Soviet Union pulled its troops out of Afghanistan and outer Mongolia and persuaded the Vietnamese to terminate their occupation of Cambodia, thus normalizing Soviet relations with the PRC.

Probably even more significant over the long run is the Kremlin's emphasis on economic diplomacy and a bold attempt at an open door policy in Far Eastern Siberia and expansion of economic interactions with the countries of the Asian Pacific region. Indicative of Moscow's new look is the effort to make the Primorsky district in and around the strategic port city a free economic zone and open it for investment by, and trade with, Japan, South Korea, and other Asian Pacific states. In so doing, the Soviets hope to attract huge foreign capital and high technology to modernize the entire Far Eastern Siberia and to step up economic ties with the Asian Pacific region.

It is with good economic and strategic reasons that the Soviets are trying a different tack in Asia. First, eastern Siberia has been stagnating economically and badly needs a transfusion of capital and high technology. The development of eastern Siberia has become a top government priority because the Kremlin is feeling the pressure from the relatively affluent and well-educated younger Russian generation, who seek to raise their living standards and improve their quality of life. Indeed, the viability of Gorbachev's leadership may hinge on whether he can deliver more goods and services to the Soviets.

Second, Moscow does not want to be left out of the prosperity of the Pacific community. Highly cognizant of the enormous economic and technological strengths of Japan, South Korea, and other Asian newly industrialized countries (NICs)—such as Taiwan, Singapore, and Hong Kong—the Soviets hope to increase economic ties and draw on their resources. Recently, Moscow applied for membership in the Pacific Economic Cooperation Council and Asian Development Bank, two major Asian Pacific economic cooperation and financial institutions that the Soviets once denounced as tools of U.S. imperialism.

Third, the Soviets have attempted to draw attention to the strong protectionist tendencies in the United States and the sharp trade friction, as well as rising economic tensions, between the United States and several Asian countries, especially Japan, South Korea, and Taiwan, and they have sought to exploit these issues. By offering an economic incentive in the form of expanded trade and economic ties, Moscow intends to move these Asian countries toward a more independent position between the Soviet Union and the United States.

In addition, several other political and strategic considerations are behind Gorbachev's daring diplomatic offensive. The USSR has little reason to be happy with its current political position in the region, as it is estranged from all the major states of eastern Asia. True, the USSR is recognized as one of the two superpowers—its colossal military capabilities in the Asian Pacific region and its bases in Indochina have enhanced Moscow's global outreach and enabled Soviet forces to rival the U.S. Seventh Fleet for superiority. The Soviets have thus far failed to translate this military might into political influence, however.

From the perspective of the late 1980s, Moscow has little, if any, impact on Asia's major economic and political decisions. The Asian nationalist revolutions have been completed; thus, there are no more liberation movements to support. Throughout Asia, power is largely in the hands of second- or third-generation figures, who are generally pragmatic and intent upon economic modernization and do not see the Soviet model of development as providing a path to the future. In fact, Soviet-style communism is widely seen as a failure—not only by the Chinese Communists who spent years seeking to adapt it to their society, but even by Gorbachev and other Soviet leaders who are tinkering with communism, trying to make it work.

The USSR is well aware of these facts and has launched a new diplomacy to improve its economic and political position. Moscow has long wanted to engage Japanese capital and technology in the development of Siberia, but its efforts have not achieved its desired objectives because of rigidity and harshness. In addition to rejecting Japan's repeated requests to settle the long-standing dispute over the Northern Territories, which the Soviets have occupied since 1945, Moscow has added insult to injury by heavily fortifying the islands. Japan considers the Soviet occupation of the islands a serious threat to its national security. Previous plans for Soviet–Japanese joint ventures have failed because Soviet leaders acted on the erroneous belief that Japan could be attracted by the prospect of participation in the development of Siberia without making major territorial or strategic concessions. Gorbachev has announced his plan to visit Japan in 1991. If he expects to improve Soviet–Japanese ties, could he bring himself to give back those small islands?

There is no evidence that Gorbachev's new thinking has extended to the Northern Territories. It may be quite difficult, if not impossible, for him to return the islands to Japan. Precisely because of this reason, opening relations with the ROK seems particularly attractive—Moscow does not have to make any concession on the territorial issue, and Seoul, because of *nordpolitik* and economic reasons, is anxious to invest in Siberia and expand economic ties with the USSR. For these reasons, the Soviets have turned their attention to the ROK.

Thus, in a speech at the Siberianeity of Krasnoyarsk on September 16, 1988, Gorbachev clearly stated that the USSR was willing to forge economic ties with South Korea.[8] The following month, Vladimir Golanov, deputy chairman of the Soviet Chamber of Commerce and Industry, visited South Korea at the invitation of Lee Sun-Ki, president of the Korea Trade Promotion Corporation, to discuss steps to strengthen the economic relations of the two nations. In July 1989, both sides established trade missions in Moscow and Seoul.[9] In June 1990, Roh and Gorbachev agreed in San Francisco to launch full diplomatic relations.

In retrospect, Seoul seems to have been a major catalyst in opening Soviet–South Korean relations. More than 6,000 Soviet athletes, artists, citizens, and officials came to the ROK to attend the Olympics, the largest Soviet presence in South Korean since 1945. Soviet officials who visited South Korea were immensely impressed by what they saw and by the generous hospitality they received from the South Korean people and officials.[10] In the wake of the Olympics, both sides have exchanged trade missions, as noted previously, and economic cooperation has been stepped up. For example, negotiations for Aeroflot and Korean Airline scheduled passenger flights between the USSR and the ROK are under way, and a direct sea transportation link between Pusan and the Soviet port of Nakhoda will soon be operational. Two-way trade has expanded rapidly since 1988, exceeding $500 million in 1989.[11]

Moscow's New Thinking about Korea

Increasingly, the Soviets see North Korea as a liability and embarrassment, a drain on their resources, and the Soviets have been assigning less and less priority to North Korean concerns. Although Moscow still maintains good relations with Pyongyang and supplies up-to-date weapons (e.g., the MiG 29 planes and the SA–5 missile launchers) to the North Koreans, in so doing the Soviets seem to be trying to reassure the North Koreans, thus retaining a moderating influence on their recalcitrant ally and redressing the military balance that has been tilting to the South's favor.

The economic situation in North Korea remains bleak, and trade deficits with the Soviets have widened in recent years.[12] In the mid-1980s, North Korea's trade with the USSR accounted for one-third of Pyongyang's foreign trade; in the past two years, the percentage has risen to more than 60 percent. According to some Soviet scholars, Moscow has advised the North Koreans on economic reforms, but to no avail.

Although President Kim Il-Sung has visited Moscow twice since 1984, Gorbachev has not seen fit to reciprocate those visits, and that may well reflect the low priority he attaches to the DPRK. Pyongyang was greatly disappointed when the scheduled visit of President Andrei Gromyko in September 1988, the first by a Soviet head of state, did not materialize at the last moment. Instead, Moscow sent the chairman of the Commission on National Security (KGB) as the replacement, but the North Koreans did not see him as an adequate substitute.[13] North Korea had high expectations that Gorbachev would visit Pyongyang in May 1989 on his way back from Beijing, but reportedly Gorbachev asked Foreign Minister Eduard Shevardnadze to tell the North Koreans that he was too busy and that he was tired of Pyongyang's complaints about Soviet participation in the 1988 Olympics and growing economic relations with Seoul.

There are unmistakable indications that the Soviet new thinking is affecting Moscow's policy toward North and South Korea. In an article in *Izvestia,* in September 2, 1989, Faina I. Shabshina, a highly respected expert on Korean affairs at Moscow's Institute of Oriental Studies, called for the establishment of formal diplomatic relations between the USSR and ROK. Shabshina stated that in formulating Moscow's policy toward Korea, the national interests of the Soviet Union also should be considered. "For a long time, [national interests] were not considered in the USSR's policy toward Korea." According to Shabshina, the Soviet Union had no policy of its own; rather, it "automatically supported the course of our ally—the DPRK." Now having begun economic ties with South Korea, it is necessary for the Soviet Union to establish relations with South Korea in other spheres—for example, in reducing tension in the Far East. Stated Shabshina, "Recognition of South Korea would also enhance the international prestige [of the Soviet Union] because it is consonant with the new political thinking."[14]

Moreover, Shabshina sees the establishment of a formal Soviet–ROK relationship as the key to the solution of the Korean problem. She argues her case on the following grounds: the existence of the ROK as a reality, DPRK policy, and peace on the Korean Peninsula.

Although the Republic of Korea represents an "illegitimate state," set up by the U.S. imperialism, it has proved "a viable and even thriving one from the economic standpoint." The most important thing is that the South Korean state has existed for more than 40 years. "It is an objective reality." This reality is recognized by the confederation plan of North Korea in which two autonomous states form a confederal state of Korea. For the idea of a confederation to materialize, "extra levers capable of transplanting it into reality are required," and, according to Shabshina, "establishment of diplomatic relations between the USSR and other socialist countries with South Korea is seen as such."

Shabshina notes the immense change in the South's political life: the demands for "the withdrawal of American troops and intensifying calls for the country's reunification." She asserts that the U.S. influence on the South's internal affairs has weakened considerably of late, but notes that the United States is "active in the spiritual and psychological sphere and seeks to exploit to the utmost the particularities of local conditions and the whole situation on the peninsula." However, "the craving for democracy and national unity is gaining strength"; hence, "the establishment of diplomatic relations between the Soviet Union and other socialist states with the Republic of Korea could . . . promote the progressive processes taking place in South Korean society."

As if to anticipate the objection of Pyongyang, Shabshina states that the "socialists' recognition of the state of South Korea does not represent a violation of their socialist duty and the principles of socialist internationalism." In as much as the Korean Peninsula is a region of extreme military and political tension, "the socialist world's recognition of the South may reduce it considerably . . . . The DPRK's solidarity with that action and active support for it," according to Shabshina, "would greatly enhance Pyongyang's standing in the eyes of the Korean nation and the world community." Obviously intended for North Korean ears, she argues that South Korea's "broad involvement in cooperation and collaboration with the socialist countries could promote gradual implementation of the idea of a confederation, the transformation of the peninsula into a nuclear-free zone and of the armistice into lasting peace, and North–South dialogue."

It is not difficult to see why the North Koreans were upset and alarmed by Shabshina's article, and they quickly made an informal protest to the Soviet Union. Igov Rogachev, Soviet vice foreign minister in charge of Asian Pacific affairs, felt compelled to make a clarification and stated that the official Soviet position remains unchanged, dismissing the *Izvestia* article merely as the view of a scholar. In private conversations, however, some Soviet officials acknowledged that the article did articulate their new thinking.[15] These officials were candid enough to say that Moscow would support cross-recognition, but its realization may take many years because of opposition by both the DPRK and the PRC.

Beijing's Policy toward Korea

For almost three decades, Beijing had pursued a very antagonistic policy toward South Korea. The Korean War, the PRC's participation in it, the legacy of the war, Sino–U.S. enmity, and the broader regional and global alignment of forces all served to color the Chinese perception of international reality and to shape Chinese policy toward Korea.

Thus, until recently, the Chinese leaders saw the ROK as a U.S. puppet and a U.S. base from which the United States could launch an invasion against China and North Korea. Moreover, the ROK once maintained strong political and military ties with the Republic of China (ROC) on Taiwan, another enemy of Beijing, although Seoul, pursuant to its "northern policy," has sought to distance itself from Taipei since the early 1980s.[16] The ROK remains the only country in Asia that still keeps official diplomatic ties with the ROC.

As time and circumstances have changed, however, so too has Beijing's policy. As a result of the normalization of relations between the PRC and the United States in 1979 and Beijing's quest for economic modernization at home, changes in Beijing's policy toward Korea have become discernible in the past decade.

In as much as a peaceful international environment is seen as crucial for China's modernization efforts, Beijing has moderated its military and economic support for the DPRK, encouraged the DPRK to hold a dialogue with the South, and supported measures to ease tensions on the Korean Peninsula. Beijing's perception of the ROK has also undergone significant changes; the Chinese increasingly recognize the advantage of economic ties with South Korea—as a valuable trading partner and as a source of capital and advanced technology.

The first official PRC–ROK contact occurred in May 1983, ironically, as a result of the hijacking of a Chinese jetliner that landed in an airport near Seoul. PRC officials went to Seoul to negotiate the return of the plane, its crew, and passengers (minus the six hijackers who were jailed for several years and sent to Taiwan). Since then, contacts between the two sides—especially athletic and economic—have expanded. In 1986, the PRC sent the largest delegation (more than 500 athletes) to Seoul for the Asia Games and took away the most gold medals. In September 1988, the PRC took part in the Seoul Olympics, notwithstanding the boycott by the DPRK.

The most impressive development in the PRC–ROK relationship, however, has been in the economic sphere. Trade, which was virtually nonexistent in the 1970s, has steadily increased in the 1980s, and it reached $3 billion in 1988, making the Republic of Korea China's fourth largest trading partner. Out of concern for Pyongyang, until recently, the Chinese maintained the fiction that trade with the ROK was "indirect." It has been an open secret in the international business community, however, that direct trade between the two sides began in the early 1980s. Furthermore, a large number of South Korean multinational corporations have established joint ventures in China.

In spite of booming trade and other economic ties, Beijing has sought to separate politics from economics and minimize political contacts with Seoul. For instance, whereas Beijing has allowed the establishment of provincial-level trade offices, it has no intention of establishing formal diplomatic ties with the ROK, notwithstanding Seoul's strong desire. Not unlike the Soviets, the Chinese also regard diplomatic recognition as an important bargaining chip for securing major economic and political concessions from the ROK.

Two other considerations are also vital in the Chinese calculus of decision. First, China's reunification has been one of the three top national priorities for the current PRC leaders—they do not wish to initiate a two-Korea policy by recognizing the ROK officially, lest other nations would use it to justify a two-China policy by restoring diplomatic ties with Taiwan. When Grenada, Liberia, and Belize established formal ties with the ROC recently, Beijing terminated diplomatic relations with them immediately.

Second, the Chinese leadership still attaches great importance to the DPRK, the only country in the world with which the PRC has concluded a treaty of mutual defense. In spite of growing economic relations and occasional flirtations with South Korea, Beijing has not diminished its diplomatic support of the DPRK and continues to oppose cross-recognition and ROK admission to the UN. In the wake of the violent crackdown against the pro-democracy demonstrators in Beijing in June 1989, North Korea was one of the very few countries in the world that openly supported the PRC amid the chorus of global condemnation. Under such circumstances, and in light of the political and ideological disarray in the socialist world, the bonds between Beijing and Pyongyang must have been strengthened. It is in this context that Kim Il-Sung visited Beijing in early November 1989 to cement North Korea's friendship with the PRC, including the new party general secretary, Jiang Zemin.

Beijing's solidarity with Pyongyang's position has (until June 1990) had the effect of constraining the Soviet initiative toward South Korea. In theory, Sino–Soviet reconciliation would give Pyongyang less scope to play off its allies. In reality, the two countries do not coordinate their policies toward Korea because the Sino–Soviet rivalry remains.

Notes

1. Ahn Byung-Joon, "North Korean Foreign Policy: An Overview," *The Foreign Relations of North Korea: New Perspectives,* Park Jae-Kyu, Koh Bying-Chul, and Kwak Tae-Hwan, eds. (Seoul: Westview Press–Kyungnam University Press, 1987), 29.

2. U.S. Department of State, *Foreign Relations of the United States,* Vol. 8 (Washington D.C.: U.S. Government Printing Office, 1971), 653.

3. Carl Berger, *The Korea Knot* (Philadelphia: University of Pennsylvania Press, 1957), 69.

4. Nikita Khrushchev, *Khrushchev Remembers: The Last Testament* (Boston: Little, Brown, 1974), 367–368.

5. Ahn Byung-Joon, "The Soviet Union and the Korean Peninsula," *Asian Affairs* 11, no. 5 (Winter 1985): 5.

6. B.C. Koh, "North Korea in 1987," *Asian Survey* 28, no. 1 (January 1988): 65.

7. This item of information was supplied to the author by a Soviet official in Moscow in September 1989.

8. *Pravda,* September 18, 1989. Although the media in Seoul gave a full coverage to Gorbachev's speech, Pyongyang was silent on his remarks about strengthening economic cooperation with South Korea.

9. The Soviets established their trade office in Seoul in April 1989, while the ROK established theirs in July 1989 because of domestic political reasons.

10. Many Soviet officials and scholars made such comments to the author during his trip to Moscow in September 1989.

11. *Far Eastern Economic Review,* September 28, 1989, p. 34.

12. According to a Soviet scholar who has the access to official statistics, the DPRK has failed to deliver goods on time in the past three years and is unable to deliver the specified volume according to their barter agreement. Their two-way trade for 1988 was approximately 1.2 billion rubles, with a deficit of 0.3 billion rubles on the North Korean side.

13. The PRC sent its head of state, Yang Shang-Kun, who commanded considerable stature, while the Soviet KGB boss "retired" not long after he returned to Moscow.

14. Faina I. Shabshina, "Can the Korean Knot be Unraveled," *Izvestia,* September 2, 1989. The English translation is from *FBIS–SOV–89–172.*

15. One of these officials is a Soviet Foreign Ministry expert handling the Korean affairs.

16. Since the early 1980s, Presidents Chun Doo-Hwan and Roh have avoided visiting Taipei during their trips to other Asian states. Ranking South Korean officials, including the two presidents, have repeatedly expressed the wish to normalize relation with the PRC.

PART THREE

Arms Control in Korea:
Issues and Prospects

11

Military Talks in Korea: An Overview

Ohn Chang-Il

Significance of Political–Military Talks in Korea

Not unrelated to the global surge of "a sense of realism" championed by the Soviet leader Mikhail Gorbachev, the possibility of serious talks on political and military matters to ease the tension between North and South Korea is now more promising than ever before. The near-abandonment of the so-called Brezhnev Doctrine now permits the East European countries to conduct their own affairs. The economic needs of Communist nations have enabled worldwide cooperation and moved nations beyond the ideological barriers between East and West.

Despite the continued promise that communism is the sure way to enhance the standard of living of ordinary people, decades of Communist rule have instead resulted in economic stagnation and an attendant scarcity of daily necessities. The exclusive role of the Communist Party has ignored the uniqueness and the creativity of the individual and thus failed to vitalize society. As a result, the people's disaffection with communism has led to new thinking about democratic forms of government. Today, Eastern Europe is trying to make democracy work.[1] North Korea, which has ruled half of Korea for nearly half a century, cannot remain aloof from these internal and external pressures nor ignore the need to resolve its long-standing political and military problems. This need has been hastened by a realistic sense of urgency from the Soviet Union.

An important declaration by South Korean President Roh Tae-Woo on July 7, 1988, the successful Seoul Olympics from September 17 to October 2, 1988, and the subsequent address delivered by Roh before the UN General

Assembly on October 18, 1988, have marked a watershed in North–South relations.

The July 7, 1988, declaration called for comprehensive trade; humanitarian, cultural, and political contacts between the two Koreas; and an end to a seemingly eternal struggle for supremacy in the international arena.[2] The sixth point of the declaration drew special attention. The South Korean government offered to help the North improve its relations with South Korea's allies, including the United States and Japan.

The Seoul Olympics held in 1988 under the banner of "Harmony and Progress" added to Olympic history. In addition to its achievement in the sheer number of the participating countries and athletes, it was also the first East–West gathering in 12 years, a period that had been tainted by political and ideological interruption. Another slogan, "Beyond All Barriers," typified the symbolic character of the Seoul Olympiad.

In his October 18, 1988, address before the UN General Assembly, President Roh proposed a six-nation consultative conference to discuss a "broad range of issues concerning peace and stability" in Northeast Asia, solemnly declaring that "South Korea will never initiate the use of force against the North." President Roh also indicated that he "is willing to discuss disarmament, arms control, and other military issues in a possible summit with Kim Il-Sung."[3]

Each of these three events, in addition to the relative economic strength of the South, may enhance the decision-making process between North and South. Indeed, it will be impossible for the DPRK regime to keep North Korea as a "Taoist state" forever.

The pragmatic segment of the North Korean leadership, composed of a handful of moderates and technocrats, could be the driving force in engaging South Korea in serious negotiations. In the 1950s and 1960s, North Korea was able to make significant economic strides without access to Western technologies. During the past decade, however, obsolescence has overtaken most of the industrial plants in North Korea, and production has begun to stagnate. Sensing the importance of introducing advanced technologies to revitalize the North Korean economy, DPRK pragmatists were able to activate a 1984 Joint Venture Law. Through this law, it was hoped that joint ventures with foreign companies would stimulate the North Korean economy, but economic conditions in that country were not favorable enough to lure foreign investment.

Unfortunately, a much larger portion of the North Korean leadership—probably headed by Kim Il-Sung, who sought to communize South Korea by force in 1950 and is likely still obsessed with the idea that the South could be "liberalized" by force—does not seem to recognize the South as a proper negotiating partner. This may be a fundamental reason why

North Korea has undertaken various subversive activities; they have been based on the concept of "indirect strategy" against the South. For example, North Korea has constructed several tunnels under the DMZ, although it talks of peace on the peninsula. Thus, South Korea has found it difficult to trust North Korea and will continue to have questions about North Korean duplicity in the future. In the long run, however, the pragmatic element in North Korea could play a role in making the current leadership recover their sense of realism and eventually see the need for North–South talks.

Needless to say, the preliminary meeting for the prime ministers' talks, which was held on February 8, 1989, was very significant. This was the first bilateral face-to-face discussion in preparation for the talks on substantial North–South issues, including military matters. It was significant because it was the first meeting at which the military representatives of both sides, along with civilian members, were present. Although it failed to produce any tangible compromise on the issues to be discussed—in large part because of North Korean intransigence on the dissolution of the "Team Spirit" exercise—this first round of preparatory meetings implicitly revealed that both parties in practice recognized the other side as a negotiating counterpart.[4] Because one of the main goals of the proposed high-level talks is to identify avenues for easing tension on the Korean Peninsula, including arms control and arms reduction, this preliminary meeting could be a meaningful step toward successful talks on peace and stability.

Success in the high-level talks would be exhilarating; the Koreans have lived separately for more than 40 years. Successful high-level talks could foster internal conditions that would allow families separated by war the opportunity to visit—even to live together freely—with estranged relatives and friends. Ordinary Koreans, too, would have the opportunity to visit historic places throughout the peninsula. At the national level, the success of the talks could end the energy-consuming, self-destructive animosity between the North and the South and provide the opportunity for both sides to concentrate on enhancing the level of prosperity for both the individual and the nation, with the ultimate possibility of national reunification. To secure these results, however, both North and South Korea must do their part. South Korea must be strong enough to convince the North that military means alone cannot secure peace and prosperity for all of Korea. North Korea should awake from the illusion that the South could be "liberalized" under Communist rule, even by force, because historical experience indicates this is unlikely.

Observations on the Proposals Regarding Military Matters

North Korea has made an extensive number of proposals on military issues. It has touched almost every conceivable aspect of military matters—from arms and troop reductions to the abrogation of the mutual defense treaty between the Republic of Korea and the United States. Because most proposals have been put forward merely for propaganda purposes, this lack of sincerity has not gone unnoticed. Most of these proposals did not even merit counterproposals from South Korea.

The most conspicuous example of such hypocrisy came when North Korea broadcast a message calling for "peaceful unification of the fatherland" on June 7, 1950, while Kim Il-Sung was simultaneously ordering military commanders to move their troops along the 38th parallel for a massive invasion of the South. In the message, North Korea proposed a meeting between the "democratic" parties and representatives of social groups of the North and South either in Kaesong or Haejoo from June 15 to 17, 1950, to discuss procedural matters and to convene a "supreme legislative body" on August 15, 1950. Rejecting the UN proposal to meet on June 10, 1950, North Korea answered with a full-scale military attack against the South on June 25, 1950.[5] Until recently, North Korean proposals on military issues have remained propagandistic in nature, with little substantiation by North Korean actions.

South Korea, on the other hand, has, for the most part, ignored North Korean proposals until the early 1970s, when the late President Park declared that North Korea should abandon its goal of communizing the entire Korean Peninsula, should it desire a peaceful unification of Korea on March 30, 1972—the graduation day of the Korea Military Academy.[6] Since then, the South Korean government has continued to propose measures to ease North–South tensions, with an ultimate goal of national reunification. Unlike the first president of South Korea, Syngman Rhee, who had urged "national unification through marching to the North," the current South Korean government under President Roh unilaterally declared that South Korea would never initiate force against North Korea. This no-first-use declaration clearly manifests the sincerity of South Korea to avoid bloodshed and solve the North–South problems by peaceful means.

North Korean proposals on military matters can be classified by several categories. The most frequent category comprises proposals made about U.S. troop withdrawals from South Korea. Officially or unofficially, North Korea has advanced the proposal several times a year since 1948, with only a few interruptions during the Korean War period. Indeed, North Korea has demanded the withdrawal of U.S. troops more than 80 times since 1948.[7] Arguing that "the forcible occupation of South Korea by U.S. troops impedes the peaceful reunification of Korea, intensifies tensions in Korea and is a constant cause for creating a danger of war," North Korea has made it clear that "the removal of U.S. forces is a prerequisite for dialogue and unification."

Furthermore, North Korea has elaborated several justifications for its position: The "occupation" of South Korea by U.S. troops violates not only the principles of international law for national integrity, but also those of self-determination set by the UN Charter, by the July 4th Joint Communique, and by the Armistice Agreement.[8] On this basis, North Korea has repeatedly demanded that U.S. troops be withdrawn from South Korea, and it is likely to continue to do so.

The next issue that North Korea has continuously pursued since the end of the Korean War is the conclusion of a peace treaty with the United States. Through Nam-Il, the chief North Korean representative to the Geneva Conference on June 15, 1954, North Korea has proposed to form a committee to foster conditions for peace in Korea. It has proposed the conclusion of a peace treaty between North and South Korea under the condition of U.S. troop withdrawal or, alternatively, through a peace treaty with the United States and the Republic of Korea. Recently, the North, arguing that the issues of U.S. troop withdrawal and a peace treaty should be settled by talks between the United States and North Korea, demanded bilateral talks with the United States, with possible representation from South Korea as an observer.[9]

In the 1980s, North Korea called for a tripartite conference in which a nonaggression "declaration" and unification would be discussed. North Korea also proposed at this time a bilateral peace treaty with the United States, excluding South Korea because it was not a signatory to the armistice agreement. Another reason for not signing a peace treaty with the South, Pyongyang still argues, is that the United States "controls" South Korea through "military command control" and that a treaty with the South would be meaningless.[10] Thus, it seems that the current DPRK leadership still rejects the South as a counterpart in negotiation and sees it as an area to be dissolved and later absorbed into the North.[11] The North Korean attempt to form a unified front by making the most of the unstable situation in the South has been another tactic employed by the North. One example of this was Kim Il-Sung's embrace of Moon Ik-Whan and other opposition leaders at the same time Kim was avoiding formal talks with the South.

Another persistent North Korean proposal has been arms reduction, including the demand to stop arms reinforcement and, recently, to stop combined military exercises. At the Geneva Conference, which was convened to solve the "militarily unsolvable" Korean problem and other thorny issues relating to Vietnam, Nam-Il, the North Korean delegate, proposed on June

15, 1989, that North and South Korea should reduce their troop strength to less than 100,000 within the year. This proposal was quickly supported by a declaration from the Supreme National Assembly in March 1955 and Kim Il-Sung's address on August 15, 1955.[12] Since then, this North Korean demand has sporadically but consistently appeared in the various statements by Kim Il-Sung in other speeches, conversations, and memoranda to the United States.[13]

At times, North Korea has suggested that, if the United States were to withdraw its troops from South Korea, the North would reduce its own troop strength voluntarily to less than 200,000, with an accompanying promise not to invade the South.[14] On July 23, 1987, North Korea issued a statement calling for a phased troop reduction by Seoul and Pyongyang to the level of less than 100,000 each and for a convening of a tripartite meeting. The statement suggested a three-stage troop cut by both sides, from 1988 to 1991, which would be followed by a phased withdrawal of U.S. troops from South Korea. It called for a total withdrawal of all U.S. forces, including all U.S. weapons, and a total dismantling of U.S. bases in South Korea after having achieved the 100,000-troop level by both Koreas.[15] According to the proposal, a tripartite talk would be held in Geneva in March 1988, and, after 1991, each side would be allowed to maintain forces below the 100,000 level without any foreign forces in South Korea.

The proposal received a cold response not only from South Korea, but also from the United States and Japan. This lack of interest is largely the result of previous North Korean insincerity in the inter-Korean dialogue. Since December 1985, North Korea had rejected all established channels for dialogue.[16] In addition, North Korea had demanded a halt to arms reinforcement since the early 1970s and an end to a joint military exercises since the mid-1980s, utilizing the latter as a good pretext for delaying or avoiding any kind of inter-Korean talks.[17] The lack of sincerity in the North Korean proposals clearly shows that Pyongyang has tried to capitalize on the unstable—and sometimes volatile—situation in the South. It has tried to place all responsibility for tension on the peninsula upon the South by presenting itself as a nation of good intentions.

One unceasing demand of North Korea has been to "denuclearize" the Korean Peninsula. At the same time, North Korea continues to maintain a huge stock of biochemical weapons—the third largest in the world—and has operated a nuclear power research center since 1962.[18] The South Korean government also confirmed in its report to the National Assembly that North Korea could produce 13 to 33 Hiroshima-type atomic bombs.[19] Regardless of its own nuclear and biochemical capabilities, North Korea has continued to insist on a nuclear-free zone for South Korea, especially since the mid-1980s.

The idea of denuclearizing South Korea was first pushed by Kim Il-Sung in his welcoming address to the Zambian president on April 5, 1980, when he put forward the idea of nuclear-free zones throughout the world, including on the Korean Peninsula.[20] ROK–U.S. combined forces—which were formed under UN authority to repel invading North Korean forces in 1950 and were given legal justification by the mutual defense treaty between the Republic of Korea and the United States in 1953—have been armed with conventional weapon systems.

It was a U.S. journalist who first raised the issue of whether one component of the ROK–U.S. combined forces was nuclear. Jack Anderson alleged that there were tactical nuclear weapons in South Korea and that neutron bombs could be deployed should the South Korean government agree.[21] Although no authoritative voices have been heard to confirm or deny these reports, the impact of this revelation has left doubt in the minds of many North Koreans. On June 23, 1983, the DPRK issued a statement calling for total withdrawal of U.S. troops and for the dismantling of any plan to deploy neutron bombs in South Korea. Again, the North Korean Foreign Ministry demanded a total withdrawal of U.S. troops and weapons, including nuclear weapons.[22] Since that time, the North has continued to call for a Korean nuclear-free zone.

In addition to the proposals mentioned above, North Korea has touched on various other military issues. It has called for the abrogation of the mutual defense treaty between South Korea and the United States (1956, 1965, 1968, 1971, 1980), for an end to the arms race (1973, 1974, 1977, 1986), for a prohibition to arms importation (1972, 1973, 1974, 1977, 1979), for dismantling civilian defense organizations (1980, 1986, 1987, 1988), and even for a total withdrawal of troops and installations from the DMZ (1972, 1985, 1986, 1987, 1988).[23] None of these North Korean proposals has had even a glimmer of sincerity. Pyongyang appears to have operated on the assumption that they would be ignored in Seoul and Washington, and they have been.

Unlike North Korea, the ROK has made few proposals, although slogans such as "unification through victory march to the north" were popular in the 1950s and 1960s. One viable proposal during that period, however, was made by the South Korean foreign minister, Byoun Young-Tae, at the Geneva Conference on May 22, 1954, which called for a free election throughout Korea, based on the then-constitutional procedure of South Korea and a discussion of military matters by a newly formed National Assembly.[24] In fact, substantial proposals have been made by the South Korean government since 1970, when, in August of that year, the late President Park called for an explicit easing of tensions and demanded that North Korea halt its military infiltrations and show good intentions by not attempting to topple the South

Korean government or slander its name.[25] Thus far, however, the South Korean government has made only 64 proposals on military matters—far less than the 236 made by the North.[26]

The most frequent proposal that the South has made since 1974 is the development of a nonaggression treaty between the South and the North. In his annual press conference on January 18, 1974, President Park proposed entering such a pact.[27] Since then, the South Korean government has continued to call for a nonaggression treaty, whereas the North has insisted on a nonaggression "declaration"—a less-binding form of agreement. One of the fundamental reasons for North Korean intransigence on the declaration appears to be that the North still does not consider the South to be a legitimate partner in a treaty relationship. Sensing this North Korean attitude, South Korea has consistently asked for a North Korean abrogation of its terrorist activities and of its attempt to communize the entire peninsula.[28] Most notably, the South proposed in 1982 that both the North and South should embark on projects to demilitarize the "remilitarized" zone, including the construction of a meeting place through which South–North contacts could be conducted.[29] So far, these South Korean proposals have gone unanswered.

The most conspicuous unilateral declaration made by the South Korean government was President Roh's proclamation in his UN address on October 18, 1988, that "South Korea will never initiate the use of force against the North."[30] In addition to this declaration, President Roh proposed a six-nation conference to establish peace and stability in Northeast Asia and a summit talk between the two Koreas to discuss a wide range of problems relating to the issues of nonaggression, disarmament, arms control, a system of peace that reflects the armistice, and a peace city in the DMZ, among others.[31] President Roh's UN address clearly indicated a South Korean willingness to discuss issues that could lead to an easing of tension on the Korean Peninsula. North Korea, however, responded to the proposal by inviting a dissident Korean student and an aged minister, embracing them as the true representatives of South Koreans who yearn for national unification.

Calling for a guarantee of human rights in North Korea, on August 15, 1989, South Korean President Roh urged North Korea to abandon its policy of unifying Korea through a Communist revolution in the South and, instead, proposed mutual recognition.[32] On September 11, 1989, in a special address before the National Assembly, President Roh proposed the creation of a North–South Commonwealth as an interim move toward unification to build "a Democratic Republic to ensure freedom, human rights, and happiness" for all Koreans.[33] In response to Roh's formula, North Korea proposed a consultative conference for national unification on September 28, 1989, at which delegates from the two governments and all political and social organizations in Korea would meet.[34] North Korea is still encouraged by various dissident elements in South Korea and continues to demand adoption of its own formula, based on its "anachronistic" strategy that is designed to communize the South "in conspiracy with South Korean dissidents," according to a statement by the National Unification Board of South Korea.[35]

Reviewing the proposals made by both sides, one can easily sense that North Korea has intentionally tried to avoid any dealings with the South Korean government, although South Korea has continuously emphasized the importance of official talks. In other words, the North has refused to recognize the legitimacy of the South Korean government, although the South has implicitly recognized the North Korean regime. As a result, while South Korea has been calling for a South–North summit and a nonaggression treaty, the North has insisted on a consultative conference among the delegations of the two governments and social organizations within Korea and on a nonaggression declaration, a less-binding form of commitment. Thus, it appears the dichotomy is still very wide.

The two different approaches have resulted in two sets of unreciprocated proposals. The basic North Korean perception of the South has been—and perhaps still is—that any political authority established in the South should be discredited and dismantled, thereby leading to absorption. In fact, North Korea once tried to communize the entire peninsula by force, but failed because the United States (under the UN flag) intervened.

Because the North Korean Communists still see South Korea as an area to be "liberated," it is quite natural that they should demand the withdrawal of U.S. troops in spite of continuous assurances that the U.S. presence in postured defensively. In fact, both sides have been talking past each other primarily for the record. Needless to say, such overtures have borne little fruit.

Conditions for Successful Military Talks in Korea

The most fundamental condition for the success of talks between the two parties in Korea is a dramatic change of perception by each side. It is impossible and absurd for either side to deny the existence of the other. The refusal by one party to recognize the other calls into question its own validity; the two factions of Korea, for whatever reasons, share the same origin in the postwar period. Any talk about reunification, including talk about military matters, requires both sides to recognize each other. Otherwise, it is nearly impossible for both parties to reach an agreement on any of the inter-Korean issues. In fact, undoing what had been done—the division of

Korea—demands painstaking effort by both sides. As long as one side considers the other an entity to be dissolved, then any agreement will be temporary in nature and have no binding force. In this regard, mutual recognition is the first step toward serious talks between North and South.

Sincerity is the next prerequisite for productive talks. Any proposal designed to camouflage military actions, such as the North Korean peace proposal made just before the Korean War, is not only counterproductive, but harmful to viable negotiations as well.

One observer has noted that "by December 1986 and certainly by early 1987, it was clear that North Korea's initiatives and flexibility encountered South Korea's indecision . . . ."[36] This may have been true; however, North Korean insincerity, and sometimes dishonesty, in putting forward proposals itself led to a lack of response from the South. Even today, South Korea cannot be sure whether North Korea is willing to discuss political and military matters sincerely because North Korean delegates are still complaining about the arrest of three people who visited North Korea illegally—Moon Ik-Whan, Im Su-Gyoung, and Moon Kyu-Hyon—without agreeing to even the title or agenda of the proposed high-level talks.[37] As a result, the North should take immediate steps to show its sincerity not only to its southern counterpart, but also to other nations concerned.

To discuss military matters, including disarmament and arms control, both North and South Korea should try very hard to enhance trust. Unless both sides feel physically secure, it is almost impossible to reach an agreement on issues such as arms reduction, limitation, and control. Because the North has attacked the South and thus created animosity between the two sites, it should seek to adopt measures—even unilateral ones—to enhance trust. In this sense, President Roh's unilateral no-first-use of force declaration at the UN General Assembly on October 18, 1988, was very significant, opening the door for substantial talks with the North and demanding a corresponding undertaking from North Korea.

Seoul and Pyongyang might start by demilitarizing their sides of the DMZ. Other steps could include joint academic research on Korean history and broadening humanitarian, cultural, and economic contacts between the two Koreas. Both sides would then be in a better position to discuss military affairs, disarmament, peace and stability, and the size of the military forces of a reunified Korea.

All in all, what is needed most in a negotiation of military issues is mutual recognition, sincerity, and understanding. Of course, these conditions are also necessary for the success of talks in other areas, the fruitful results of which may lead to more serious military negotiations. Factors beyond the Korean Peninsula also contribute a set of conditions, either favorable or unfavorable, for military talks. Intra-Korea agreements on military issues, however, are far more important for the future of Korea than any extra-Korea arrangements.

Prospects for the Future

In 1990, two channels are open for North and South Korea. The first is the preparatory meeting for the "yet-to-be-named" high-level talks, which has just concluded. This meeting has failed, after several rounds, to produce even a title or agenda for the main talks. The other channel is the high-level Red Cross talks, which have thus far sought primarily to promote cultural exchanges. Despite their meager results to date, both channels should be kept open.

Based on the U.S. experience in the negotiations for the armistice during the Korean War (1950–1953) and the lack of progress in the various talks now proceeding, it is fair to say that even an agreement to discuss substantive matters (including military issues) is likely to be reached only after a deeper mutual commitment of political will has been developed. Even though the UN Command had a good bargaining chip at the armistice conference—that is, the superior fire power of UN forces—it took more than two years to reach an agreement.[38] Whenever the Communists were intransigent on a certain item, the UN Command intensified its military operations. Now, the South no longer possesses this type of military leverage. Instead, it is reduced to reliance on humanitarian and economic incentives, the steady erosion of the DPRK's relative position, and the hope for a moderating change in the North Korean leadership.[39]

Thus, it appears to be the North that holds the key to a breakthrough of the current impasse. A continued flow of insincere proposals from Pyongyang will lead only to continued stalemate. The North must accept the fact that if they want to make peace, they must make it with Seoul, not Washington. They must publicly repudiate the use of terror and subversion and abandon the idea of a Korea unified under communism. Only when the North Korean leadership has addressed these issues sincerely can serious negotiations begin.

Notes

1. The *Korea Times,* October 6, 1989. The picture, showing several young Czechs looking at the mass of East German cars abandoned as the East Germans fled to the West, is quite impressive. See *The Korea Times,* October 7, 1989.

2. For the text of the July 7 declaration by President Roh Tae-Woo, see the *Korea Times,* July 8, 1988; *Dong-A Ilbo,* July 7, 1988. For commentary,

see "Roh's 7.7 Declaration," and "Seoul Leaves Door Wide Open to P'yang," *Diplomacy* 14, no. 7 (July 1988): 5, 8–10.

3. For the text of UN address (October 18, 1988), see *Dong-A Ilbo,* October 19, 1988.

4. *Dong-A Ilbo,* February 8, 1989. The North Korean representatives urged that the discontinuance of the Team Spirit exercise be the precondition for the talks, either preparatory or high-level.

5. *Military History of Korea* (Seoul: Military History Department, Korea Military Academy, 1988), pp. 207–211.

6. Republic of Korea National Unification Board, *Comparative Review on the Major South—North Proposals for Unification and Other Major Topics, 1945—1986* (hereafter *Review on the Major South—North Proposals*) (Seoul: ROK National Unification Board, 1984, 1987), 120.

7. Song Dae-Sung, "Review of the Feasibility of Arms Control and Reduction in Korea," *Korean Journal of International Relations* 29, no. 1 (Fall 1989): 94.

8. See *Aide-Memoire of the Foreign Ministry of the Democratic People's Republic of Korea,* October 7, 1974 and July 25, 1981; the Joint Statement of Political Parties and Social Organizations of January 18, 1983, is quoted and summarized in Young C. Kim, "The Politics of Arms Control in Korea," *Korean Journal of Defense Analysis* 1, no. 1 (Summer 1989): 114–115.

9. For the address of Premier Lee Jong-Ok at the 6th Summit Meeting of the Nonaligned Nations, September 5, 1979, see the statement of the North Korean Supreme People's Conference, January 10, 1984, *Review of the Major South—North Proposals,* 127, 162.

10. Conversations between Kim Il-Sung and the Peruvian Representatives for People's Revolution in America, July 1–5, 1983; *Decision of the Supreme People's Conference,* October 1, 1984, pp. 166–167. Kim's annual messages, January 1, 1985 and January 1, 1986, pp. 311, 393. In these messages, Kim reiterated North Korea's position to discuss the issue of a peace treaty and a North–South nonaggression declaration. In his letters to the ROK defense minister and the UN commander (June 9, 1986), the chief of North Korean Armed Forces, Oh Jin-Woo, proposed a military meeting of the three to discuss military matters, including an end to the joint military exercise between South Korea and the United States and arms reinforcement, arms reduction, and other measures to ease tension in Korea, pp. 413–414.

11. The intensity of this dimension in North Korean proposals has been somewhat subdued since the middle of the 1980s; however, the political action of the North Korean authority has shown a different picture.

12. *Review of the Major South—North Proposals,* 115.

13. Ibid., 116–123.

14. The memorandum to the 25th UN General Assembly, September 26, 1973, *Review of the Major South—North Proposals,* 124.

15. The *Korea Herald,* July 24, 1987; *Chosun Ilbo* and *Dong-A Ilbo,* July 24, 1987; Kim, "The Politics of Arms Control in Korea," 117–118.

16. The *Korea Herald,* July 24, 1987; *Chosun Ilbo,* July 24, 1987; *Dong-A Ilbo,* July 24, 1987.

17. Song, "Review of the Feasibility of Arms Control and Reduction in Korea," 94; *Review on the Major South—North Proposals,* 121–127, 137–145, 153–168.

18. For information on North Korean biochemical weapons, see "The Search for a Poison Antidote," *Time,* January 16, 1989, p. 22; "North Korean Bio-Chemical War Capability, the Third in the World," *Hangook Ilbo,* January 13, 1989; "Nuclear Weapons of the Poor: 22 Countries Have Biochemical War Capabilities, including North Korea," *Chosun Ilbo,* January 11, 1989.

19. The *Korea Times,* October 7, 1989.

20. *Review of the Major South—North Proposals,* 125.

21. According to the article, there were then 133 nuclear bombs, 63 nuclear shells for 8-inch howitzers, 33 nuclear shells for 155-mm howitzers, and 21 nuclear mines. In particular, nuclear mines were to be laid near the DMZ to the north of Seoul and would be detonated by a remote-control device. See *Joong-Ang Ilbo,* May 3, 1983.

22. *Review of the Major South—North Proposals,* 146.

23. Ibid., 115–431; Song, "Review of the Feasibility of Arms Control and Reduction in Korea," 94.

24. *Review of the Major South—North Proposals,* 146.

25. Ibid., 149.

26. Song, "Review of the Feasibility of Arms Control and Reduction in Korea," 94–95.

27. *Review of the Major South—North Proposals,* 156.

28. Song, "Review of the Feasibility of Arms Control and Reduction in Korea," 95.

29. Ibid.

30. See *Dong-A Ilbo,* October 19, 1988.

31. Ibid.

32. The *Korea Times,* August 16, 1989.

33. The *Korea Times,* September 12, 1989.

34. The *Korea Times,* September 30, 1989.

35. See the statement of Choi Byoung-Bo, spokesman for the National Unification Board, in the *Korea Times,* September 30, 1989.

36. Kim, "The Politics of Arms Control in Korea," 125–126.

37. At the end of the third preliminary meeting on October 12, 1989, North Korean delegate, Paek Nam-Jin said that the North would push for the release of the three at the next meeting, too. See the *Korea Times,* October 13, 1989.

38. See Walter G. Hermes, *The Truce Tent and Fighting Front* (Washington, D.C.: Government Printing Office, 1966).

39. See the remarks of the director of the IISS who visited South Korea on October 8, 1989, *Dong-A Ilbo,* October 9, 1989.

12

Inter-Korean Military Negotiations and U.S.–South Korean Security Cooperation

Park Tong-Whan

For decades, inter-Korean military relations have greatly influenced the security ties between Seoul and Washington. In fact, one of the most important determinants of the bilateral alliance has been the intense hostility between the two Koreas. There were other reasons why the United States wanted to maintain its military presence on the Korean Peninsula, including the regional and global balance of power it sought, but the continued threat from North Korea has undoubtedly been the driving force for U.S.–South Korean cooperation in security affairs.

Although the inter-Korean rivalry and the U.S.–South Korean alliance have combined to produce a state of fragile stability on the Korean Peninsula, there began to emerge signs of shift in each of the two relations. Seoul and Washington have long been discussing ways to change the nature and makeup of their common defense against Pyongyang, their primary target, and against Moscow and Beijing, their secondary targets (from the perspective of the U.S.–South Korean alliance). In light of Washington's changing mood about global strategic competition, the time will come soon, if it is not already here, when the U.S. security umbrella cannot be taken for granted.[1] At the same time, one can surmise that the military relationship between Pyongyang and Seoul may see a turning point in the 1990s. Under the burden of extensive armament, the two Koreas have paid the price in heavy defense expenditures—money that could have been invested in the civilian sector. Because this burden has been especially painful for North Korea, a reduction in tension would have a positive multiplying effect on the North Korean economy.

How can one establish a linkage between the inter-Korean rivalry and the U.S.–South Korean alliance when these two phenomena are undergoing, or are likely to undergo, major structural shifts? Because the main purpose of this chapter is to formulate directions for cooperation between Seoul and Washington in the context of change in inter-Korean rivalry, the approach taken here is to treat bilateral security ties between Seoul and Washington as the dependent variable or a cluster of dependent variables. Thus, this chapter begins with an analysis of the determinants of the U.S.–South Korean military relationship, with special emphasis given to the influence the inter-Korean rivalry on this alliance. Then, a possible agenda for military negotiations between the two Koreas is examined. Finally, the areas and directions in which Seoul and Washington may cooperate to promote peace and prosperity on the Korean Peninsula are identified.

Determinants of the U.S.–South Korean Military Relationship

Where is the U.S.–South Korean relationship headed? To answer this question, it is necessary to investigate changes in the determinants of the bilateral military relationship. Roughly put, there are two sources—internal and external—from which the determinants of the U.S.–South Korean military relationship originate. The former consists of domestic changes in South Korea and the United States, and the latter consists of three parts—relations on the Korean Peninsula, the four big powers in Northeast Asia, and the global system itself.

With regard to the domestic source, pressure has been mounting in both South Korea and the United States for a reconfiguration of the bilateral security arrangement. Plagued by twin budget and trade deficits, the United States has begun to reappraise its alliance commitments. As Walter Lippmann wrote during World War II, the United States has successfully managed its foreign policy by "bringing into balance, with a comfortable surplus of power in reserve, the nation's commitments and the nation's power." Unfortunately, the current generation of U.S. leaders is worried whether the United States can now cope with what Samuel Huntington described as "the Lippmann gap." Hence, it is only natural that many Americans voice their resentment, through the media and through Congress, about the undue burden of defense the United States is asked to assume, while some wealthy allies enjoy a free ride.[2]

As was the case with Western Europe and Japan, South Korea's economy was able to grow under the international free trade regime, which in reality meant a generous opening of the U.S. market to imports from its allies' fledging industries. Although South Koreans remain appreciative of U.S. leadership and assistance during the formative stage of their nationhood, they also regret the fact that the United States' door for commerce was shut much sooner for them than it was for the Japanese or West Europeans. Given this background, it is understandable that some South Koreans feel that the U.S. government lacks sensitivity in handling security-related negotiations. To them, the security umbrella provided by the United States is vital to South Korea's continued economic growth, let alone survival, and this security should not be subject to the whim of U.S. domestic politics.

Turning to the external determinants of U.S.–South Korean military relations, there exist three types of threat affecting the security of South Korea: the inter-Korean rivalry, the regional balance of power among the four big nations in Northeast Asia, and global changes.

With regard to the hostility on the peninsula, the two Koreas have been locked in a mutually destructive arms race since the Korean War. Despite current trends toward a superpower detente and the wave of democracy in Eastern Europe, military tensions remain excessive on the Korean Peninsula. Almost 1.5 million troops face each other along the DMZ, and, since 1953, more than 1,000 South Koreans and 90 Americans have died in border incidents. To South Korea, the threat is very real indeed. North Korea remains the most closed and isolated state in the world, and it maintains its commitment to reunify the peninsula by force. North Korea is known to have the military superiority needed to carry out its threat. Excluding the war-fighting capacity of U.S. troops in South Korea, it is estimated that an overall parity in cumulated military stock between the two Koreas will not be reached until well after 1997. It should also be borne in mind that the Soviet Union continues to upgrade Pyongyang's military hardware in spite of Gorbachev's rhetoric of peace.

At the regional level, the changing balance of power among the United States, the Soviet Union, China, and Japan makes the future of Northeast Asia very unstable. All four countries are presently undergoing major domestic changes that will have critical implications for their foreign policies. In the United States, there has been a definitive change in foreign policy because of U.S. economic problems and the attendant return to neo-pragmatism. Changes have been visible not in Washington's goal of preserving U.S. security interests in Northeast Asia, but rather in the foreign policy instruments with which such goals are to be implemented. In short, the U.S. role will become more supportive than directive. Allies will be asked to fend for themselves, receiving U.S. aid only when needed.

In contrast, Soviet foreign policy appears to be committed to the opposite direction: building a modernized state, with the aim of achieving hegemony in the global political economy. Its domestic reforms are all geared toward socioeconomic growth, and its gesture of arms reduction is designed to free scarce resources from the military sector. It should be noted that the Soviet move toward global detente may not necessarily apply to Northeast Asia, however. If anything, its political and military presence in the region has been increasing, including its move to become a full-fledged member of the Pacific community from both the economic and military standpoint. Thus, it is quite fitting that Moscow wishes to cultivate friendly relations with both North and South Korea. Moscow needs Pyongyang's cooperation to strengthen its military posture as an Asian power. Simultaneously, it seeks to use the emerging Seoul connection (now formalized by an agreement on diplomatic relations) to increase its commercial ties with the booming economies of the Pacific Basin.

China's foreign policy direction is somewhat more difficult to predict. Until the June 1989 massacre at Tiananmen, China watchers were united in painting a rosy picture of Beijing's policy of liberalization and modernization. Now, with Deng Xiaoping's semi-retirement, the critical question is whether the present hard-line policies are merely a temporary setback or a harbinger of more serious structural changes. The answer appears to be a combination of the two. On the one hand, China cannot afford a challenge to its Communist leadership; hence, law and order must be given priority, even at the high cost of slowing its economic cooperation with the West. On the other hand, China has been trying to become rich and powerful in its own way; the pendulum-like swings between the doctrines of revolution and pragmatism can be seen as the political tools employed in its path to superpowerdom. Hence, China's foreign policy toward the Korean Peninsula will follow a line similar to that of the Soviet Union—an attempt to simultaneously woo Pyongyang politically and deepen economic interactions with Seoul.

Japan is also experiencing turmoil in its internal politics. For the first time in the 34-year history of one-party dominance by the Liberal Democratic Party (LDP), opposition groups are in command in the Lower House. With the loss of control in the Upper House, the LDP will face increasing challenges to its policy of security dependence on the United States. Fortunately, Japan's changing political face will have few consequences for the Korean Peninsula because the Tokyo government is expected to maintain its equidistant foreign policies toward Pyongyang and Seoul.

Finally, at the global level, two developments will seriously affect Northeast Asia—the maturing of the Pacific era and the rising importance of the NICs in the international political economy. In the Pacific Basin, Korea is located at the intersection of continental and maritime powers. Historically, this location has served as the setting for many battles because the peninsula serves as a bridge or beachhead for opposing powers. As a new international order is established in the Pacific Basin, it is not yet certain that the transition will be entirely peaceful.

What can be deduced from the analysis thus far is that the security situation in Northeast Asia has been changing, and there are two discernible trends. One is the continuing U.S. military presence in South Korea, which has become important not only from the perspective of deterring Pyongyang, but also from that of maintaining stability in Northeast Asia and the international system. The other is that in the new international order of the Pacific Basin, economic security is as valuable as—if not more valuable than—military security.

Given this picture of the Northeast Asian international system, it can be hypothesized that the future of U.S.–South Korean military relations will be affected most strongly by the inter-Korean relationship and, to a lesser degree, by U.S. engagement in the region.[3] The remaining determinants, whether internal or external in nature, are expected to make only minor changes in the U.S.–South Korean military relationship, largely because the other three powers—the Soviet Union, China, and Japan—would favor the maintenance of a status quo on the peninsula, at least until they can claim hegemony in regional affairs. In contrast, North Korea's intentions are extremely difficult to discern, although it can be assumed that North Korea will resist liberalization and de-communization until the last possible moment.

At the same time, one can envision a significant change in the nexus between the inter-Korean military rivalry and the U.S.–South Korean security relationship. That is, the linkage will become genuinely more bidirectional than unidirectional. The inter-Korean military relationship will both influence and be influenced by Seoul–Washington military ties, based on a calculation of relative capabilities and constraints, rather than political rhetoric.

In the past, the predominant pattern was such that the United States and South Korea responded and reacted to threats from North Korea, whereas Pyongyang went about its military buildup without concern for the other side. That the Pyongyang government has continued the propaganda blitz against Yankee imperialists was, in a sense, to satisfy its domestic audience.[4] In the future, Pyongyang's attitude toward Seoul and Washington is expected to be more circumspect. This prediction is based on South Korea's status as an economic giant, compared with the North, and its continued investment in defense, which will soon make South Korea's military a force of great threat. It is apparent that South Korea will no longer remain a military underdog that North Korea can look down upon. The result of this development is that, from now on, Seoul and Washington should move with more caution in dealing with Pyongyang because their policies will carry more weight in the latter's decision-making process.

Agenda and Direction

In the history of dialogue between the two Koreas, security issues have seldom been subjected to serious bilateral negotiations. Instead, the two Koreas have frequently made unilateral proposals and pronouncements, whose intended targets were their domestic audiences and the world community. It is unlikely that the pattern will change radically in the near future. It should be noted, however, that these declaratory statements may become useful as a prelude to substantive negotiations when the two sides are ready to negotiate seriously. It is believed that the 1990s will be the decade with ample opportunities for a serious negotiation. This forecast is based not only on a systematic observation of recent political developments in Northeast Asia, but also on a historical imperative: Seoul and Washington may never see a better opportunity to induce Pyongyang to the negotiating table. Because it is evident that the current leadership in Pyongyang is unwilling to initiate a Gorbachevian *glasnost* for domestic political reasons, Seoul should take initiative to bring about detente on the Korean Peninsula. Indeed, Pyongyang's decision makers may accept an offer of peace from the South if it is carefully designed not to undermine their grip on political power. An offer from the South could range from such tangible items as arms control and disarmament to political gestures aimed at promoting mutual trust.

Taking the peace initiative will surely require some real sacrifices on the part of Seoul and Washington, but these short-term sacrifices will be more than offset by the prospect of long-term savings that will accrue from a more stable and peaceful Northeast Asia. Specifically, there are three areas in which Seoul and Washington may launch such an initiative: arms control and disarmament, nuclear weapons, and the withdrawal of U.S. forces from South Korea. These three areas have been the target of constant bickering by the North, and Pyongyang would find it difficult to evade these issues, should the inter-Korean dialogue begin in earnest. A description of each issue will be followed by a discussion of the means of cooperation between Seoul and Washington.

Arms Control and Disarmament

Given the long time span during which the two Koreas have been locked in a system of confrontation, it is expected that the task of reducing bilateral tension would be extremely difficult.[5] There is no doubt, however, that a prerequisite for tension reduction is some form of arms control and, at a later stage, disarmament. Arms control does not necessarily involve disarmament. Although the objective of disarmament is to reduce military capabilities, arms control is a mechanism that produces agreements on the use of military forces and weapons—types, how and where they are deployed, their characteristics, safety conditions to prevent accidents, and the like.[6] Arms control policies thus imply collaboration between the adversaries through formal agreements, tacit approvals, informal cooperation, or unilateral moves made with the expectation that the other side will reciprocate.[7] Hence, the main objective of arms control is to stabilize the military relationship.

Perhaps the reason that arms control has received so little attention in Korea is its conceptual confusion with disarmament. In light of the tension between the two Koreas and among the major powers in Northeast Asia, it must have been impossible for Pyongyang and Seoul to discuss substantive disarmament. Even regarding arms control, whose importance can be clearly justified, the two Koreas have made little progress. Simply, there have existed too many obstacles to arms control between Seoul and Pyongyang.

First and foremost, both sides have adhered to the belief that negotiations should be conducted only from a position of strength. Although the doctrine of "peace through strength" appeals strongly to each side's domestic audience, this tactic will very seldom lead to a successful agreement on arms control. Obviously, it is impossible for both sides to simultaneously gain an upper hand in their bilateral relationship. Closely tied to this one-upmanship is the inherent distrust of one's enemy. Long recognized as the most formidable barrier to arms control, this mirror image syndrome of distrust has prevailed in both North and South Korea since the division of the peninsula after World War II. As long as distrust persists between the two countries, the problem of verification will remain a thorny issue in any potential arms control negotiations. Although surveillance satellites of the superpowers could provide both sides with up-to-date information about the movement of troops and weapons above ground, posing a grave danger to the military balance will be those activities that may evade even the keenest lenses, such as the fortification of underground bases and the digging of infiltration tunnels.

Another factor that hinders arms control agreements is the difficulty of devising a formula that will not handicap either of the parties involved. Because the two Koreas perceive different security requirements and possess different weapon systems, it is not an easy task to establish qualitative comparability of military power. Surely, the North is ahead of the South in virtually all areas of military capability, but does this static disparity automatically imply dynamic superiority on the battlefield? It has been proven time after time that wars are not necessarily won because of a preponderance of weapons and troops, but, rather, because of better utilization.

One must also include in the calculus of the military balance on the Korean Peninsula the potential and real presence of the superpowers. How would one measure, for instance, the deterrent capability of tactical nuclear weapons held by U.S. troops in South Korea? Is the United States or the Soviet Union more interested in promoting arms control than a military balance in Northeast Asia? If so, to what extent? Given the conflicting interests of the nations involved, one cannot expect an arms control proposal in Korea to satisfy all.

A further obstacle to arms control is that defense policies are not shaped solely on the basis of external threat. Bureaucratic and domestic political variables strongly influence the types and levels of weapons procured. In both Koreas, the military sector takes up the biggest piece of the budgetary pie. It also constitutes the single largest organization among the adult population, thus making it a powerful interest group in national decision making. In addition, one should note that interservice competition can at times become quite intense. Consequently, the military in both North and South Korea can be seen as a giant entity with its share of internal conflict and its own mechanism for settling such conflict.

A final factor pertinent to the Korean case is that both sides may fear arms control more than they fear an arms race. Although it is a tragic irony, Pyongyang and Seoul have established a certain modus vivendi as a result of their long history of bilateral competition. Arms control is unknown territory, however. The Koreans are not familiar with the risks associated with arms control, and thus the trails leading to it appear more threatening.

The lack of progress in arms control does not mean that the two Koreas have neglected the subject. On the contrary, numerous proposals have been advanced by Pyongyang and Seoul since the formation of two separate governments in 1948. In fact, Pyongyang has made about four times as may proposals as Seoul regarding arms control, and this reveals two important points. One is that the North has undoubtedly maintained the initiative in the discussion of arms control on the Korean Peninsula. The other is that Pyongyang's true intentions were not necessarily arms control; instead, the "peace offensive" was designed to confuse the South Koreans.

That the domestic and international conditions may not be favorable to arms control on the Korean Peninsula at this time is no reason to be pessimistic about the future. In a sense, the long history of hostile inter-action has created physical and psychological barriers that are difficult to dismantle in a short period of time. The Koreans have become so accustomed to life in a divided state that they may even feel uneasy with the idea of rapprochement. Because the foremost stumbling block to arms control is psychological, attempts should be made to install such nonmilitary steps as confidence-building measures. Once the psychological resistance to arms control is lowered, the remaining obstacles should be more easily overcome because they largely center on more technical aspects of the arms race.

Consequently, the most important contribution the United States can make toward arms control and disarmament on the Korean Peninsula is to help the two Koreas build mutual trust. Just as a third party can often intercede to rebuild the relationship between two quarreling individuals, so too can the United States promote a setting in which the two Koreas can start a serious dialogue. There are a number of specific measures the United States can take toward that end. First, Washington can offer its electronically gathered data to both Seoul and Pyongyang for the verification of any arms control accord. The data will need to be doctored to conceal sensitive technical capabilities, but could be sufficiently detailed to spot any violation of the agreement. In addition, Washington may persuade Moscow to do likewise, thus increasing the reliability of the information provided.

Second, the United States can make a public pronouncement that its troops will serve as a buffer between the two Koreas while the Koreans work out their differences. The statement may not come as a surprise to Pyongyang and Seoul, although each will be somewhat disappointed by it. For North Koreans, the U.S. military presence has been a powerful incentive to maintain their garrison state, and any downgrading of the U.S. military threat will have a dampening effect on their sociopolitical control. Such a statement by Washington will be considered by South Koreans as a turning point in their international relations. They will realize that their security dependence on the United States has finally come to an end, and a new era of foreign policy has dawned. Thus, they will try to maximize the remaining years before seeking a more independent security posture in the global community.

Third, and perhaps most important, Washington can use its leverage with Moscow and Beijing to encourage these two patrons to exert pressure on Pyongyang to meet seriously with Seoul. As demonstrated during the 1988 Seoul Olympics, the big powers can influence Pyongyang with both carrots and sticks. Because it is also in the interest of these Communist giants to have peace on the Korean Peninsula, a little prodding from the United States is likely to bear favorable results.

Nuclear Weapons on the Korean Peninsula

Despite the U.S. government's policy of "neither confirming nor denying" the presence of nuclear weapons on the Korean Peninsula or because of such a policy, the world is led to believe that the United States indeed maintains a stockpile of various nuclear weapons there. The presence of the structure of weapon storage, special weapon support systems, emergency action consoles, and permissive actions links, which have been put in place over the past 30 years, add credibility to the presumed presence of a nuclear arsenal. Although this has lent a powerful element of deterrence, the strategic utility of nuclear weapons has come under increasing attack in both the scholarly and decision-making communities of Seoul and Washington. As General Menetrey, commander of U.S. forces in South Korea, has said, the United States envisions no situation in which the employment of nuclear weapons would be used for South Korea's defense. Thus, the only other reason for maintaining them would be deterrence against the Soviet Union or China.

With the increasing military capabilities of the two Koreas, the issue of U.S. nuclear weapons on the peninsula began to have implications far beyond the intended goal of deterrence. First of all, Pyongyang has come to regard them as the ultimate threat to the viability of North Korea. North Koreans may see U.S. nuclear weapons as additional insurance for South Korea, while the latter increases its own military capability to match that of the North. As the insurance policy matures, North Koreans may begin to worry that the South could launch a preemptive strike against the North. It is not surprising to hear, therefore, that North Korea is allegedly building a plutonium reprocessing plant near Yungbyun. Should North Korea be able to fabricate a small atomic device, it will certainly boost Pyongyang's stature tremendously, both domestically and internationally. North Korea will become a member of the prestigious nuclear club, commanding attention from powers both big and small. With its new status, Pyongyang could even fend off external pressures for liberalization, thus maintaining its totalitarian system. Domestically, it would strengthen the hand of the present leadership and facilitate the political transition from Kim Il-Sung to his son, Kim Jong-Il.

A North Korea bomb would have a truly terrifying effect on the South. The fear North Koreans presently have about U.S. nuclear weapons will be minuscule compared with what would be felt by the South Koreans should North Korea develop the bomb. South Koreans would likely react to such a development in two ways. One would be a "me too" psychology, in which those on the right would demand an acceleration of South Korea's own program of nuclear weapons development. The other—a more leftist— response, would be to level all blame on the presence of U.S. nuclear weapons on the peninsula and to demand the severance of military ties with Washington.

It is no secret that South Korea has attempted to develop its own nuclear weapons capability. Based on the assumption that possession of nuclear arms would enhance Seoul's security posture, the late President Park Chung-Hee launched plans in the mid-1970s to acquire a spent-fuel reprocessing plant from France, only to have this plan foiled by U.S. interdiction. Even in President Chun Doo-Hwan's Fifth Republic, Seoul has reportedly shown interest in obtaining reprocessing technology. In 1984, a proposal was allegedly made by the Canadian Atomic Energy Agency to recycle the spent fuel from a U.S.-made light water reactor in South Korea into mixed oxide fuel, which would constrain weapons-grade plutonium for the Canadian heavy water reactor at Wolsung. Again, the proposal was blocked by the U.S. government. The search for indigenous nuclear weapons will not be active in the Sixth Republic under President Roh Tae-Woo. Deeply committed to rapprochement with northern countries, the Seoul government will not take any action to threaten its *nordpolitik*.

Given these conflicting developments in North and South Korea, what are the options available to Washington to promote peace on the peninsula while maintaining deterrence against the Communist powers? One option that may be worth considering is removing the nuclear issue entirely from the agenda of inter-Korean negotiations and the domestic opposition in South Korea. All it takes to achieve this goal is to move the nuclear weapons offshore, while reaffirming a commitment to deterrence. Then the U.S. nuclear arsenal will be about the same distance from the Korean Peninsula as is the Soviets', and it would continue to maintain a sufficient level of deterrence. Although the added cost to the United States is minimal, the effect would be dramatic— the creation of a de facto nuclear-free zone on the Korean Peninsula.

Of course, the United States' offshore nuclear strike force should remain visible, as would a carrier task force, or should patrol Korean shores undetected, as nuclear missile submarines. For additional precaution, a solid presence of conventional deterrence would be required, that is, a sizable ground troop presence with a command, control, communications, and intelligence (C^3I) capability to nullify North Korea's advantage in the forward deployment of its forces and South Korea's disadvantage in having its capital so close the DMZ. Other measures to ensure the absence of nuclear weapons would include the verification of nuclear power plants via satellites and on-site inspections by the International Atomic Energy Agency.

U.S. Troops in South Korea

Turning to the final and most critical issue in inter-Korean military relations, what will happen to U.S. forces in South Korea when Northeast Asia undergoes major structural changes in the 1990s? The original purpose of stationing U.S. troops along the DMZ was to make them serve as a tripwire, guaranteeing an automatic U.S. involvement in the event of a North Korean attack. U.S. troops in South Korea have been fulfilling that function successfully since 1953. With the changing security climate of the Pacific Basin, however, U.S. forces in South Korea have begun to assume roles far beyond the original tripwire purpose. They have become an instrument through which a range of foreign policy signals can be transmitted and received. How will these changes then affect the future of U.S. forces stationed in South Korea?

First, on the question of how much longer U.S. troops will remain on the Korean Peninsula, it can be forecast that they will be there for a long time to come, even beyond the year 2000, barring such revolutionary developments as Korean reunification or a U.S.–Soviet entente. The rationale underlying this prediction is that U.S. troops ensure peace in Northeast Asia and serve as a watchdog for the rapidly cumulating wealth in South Korea. In addition, U.S. forces in South Korea are a critical component in the U.S. strategic net that links Western Europe, Southeast Asia, and the Pacific. Unless the United States decides to pull back its troops from Japan or West Germany, the complete withdrawal of U.S. soldiers from the Korean Peninsula is virtually unthinkable.

Second, how many U.S. troops will remain in South Korea? A prudent guess is that no significant cutback will be possible. The current level of 43,000 is totally inadequate for *defense* against a North Korean attack. Except for the Korean War period, it should be remembered, the United States stationed its forces in South Korea for the purpose of deterrence, not defense. As a symbol of deterrence, the number of ground troops need not be enormous, but it should be sizable enough to have the tripwire effect. It is often suggested in U.S. military circles that some fat could be trimmed off the administrative side of U.S. forces in South Korea, thus saving money and, at the same time, satisfying U.S. public opinion. One could surmise that at least a combat division is required, while the air force needs the level of equipment and personnel that would enable a crippling second strike.

Third, in what form will the United States continue its military presence in South Korea? Although the principle of deploying U.S. troops near the DMZ will remain unaltered, the structure of command and control for combined defense will undergo major changes. Created in 1978, the Combined Forces Command has withstood a number of challenges, including its alleged implication in the Kwangju Democratization Movement. The current wave of anti-Americanism in South Korea, however, has focused significant attention on the U.S. military presence in South Korea and finds an easy target in the "unfair" mechanism of the combined command system. It was a sensible decision for Seoul and Washington to agree to the constructive reform of the command mechanism and to embark on the removal of the most visible sign of a U.S. military presence from the capital city of Seoul.

Fourth, the area that will see the largest change is burden sharing. Sharing the defense burden has never been determined by a uniform formula; rather, it has been arrived at by subjective perception and objective evaluation of security interests and by the ability of each ally to pay. The arrangement thus varies from case to case: from Japan, which pays the lion's share of the cost to support U.S. forces on its soil, to the Philippines, which receives significant compensation from the United States for the use of military bases. The Seoul government has contributed significantly to the maintenance of U.S. forces in South Korea and continues to enlarge its share.

What has been discussed thus far reinforces the observation that U.S. troops in South Korea have been, and will remain, an extremely sensitive issue not only in inter-Korean military relations, but also in the security ties between Seoul and Washington. It cannot be resolved by consultation between Seoul and Washington alone. Likewise, no agreement between the two Koreas can leave out the United States. Its resolution will become possible only when the parties involved pursue a two-front approach: both inter-Korean dialogue and negotiation between Seoul and Washington.

In the past, Washington was able to make virtually unilateral moves regarding its military presence in South Korea largely because there existed no link between these two sets of relations. It is also obvious that the United States did not see the need to nurture one. Pyongyang did not make any serious attempt to link these two relationships either. Knowing that it cannot will the U.S. soldiers away from the peninsula, Pyongyang has been exploiting the politics of this triangular relationship. It should be noted that North Korea's incessant call for a three-way dialogue among Washington, Seoul, and Pyongyang has been intended to isolate South Korea and to deal with the United States on a coequal basis. For its part, Seoul has been in no position to tamper with the security arrangement with the United States, particularly with those U.S. troops stationed along the DMZ.

Consequently, the most important change to be made in handling the issue of U.S. forces in South Korea is in the attitude of the three nations involved. To bring about a lasting peace on the Korean Peninsula, the three countries need to develop a plan for the constructive use of U.S. troops in South Korea, one that departs from the practice of using them as a tool for political maneuvering. For the United States, it will be necessary, although difficult, to make the candid admission that South Korea is different from Japan, and Washington will continue to be hesitant about reducing its military presence even when it is prudent to do so.[8] Pyongyang and Seoul should also make it known that U.S. troops on the peninsula have multiple roles to play, some of which are advantageous and some of which are not in their national interest. Only from this changed perspective can concrete steps be taken toward the constructive disengagement of U.S. troops, thus building the foundation for mutual trust and cooperation between the two Koreas.

Conclusion

At no time in the 40-year history of the U.S.–South Korean security relationship have the two allies faced challenges of the magnitude they now do. Domestic and international changes of a revolutionary nature are forcing the two countries to cope directly with the new issues, as well as address old issues in a new form. Arms control and disarmament, nuclear weapons on the peninsula, U.S. troops in South Korea—these are the most critical of the issues that have constantly troubled the key players in Northeast Asia. What makes them doubly painful at this juncture is that these issues have gone past the stage of verbal exchanges. It is now time for definitive action to achieve their resolution.

Furthermore, in the process of tackling these issues, a structural change will be needed in the regional balance of power in general and in the triangular relationship among the two Koreas and the United States in particular. Until now, the two "legs" of the triangle—namely, the inter-Korean relationship and the Seoul–Washington alliance—have not had any formal bridging mechanism despite the enormous political and military impact each had on the other. This is the reason that those military issues have remained unsettled. If anything, those issues were often used as tools to legitimize authoritarianism or anachronistic foreign policies.

It has been widely held that the lack of an organic link between the two "legs" has greatly handicapped Seoul's foreign policy because Seoul has had to counter the threat from Pyongyang and, at the same time, accept the largely unilateral behavior of Washington in security affairs. This situation must change before a serious attempt can be made to resolve these military issues, and the place to begin is with the attitudes of the parties involved. Because the most logical point of connection between the inter-Korean relationship and the Seoul–Washington linkage is South Korea, it is imperative that both the United States and North Korea first recognize this as undeniable. In other words, Pyongyang and Washington need to regard Seoul as an independent entity in the negotiation process and accord it with proper authority to handle substantive issues.

Certainly, it will not be easy to change the modus operandi of the triangular interactions among Pyongyang, Seoul, and Washington, but the alternative will be continued instability in Northeast Asia, which favors no one. North Korea would be forced to maintain its course of almost suicidal military buildup, thus pushing to the limit its overburdened economy. Similarly, the United States would continue to be irritated by the sore spot in global detente, as long as tension remains high on the Korean Peninsula. For its part, South Korea would have to live with the constant threat from the North, no matter how diligently it built its military or how fervently it cultivated its friendly relations with its Communist neighbors.

At long last, the cold war era is about to end. It is a sad irony that one of the most painful legacies of bipolar confrontation, the DMZ, is not likely to be erased from the map in the near future. Although a product of such confrontation, the North Korean system has developed a life of its own and defies the force of global change toward coexistence and reconciliation. What is required of Seoul and Washington, therefore, is not a hasty attempt to open Pyongyang's door, but a gradual approach toward evolving change in North Korea. To that end, the U.S.–South Korean security cooperation will also need to evolve into a more mature and interdependent relationship as well.

Notes

1. For a discussion of the changing mood in the United States about overseas military involvement and its impact on the Korean Peninsula, see Park Tong-Whan, "U.S.–Korean Security Relations in the 1990s: The Emergence of a New Partnership in the Pacific," Paper presented at the International Seminar on the Strategic Importance of U.S. Troops in Korea, Seoul, South Korea, November 27, 1987.

2. For a comprehensive historical analysis of how the United States' overseas military commitments have evolved, see John Lovell, "Cutting Back: The Future of United States Military Alliance Commitments in the Context of Past Experience," unpublished manuscript, 1989.

3. For an empirical test of the model in which the U.S.–South Korean military relationship was subjected to a multiple regression analysis against a pool of independent variables, including the inter-Korean military relationship, the U.S.–South Korean political relationship, and the U.S.–South Korean economic relationship, see Park Tong-Whan, "Alliance, Extended Deterrence, and Interdependence: Trends and Determinants of the Military Relationship between Korea and the U.S.A.," *Korea Journal of Defense Analysis* 1, no. 1 (Summer 1989): 167–192.

4. For an analysis of the pattern of action–reaction in the military competition between North and South Korea, see Park Tong-Whan, "Arms Race Between the Two Koreas: An Empirical Examination," *Journal of East Asian Affairs* 2, no. 1 (Spring/Summer 1982): 70–89; Park Tong-Whan, "Political Economy of the Arms Race in Korea: Queries, Evidence, and Insights," *Asian Survey* (August 1986); Park Tong-Whan, "Arms Race and Arms Control in Korea," *Korea and World Affairs* 10, no. 2 (Summer 1986): 404–422.

5. A more detailed discussion of the argument in this section is in this section can be found in Park Tong-Whan, "Threat Assessment and the Possibility of Arms Control and Reduction on the Korean Peninsula," *Proceedings of the Fifth ROK–U.S. Defense Analysis Seminar,* 2 (Seoul: Korea Institute for Defense Analysis, 1989).

6. Bruce Russett and H. Starr, *World Politics: The Menu for Choice* (San Francisco: Freeman, 1981), 380.

7. James E. Dougherty and R.L. Pfaltzgraff, Jr., *Contending Theories of International Relations: A Comprehensive Survey,* 2nd ed. (New York: Harper & Row, 1981), 395.

8. One need not be reminded that the U.S. Congress and the American public have made few demands for the withdrawal of more than 60,000 U.S. troops in Japan. One can surmise three underlying reasons for this phenomenon: Japan has far more value as a partner than any of the United States' other allies, the primary threat to Japan is from the Soviet Union, and the United States is worried about the potential rearmament of Japan when the U.S. security umbrella is removed.

13

Operational Arms Control in Europe: Implications for Security Negotiations in Korea

James Goodby

Operational Arms Control Measures

Negotiations within the framework of the Conference on Security and Cooperation in Europe (CSCE) have yielded accords that, in the context of large-scale political change in Europe, have the potential to transform the security relationships between opposing military forces in Europe. This chapter will review the recent European experience in negotiating operational arms control agreements with a view to considering its relevance to arms control and related security negotiations in Korea.

"Operational arms control" is the most recent term given to a form of arms control that has had a long and little-noticed history. Other, perhaps more familiar terms include "confidence- and security-building measures," "risk-reduction measures," and "stabilizing measures." Examples of this form of arms control include:

- U.S.–USSR Hot Line Agreement (1963, with upgrades in subsequent years),
- U.S.–USSR Nuclear Accidents Agreement (1971),
- U.S.–USSR Incidents at Sea Agreement (1972),
- Helsinki Final Act (1975),
- Stockholm Document (1986),
- U.S.–USSR Nuclear Risk Reduction Centers (1987),

- U.S.–USSR Agreement on Notification of Missile Launches (1979, expanded in 1988),
- U.S.–USSR Agreement on Prevention of Dangerous Military Practices (1989), and
- U.S.–USSR Agreement on Advance Notification of Strategic Exercises (1989).

Noteworthy about this list is the preponderance of bilateral nuclear-related agreements, rather than multilateral conventional arms agreements, and the increasing frequency with which operational arms control agreements have been concluded in the past three years. The reasons for so many nuclear agreements are traceable to concerns about fast-moving crises involving nuclear weapons and to the fact that negotiations on strategic nuclear arms have dominated the arms control scene since the early 1970s. The relatively large number of such agreements in recent years can be explained by greater political interest in this form of arms control in Washington, Moscow, and elsewhere.

An explanation of what such understandings are supposed to accomplish may help clarify both the preoccupation with nuclear matters and the heightened interest in operational arms control. As its name implies, operational arms control is intended to deal with the operations of military forces—with troop movements and missile launchings—rather than the numbers of troops or missiles. Operational arms control can deal with these operations, in principle, both by generating information about them and by limiting or constraining them.

Constraints, however, have not met with much success in negotiations to date. Generating information generally entails providing data to potential military adversaries in advance of the actual operation. Thus, agreements on missile launchings and troop maneuvers require advance notification through a specified channel in some prescribed form, that is, a minimum period of time for advance notice and facts about the operation, such as its purpose and size. Some agreements deal only with the means of communication (the Hot Line) while others, in addition to furnishing information, provide mechanisms for clarifying, resolving, or preventing military contingencies (e.g., Prevention of Dangerous Military Practices, Incidents at Sea, Stockholm Document). Such mechanisms can include direct observation of military operations, either in connection with pre-notified events or on demand, even in the absence of a notification. The latter serves to verify operational arms control agreements.

The general theory behind this type of arms control is similar, in some respects, to the theory of arms control in general. Schelling and Halperin defined the term in 1961 to mean "all the forms of military cooperation between potential enemies in the interest of reducing the likelihood of war, its scope and violence if it occurs, and the political and economic costs of being prepared for it."[1] This definition quite clearly encompasses operational arms control.

There are some differences, however, in the philosophy of operational arms control as opposed to arms limitation negotiations. In general, traditional arms limitation agreements deal with reduction or limitation of levels of forces, while the purpose of operational arms control is to deal primarily with reduction or limitation of risks posed by the possibility of accident, misperception, or intended surprise attack. Traditional arms control negotiations typically try to establish long-term stability by providing greater predictability about the types and levels of forces that will be maintained over a given span of time. On the other hand, operational arms control measures are aimed at establishing a framework for clarifying the nature and purpose of military operations and for enhancing or restoring stability during fast-moving crisis situations.

The hope that lies behind operational arms control is that greater openness about military operations will act to deter surprise attack and to reduce the possibility of misinterpreting the intentions of military operations. The obligation imposed by risk reduction measures is not fulfilled by dismantling hardware, but rather by dismantling excessive secrecy. Furthermore, the idea behind having means of communications and prearranged contingency procedures in place is that crises can be prevented or contained more effectively if methods of communication do not have to be improvised under the pressure of events.

As can be seen from the preceding discussion, the "units of account" in operational arms control and, therefore, the key questions to be answered and verified, are not static indicators such as numbers of tanks and divisions but rather

- How ready for combat are these forces?
- What do training practices reveal about their purpose and intention?
- What is the overall scale and scope of a nation's military activities?

One defect of risk reduction measures must be acknowledged and assessed: The intentions of an adversary can change rapidly; intentions are nebulous, in contrast with capabilities, which can be measured and quantified. Nonetheless, intentions do form an important part of assessing an adversary's overall force posture and the way one should respond to this posture. Intentions are an element, in fact, to which governments devote much time and resources in their evaluations of external threats.

It is probably correct to say that operational arms control measures now in place do a better job of dealing with prevention of the war that no one wants than with the war that someone might surreptitiously plan behind the deceptive facade of cooperative behavior. The next generation of operational arms control measures may do more to deter or detect preparations for surprise attack, but even the present generation of measures are useful. The measures in place in Europe as a result of the Stockholm Document of September 1986, for example, may help prevent future crises. They have already helped to promote greater openness and to encourage habits of cooperation between adversaries. All this is necessary and very useful as a first step, but still not sufficient. Nonetheless, these measures are contributing in a variety of ways to a more stable equilibrium in Europe.

Helsinki and Stockholm Accords

Some of the experience gained in negotiating and implementing operational arms control in Europe may be relevant in the Korean situation. There follows, therefore, a brief description of the Helsinki and Stockholm accords. The first generation of European operational arms control measures were put into effect by the Helsinki Final Act of 1975, the first substantive document to emerge from the "Helsinki process" or, more formally, from the process started by the CSCE. The CSCE includes all of NATO, all of the Warsaw Pact, and all neutral or nonaligned nations of Europe. Two measures were central to the Helsinki security provisions. One called for prenotification 21 days in advance of certain military maneuvers involving more than 25,000 troops; the other measure called for the invitation, on a voluntary basis, of observers to those maneuvers. Voluntary notification of smaller-scale exercises involving fewer than 25,000 troops was suggested. The zone of application extended only 250 kilometers into the western part of the Soviet Union.

By early 1984, when the Stockholm Conference convened, there had been nearly 100 notifications of military activities in Europe involving more than 2 million troops. Observers had been invited to about 50 exercises. NATO countries had extended more than 30 invitations; the United States alone had invited Warsaw Pact observers to 10 exercises. The Warsaw Pact had announced more than 20 maneuvers, but invited NATO country observers to fewer than half of these. U.S. observers had been invited to Warsaw Pact maneuvers only twice, and not at all after 1979. The NATO countries had notified CSCE participants of 29 smaller-scale exercises. The Warsaw Pact had notified them of four.

The Final Act expressed concern about military operations in which "participating states lack clear and timely information about the nature of such activities." The provisions of the Helsinki Final Act for advance notification and observation of military maneuvers, however, were hardly meaningful in a military sense: The level of activity that would trigger a notification was quite high, the zone of application covered only a narrow strip of the USSR, invitation of observers to watch military activities was voluntary, and there was no real system of verification. Even these simple ideas were not applied uniformly or to the fullest extent possible.

The Conference on Confidence- and Security-Building Measures and Disarmament in Europe (CDE) convened in January 1984 and adjourned in September 1986. It was a part of the CSCE, and the mandate for the conference was adopted in September 1983 by the 35 participants in the CSCE review meeting in Madrid. The mandate specified that "the conference will begin a process of which the first stage will be devoted to the negotiation and adoption of a set of mutually complementary confidence- and security-building measures designed to reduce the risk of military confrontation in Europe." In the vocabulary used in this paper, "confidence- and security-building measures" refers to operational arms control measures, although the mandate was not specific in its definition.

A widespread desire to move beyond the rudimentary measures of the Helsinki Final Act was already evident in the Madrid review meeting. The mandate negotiated there ensured that the zone in which operational arms control measures would be applied would include the whole of Europe, from the Atlantic to the Urals—a very important development in addressing the strengthening of security in Europe. The mandate also stipulated that operational arms control measures would be militarily meaningful, politically binding, and verifiable.

In September 1986, the 35 participants in the Stockholm Conference agreed to a series of operational arms control measures designed to meet those stipulations. Some of the more important improvements and innovations of the Stockholm accord were as follows:

- The threshold for notifications was significantly lowered as compared with the Helsinki Final Act and now included equipment and structural criteria as well as a personnel criterion for notification.
- The scope of military operations to be covered was expanded beyond that of the Helsinki Final Act by including various types of ground-force operations, such as alerts, amphibious landings, parachute assaults, and troop concentrations. Notification would be provided of movements of ground forces from bases outside the zone to locations within Europe. Information would be provided regarding air and naval operations functionally related to ground-force activities, including information about air sorties.

- Observers could include nationals from all participants; they would be invited to all activities above a certain size for which notification was required. The minimum size of activities to which observers would be invited is higher than that of notification, that is, there would be fewer observer invitations than notifications.
- A forecast of notifiable military activities would be provided.
- Notifiable military activities involving more than 75,000 troops would not be carried out unless two years' notice has been provided; activities over 40,000 troops should be announced two years in advance and would not be carried out unless at least one year's notice has been provided.
- Verification, including mandatory on-site inspections, would be required, with the mechanics of carrying out verification operations spelled out in the accords.

On-Site Verification

The Stockholm Document led to a successful ground-breaking experience not only with operational arms control measures throughout the continent of Europe, but also with cooperative verification measures. The experience with on-site inspection has been very encouraging.

In August 1987, the United States conducted the first on-site inspection in the Soviet Union under the terms of the Stockholm Document. This made it the first challenge on-site inspection ever conducted in the USSR.

On-site inspections are not the same as the routine observation of military exercises that must occur any time a military exercise is pre-notified. Rather, these are special inspections during which inspectors are granted access to an area to conduct an inspection that the requesting nation has reason to think is relevant to the operation of the Stockholm accord. In accordance with the terms of the document, there is no need for explanation and no right of refusal.

The regime established by the Stockholm Document also is proceeding well in other respects. Notifications of military activities and the provision of annual calendars of planned military activities are all taking place as envisaged under the terms of the Stockholm Document.

As noted above, these measures no doubt are more effective in dealing with a war that no one wants—war resulting from accidents or misperceptions—than they are in preventing a deliberate surprise attack. The measures now in place in Europe should be of some help even in that case, however, and might offer some benefit on the Korean Peninsula.

NATO faces some of the same defense problems that exist in South Korea. Opposing NATO are forces superior in personnel and in numbers of tanks, armored personnel carriers, and artillery. There are two situations that could permit the Warsaw Pact to exploit this superiority: a "standing start" attack—that is, no reinforcements and no warning—or a short-warning attack in which the Pact has undertaken a surreptitious buildup that NATO has been unable to match. Most analysts regard the second alternative as the more plausible scenario.

A surreptitious buildup might be detected by national technical means very quickly, but in such a situation, there is always room for doubt as to what is really happening. Operational arms control should be able to deal effectively with such a situation if the relevant measures are well conceived and functioning properly. Such measures could act to supplement and corroborate intelligence indicators, and they could also serve to complicate military planners' calculations, thus serving as an additional modest deterrent to surprise attack. (See table 13.1 and table 13.2.)

To visualize how this might work, simply postulate that the Stockholm measures—and perhaps others even more demanding—were in place on the Korean Peninsula. South Korean or U.S. observers would be present at any significant North Korean military exercise, and special on-site inspection teams could make short-notice visits to sites in North Korea where military activities were taking place that seemed to warrant a closer look.

If one of the current NATO proposals to strengthen the Stockholm system were in place in Korea, data concerning the strength of North Korean forces would be available, as would the means to check its accuracy. It is not difficult to conceive of other measures—sensors at critical places in North Korea and permanent liaison officers at major North Korean military headquarters, for example—that would strengthen still further the existing Stockholm measures and the follow-on NATO proposals. A list of operational arms control measures that might be relevant in Korea can be found in Table 13.2. Obviously, careful analysis of all such proposals should be made to determine their utility in the Korean situation, and a careful assessment should be made of their acceptability in South Korea. It seems likely, however, that such measures could help deter or detect preparations for a surprise attack by North Korea. The immediate question is whether there is any chance of successfully negotiating such proposals with North Korea. Experience in Europe cannot answer this, but some insights can be gained from considering the situation there.

Table 13.1 Political Measures

Confidence-Building	Improving Relations
1. periodic meetings with an open agenda between ministers of the North and the South	1. declaration on nonaggression/ renouncing the threat or use of force
2. summit meetings and meetings of prime ministers	2. developing diplomatic and other contacts between North and South and their major allies
3. cessation of propaganda directed against either the ROK or the DPRK	3. concluding a peace treaty
4. upgrading telecommunications links between Seoul and Pyongyang	4. international guarantees
5. restoring family and human contacts	
6. removing barriers to cooperation in humanitarian, cultural, and sports activities	
7. developing economic relations	
8. cooperation in the Military Armistice Commission (MAC)	
9. observers at military exercises	

Table 13.2 Arms Control Measures

Operational Steps	Structural Steps
1. advance notification of certain military activities	1. as an initial step, reduce the ground forces of North Korea and South Korea to parity at levels below those currently maintained by South Korea
2. invitation of observers to notifiable military activities	
3. a forecast of military activities to take place during the subsequent calendar year	2. in a comprehensive reduction program, reduce all armed forces in three stages to parity at 100,000 troops
4. mandatory on-site inspections on demand	3. reduce U.S. ground forces stationed in South Korea
5. a prohibition on conducting military operations above a certain size unless notified in an annual forecast	4. as part of a comprehensive reduction program, withdraw U.S. armed forces from South Korea
6. exchanges of data	
7. limitations on the sizes and types of military exercises	5. prohibit stationing of nuclear weapons in Korea
8. make the DMZ a truly demilitarized area	6. reduce the level of the military threat to senior command authorities
9. prevention of dangerous military activities	7. verification
10. continuous monitoring of garrisons, weapon depots, and lines of communications	
11. positioning liaison officers at major commands	

Applying the European Experience to Korea

The fundamental fact about the European experience with operational arms control is that operational arms control, like other forms of arms control, is tightly linked to developments of a broad political nature. The negotiations that produced the Helsinki Final Act became possible only after basic political questions had been addressed and resolved. The Berlin Quadripartite Agreement is an outstanding example of a development that enabled the CSCE process to begin. The success of the Stockholm conference likewise can be attributed in part to political changes in Moscow associated with the rise to power of Gorbachev.

At the same time, the negotiation and implementation of agreements on operational arms control can contribute to the evolution of the political situation. For example, it is clear that the successful negotiation in Stockholm led to the establishment of the two arms control forums now actively negotiating conventional arms agreements in Vienna. Although it is difficult to quantify, it is also very likely that the climate of U.S.–Soviet relations was improved by the agreement in Stockholm and that this contributed in some measure to the quite remarkable developments in U.S.–Soviet relations during the last two years of the Reagan administration.

One could speculate, looking at the pace of transformation of the political and economic landscape in Asia, that events are moving in a direction that would be conducive to negotiations. Thus, the changes in political conditions that were the necessary accompaniments to success in East–West negotiations in Europe may also be occurring in Asia.

Against the possibility that the political environment does develop in such a positive way, one should examine specific aspects of the European experience that might be useful in the Korean context. The following points are drawn from the European experience:

1. *An overall conceptual framework is useful in improving security and cooperation.* The Helsinki Final Act resulted from bargaining between East and West about the sanctity of frontiers imposed at the end of World War II—demanded by Moscow—and the conditions required for a Europe whole and free—demanded by the West. The framework created by the Final Act defined certain principles that guided relations among the participants and prescribed a number of conditions that the participating governments were expected to observe with respect to their own citizens. Included in the Final Act was the notion that cooperation in military matters could improve security for all.

Thus, the Final Act set standards and outlined a blueprint for what Europe should be. Even though many of those standards are only now being fulfilled in parts of Eastern Europe, the Final Act provided a valuable reference point for Western diplomacy on a broad range of subjects. Even though accords now in place were negotiated incrementally—operational arms control being one example—it was helpful to have these negotiations take place within a framework that provided some direction for European development.

2. *A step-by-step negotiating process is a practical way to proceed.* The task of overcoming the evils of an unjustly divided Europe was too great to be accomplished in a single negotiation; in any event, some negotiations had to await favorable political developments before they could succeed. Practical considerations, therefore, dictated that within the broad framework defined by the Final Act a series of follow-on negotiations gradually would expand the scope of the obligations and make them more demanding. This approach permitted progress to be made when it was possible, while putting off to another day those issues that were not ripe for settlement.

3. *Agreement is possible even between parties deeply divided on their views of ultimate objectives.* There is little doubt that Moscow's objectives, both in the original CSCE negotiation and in the Stockholm conference, were quite different from those of the West. It is not extreme to say that the objectives of Moscow and of the West were mutually incompatible. Yet through a process of striking a balance among the interests of the various parties to the process—neutrals included—it proved possible to reach a mutually satisfactory agreement. Thus, although part of the process involved deferring some propositions to future negotiations, a very important factor was the calculation of long-term effects. Each country, of course, made its own judgment about this.

4. *Initial agreements will probably create favorable conditions for follow-on agreements.* The experience in Europe was that agreement through the CSCE led to additional agreements. The Stockholm Document made it possible to establish the CSBM conference and the CFE conference in Vienna. Not only is a certain amount of momentum imparted to the negotiating process by a successful agreement, but concrete conditions are also established that make follow-on negotiations feasible.

5. *Organizing the work according to generic ideas without reference to acceptability is a valuable negotiating technique.* Both in the CSCE and in the Stockholm conference, one of the first steps was to categorize proposals so that similar ideas could be compared. Thus, in the CSCE,

proposals were grouped according to whether they focused on security, economics, or human rights. At the Stockholm conference, ideas were organized into groups dealing with information, verification, constraints, notification, and observation. This technique tended to create the context for an agreement; the detailed negotiations then could take place within a framework that was generally agreed upon.

What might these experiences mean in the Korean context? First, it might be useful to develop a general conceptual approach to guide the development of security and cooperation on the Korean Peninsula throughout the years ahead. Those objectives should probably include reunification of the Korean nation. Although this is an ambitious goal, no long-term blueprint for the political future of Korea would be complete if it did not require that peaceful reunification of Korea be a matter of the highest priority in discussions between the South and the North, even though other political, economic, and security measures must necessarily be negotiated and implemented for reunification to be consummated.

Reunification

Reunification, naturally, must be addressed with the meticulous care it deserves. It is reasonable to assume that the sequence of steps necessary to bring about reunification will be discussed as the juridical form of reunification between representatives of the governments of the two parts of Korea. It cannot be said too often that the Koreans themselves must resolve these problems step by step through North–South dialogue and that, following the principle of national self-determination, the Koreans themselves must decide what form reunification ultimately should take. Of course, other states should encourage the process of dialogue and seek to create favorable conditions.

Time will be required to explore the several avenues to reunification. Other steps in the political, security, and economic fields almost certainly will have to be put in place before reunification can be achieved. Reunification itself can mean many different things conceptually—ranging from the symbolic to full integration into a unitary state. A complete exploration of reunification—steps to realize it and forms it might take—would provide a useful context for discussions of other subjects and indeed might illuminate ways these other issues might be resolved.

It is not a matter of setting preconditions or engaging in procrastination to suggest that the beginning of the negotiating process should be to develop a modicum of confidence between the parties and that the end of the process might be some form of reunification. Topics relevant to building political confidence should be taken up first in order of priority; successful conversations in building confidence would reflect the first small changes in the current Korean scene. Confidence is a subjective condition that in this case means, first, that the parties are prepared to recognize one another as valid interlocutors; second, that they are prepared to discuss their differences; and, third, that they have found some reason to believe it useful to continue the conversations. (See table 13.1.)

Between reunification, at one end of the scale of complexity, and confidence-building at the other, lie a large number of subjects that present relatively complicated negotiating issues. It will take some time to resolve those issues, and, furthermore, some of the parties probably will want to link the issues in some fashion. Reunification probably will be the last major change in Korea, but it could be discussed very early on—just as soon as minimum conditions of confidence among the parties have been established.

A second conclusion derived from European experience is that putting agreements into place incrementally would contribute to the longer-term goal of reunification and to the short-term goal of enhanced security. Although it is important to develop some mutual understanding about where the negotiating process might lead, it is impractical to think that every detail of a future security system in Korea could be worked out in advance. It would also deprive Korea of much-needed improvements in stability and security to refuse to proceed at least part way toward a cooperative security system on the peninsula. For example, political confidence-building measures and some operational arms control measures could be negotiated and put into effect prior to negotiation.

A third conclusion is that even though the objectives of the governments of North and South Korea may at present differ dramatically, it is probable that the negotiating process would lead to an agreement that each side would find served its own interest. The ingredients for successful negotiations may already exist. Almost certainly both North and South would be prepared to discuss

- principles of reunification,
- reductions to parity in armed forces,
- limits on importing advanced weaponry,
- installing operational arms control measures to prevent surprise attacks,
- redeployment of forces with the objective of reducing the threat to principal command authorities, and
- provisions for the gradual phase-down of the U.S. troop presence in South Korea.

A fourth conclusion, based on the European experience, is that preliminary agreements between North and South Korea could pave the way for more far-reaching agreements. Thus, an agreement just on operational arms control, for example, could make it easier over the long run to negotiate troop reductions or the more delicate question of integrating the economies of North and South Korea.

A fifth conclusion is that negotiating such ideas as those just cited could be facilitated by the technique of grouping all relevant ideas into categories so that comparisons could be made and the possibility of accommodation examined. For example, it would be possible to divide all proposals into "political measures" and "arms control measures." Each of these categories in turn could be divided into two other notional groups: "confidence-building" and "improving relations" in the case of "political measures"; "operational" and "structural" categories could be devised for the "arms control measures." Tables 13.1 and 13.2 show how various ideas might be distributed among these categories. To repeat, the merit of this negotiating approach is that, although it gives no ranking to one proposal over another, the act of inventorying and categorizing proposals does begin to establish a framework for an ultimate agreement.

One area in which the European experience is *not* particularly relevant to Korea is the negotiating forum. In Europe, large multilateral institutions—such as NATO, the Warsaw Treaty Organization, and the CSCE—have provided the basis for establishing forums for negotiations on security matters. In Korea, such institutions do not exist. It is not clear that large multilateral forums would serve any useful purpose in a situation in which three authorities—North Korea, South Korea, and the United States—are the principal parties involved. The possibility of guarantees on the part of other countries in Northeast Asia has been raised, but that is a prospect that could be faced when the time comes.

It also is possible that no one forum or means of communicating among the principal actors would be convenient for the whole range of proposals that might be under discussion. The interested parties should consider which method best suits their need in the case of each proposal. They need not adopt a single method for all proposals, however. Many of the proposals could be dealt with, at least initially, through North–South dialogue. Indeed, some proposals must be addressed through bilateral North–South channels. A North–South nonuse-of-force agreement is one example; political confidence building measures are other examples. For most of the measures, however, the parties could work with a combination of the Military Armistice Commission (for technical matters like demilitarizing the DMZ), tripartite U.S.–North–South talks (for relating verification requirements to various operational arms control arrangements, for example), and diplomatic channels (for initial exploration of almost any proposal).

One model, suitable for many purposes, would have the South and North record some tangible progress in confidence-building. Then, the United States would be invited to join an agenda-setting conference for subsequent negotiations. This tripartite steering committee could then reassemble from time to time to review progress and to adjust the work program as developments warrant.

This discussion of the dissimilarities between Korea and Europe regarding negotiating forums serves as a useful reminder that, in many respects, the situation between the two regions is not comparable. Anyone seeking to extract lessons from the European experience with the idea of applying them without any modification to the Korean situation is almost certainly acting unwisely. The insights gained from negotiations in Europe, such as those described in this chapter, may help stimulate thinking about solutions to security problems in Korea. More than this should not be expected or desired, for Korean problems must have their own answers if they are finally to be resolved.

Notes

1. Thomas C. Schelling and Morton H. Halperin, *Strategy and Arms Control* (New York: The Twentieth Century Fund, 1961), 2.

14

Lessons for Korea from Conventional Arms Control Talks in Europe

Robert E. Hunter

Introduction

The truly revolutionary seems ready to happen soon: an agreement between states of the Warsaw Pact and states of the North Atlantic Treaty Organization to reduce conventional forces deployed in central Europe. Long hoped for and long negotiated about, during recent months the likelihood of such an agreement has gone from only a few percentage points to almost certainty. The Soviet Union has gone further in its proposals than virtually anyone thought possible when it agreed to major asymmetrical reductions in deployed forces. And, in May 1989 at the NATO summit in Brussels, U.S. President George Bush not only accepted the Soviet offer, but went one better by endorsing the principle that tactical aircraft and helicopters—long a special reservation of the Western powers—also be included in the cuts.

Furthermore, Bush called for an agreement to be concluded within six months to a year (a timetable that is not likely to be observed in terms of a completed agreement)—thus changing the negotiating picture from one of laggard efforts on both sides to almost a race for completion. Indeed, debate is already under way about what should happen in the next phase of the conventional arms talks in Vienna—the so-called Conventional Forces in Europe (CFE) talks—almost as though phase one were a foregone conclusion.

How did this come about—this apparent competition between East and West in Europe, between the United States and the Soviet Union—how were these adversaries able to agree upon reductions in the most potent conventional competition anywhere on the face of the earth? To answer this question, it is necessary to begin at the beginning—with the militarization of conflict in Europe.

The Structure of Cold War in Europe

When the North Atlantic Treaty was signed on April 4, 1949, there was no imminent danger of a Soviet invasion of Western Europe. Indeed, the treaty was designed for a basic political purpose—as a form of insurance. It was to indicate clearly that the United States was committed to the European continent and would back this commitment, if need be, through the use of military force. At the time, this commitment was not seen as a direct deterrent to conflict or to an immediate military challenge, but rather it served as an underpinning of the European Recovery Program (the Marshall Plan). This, at least, was the widespread view in Western Europe, although in the United States there was a greater sense of the military dimension of providing security for Europe. In effect, to achieve a U.S. political commitment to Europe, the new allies agreed to accept a U.S. definition that security, in the final analysis, should be denominated in large part in military terms.

In fact, the signing of the treaty did not lead to the development of a true military alliance for some time. It was only at the end of the following year that the U.S. Congress voted funds to provide for a permanent U.S. military presence on the European continent. And the "O" in NATO—Allied Command Europe—did not come into being until April 2, 1951, just short of two years after the treaty was signed. Indeed, the event that led to this transformation of a largely political treaty into one with a serious military component was the Korean War. The unprovoked attack by the People's Republic against the Republic of Korea seemed to indicate a broad-scale Soviet attempt to tip the East–West balance through military force. Whether that was Moscow's intention in Europe was not clear, but hostilities in Asia gave enough impetus to concerns to lead to serious military effort by the allies in Europe.

Thus, it seemed clear that the North Atlantic Treaty had to be given some muscle through the creation of a military force and of a fortified line in central Europe—along with sufficient personnel and weaponry to make this force credible. This requirement imposed a special demand. Because the allies were neither able nor willing to provide such a level of conventional military power on their own, they soon came to the conclusion that they would need to include forces from the Federal Republic of Germany. This need led to considerable debate about the best means for including these forces, without reviving fears of German military power. For their part, the Soviets tried to manipulate the debate in the West and in the Federal Republic, in particular, including a surely disingenuous offer in 1952 to exchange the reunification of the two Germanies for the permanent demilitarization of the Federal Republic.[1]

In 1954, the chosen instrument of the West European states—a European Defense Community (EDC)—collapsed, in large measure because it would involve too great a ceding of sovereignty. Instead, six key West European states turned in 1956 to the Treaty of Rome, an effort to proceed with a functional means of European integration through a less-encompassing form of ceding sovereignty, but with the same basic political purpose as EDC—finding a means for dealing with German power and for making war between Germany and its neighbors impossible. Following the collapse of EDC, the Western allies responded with a two-step approach: the expansion of the 1948 Brussels Treaty and its Western Union (the forerunner of NATO) into the Western European Union through the addition of two defeated Axis powers, West Germany and Italy, to the original five members (Britain, France, and the Benelux states), and the inclusion in NATO of both West Germany and Italy.[2] This was not the perfect solution from the standpoint of the Federal Republic's Western neighbors, but it served its basic purpose.

In response, the Soviet Union augmented its web of treaties with East European satellite states—treaties that bound them more tightly to the regional superpower than was true on the Western side—and formally acknowledged a rearmament of East Germany that had already become a fact. Thus, in 1955, a new treaty was concluded at Warsaw, along with the creation of a Soviet-led military command, which completed the formal division of Europe. The expansion of NATO and the creation of the Warsaw Pact also resulted in this division's being militarized, superseding the predominance of political and economic conflict.

The most important aspect of this process, however, was not a rising risk of conflict—indeed, it could be argued that the completion of the alliance systems actually reduced that risk—but the creation of a higher degree of predictability and confidence about the nature of confrontation in central Europe. It was to be military. It included forces on both sides, forces with a considerable ability to fight. The lines were clearly drawn, and the crossing of a line was clearly invested with significance. At the same time, militarizing the confrontation also resulted in freezing political divisions. Henceforth, any effort to change the political *status quo* also had to deal with changes to the military *status quo;* indeed, dealing with the latter came to be seen as a prerequisite for dealing with the former—something that has been key to understanding the nature and conduct of East–West conventional arms control talks since the early 1970s. Today, that relationship is changing again. One of the salient and potentially most destabilizing features of events in Eastern Europe is that the politics of East–West relations are changing faster than have the military aspects of those relations that, to date, have not changed much at all.

Unlike the militarization of the political conflict in Korea, however, which has continued following the 1953 armistice, in Europe there was no open fighting upon which the military division was based, no record that argued strongly that fighting was likely but for the creation of militarized alliance systems. This difference has proved to be important in later efforts to reduce the nature of military conflict. In Europe, it was not inevitable that political and economic conflict would gain this military dimension, but, once it did, the particular logic of military relationships imposed itself upon all the parties.

The Logic of European Military Confrontation

This logic continues to this day. For the Western allies, there has been an emphasis on the Warsaw Pact's ability to launch a successful attack in central Europe, not on whether the Soviet Union and its now only nominal allies have ever had any intention of so doing. This emphasis on military capabilities rather than on political intentions has always had more proponents in the United States than among virtually all of the European allies, but usually this difference of attitude and perception has not been of critical importance to the conduct of the alliance.

Fulfilling the logic has never been easy for the allies. Even before NATO was expanded and the Warsaw Pact formally came into being, it was clear that—even with West German forces—it would not be possible to mount a robust defense of Western Europe along the Central Front with the personnel and weapons that the various allies were prepared to contribute. Ineluctable facts of geography also made this course difficult—if not impossible—to pursue. Most important were the lack of strategic depth in Western Europe, both in absolute terms and in relationship to that available on the other side, and the fact that the United States was some 3,000 miles away from the inner-German border, across an ocean, whereas the Soviet Union was only about 300 miles away.

Thus as early as 1956, the allies were forced to look beyond conventional forces to be certain of being secure against a possible conventional military attack by the Warsaw Pact. That meant some role for nuclear weapons and, in practice, nuclear weapons of the United States (at that time, Britain had only a fledgling force and France had yet to join the nuclear club). Of course, there had always been U.S. nuclear weapons in the background from the time U.S. strategic bombers had been moved to England at the end of the 1940s. There had been no formal relationship between the possible use of U.S. nuclear weapons and the conduct of a conventional war, however. That relationship was codified in 1956, along with the decision to introduce U.S. tactical nuclear weapons into Western Europe.[3]

At the time, the shorthand for U.S. strategic doctrine came to be known as "massive retaliation," but that was never acceptable, either to the United States or to its allies, in large measure because the initiation of nuclear force in response to acts by the other side would be far out of proportion to the possible nuclear response. As a result, massive retaliation was neither politically acceptable—in Europe or the United States—nor likely to be credible to the Soviets. Thus was born the series of debates that continue to this day about the appropriate relationship between conventional and nuclear weapons in the defense of Western Europe.

By the early 1960s, it was clear that new arrangements had to be made. In 1962, the U.S. secretary of defense promulgated what became known as the McNamara Doctrine, under which the United States proposed to abandon a commitment to massive retaliation in favor of a more graduated escalation to nuclear war in response to events in Europe.[4] Opposed at first by most of the European allies, which were concerned that this new formulation implied a diminution of the U.S. political and security commitment to Europe, the McNamara Doctrine was in fact adopted formally by the alliance in 1967 through the NATO Military Committee document MC 14/3—a document that continues in force today and is known as the doctrine of "flexible response."

At its simplest, this doctrine holds that the Western allies will attempt to defend themselves against a Warsaw Pact conventional attack with a conventional response, but, if that defense fails, the West could (or would, depending on how the flexible response doctrine is construed) initiate the use of nuclear weapons—in practice, those of the United States. Further, according to the doctrine, if the Warsaw Pact still did not cease its aggression, escalation would continue through the level of a general strategic war involving the United States and the Soviet Union.

Throughout the more than two decades since 1967, the NATO alliance has gone through a number of political crises regarding this set of propositions. On the one hand, the nuclear component of Western doctrine has, from time to time, led to public protests and political concern about the possible use of nuclear weapons and the deployment of such weapons on the Continent pursuant to the doctrine. On the other hand, there has been a succession of debates about the credibility of the U.S. willingness to use nuclear weapons on Western Europe's behalf. These so-called "decoupling" crises have derived from the implication that, faced with the prospect of initiating use of nuclear weapons that would lead to its own destruction, the United States might not see its security as identical to that of its allies. These crises have related less to the issue of deterring the Soviet Union, which most analysts see as a relatively simple problem, than to the problem of reassuring the Western allies, of the United States' fealty.

Throughout the years, debates—essentially political, not military—have taken on an almost theological quality, but they have been important nonetheless. They have been complicated by an additional factor: The logical potential resolution of the dilemma—to increase conventional military forces—has not been available. Not only have the allies, including the United States, been unwilling to raise and support the forces needed to defend Western Europe solely with conventional weapons (allowing for the geographic factors cited above), but also there has been reluctance in Europe, especially on the part of the West Germans, to see a non-nuclear defense of Western Europe made possible. From their perspective, any war in central Europe—that is, West Germany—would be a war of utter destruction. West Germany has thus opposed calls for a doctrine of "no first use" of nuclear weapons, preferring to run a greater risk that any war will rapidly become a nuclear war to have a lower risk that there will be any war at all.

Implications for Korea

It has been important to review these issues as a background to conventional arms control talks in Europe, because they so clearly do not apply, at least not in the same way, in the case of the Korean Peninsula. To be sure, there is a U.S. nuclear guarantee to the Republic of Korea and, presumably, appropriate U.S. nuclear weapons deployed to back it up, but the guarantee does not serve the same purposes. For one thing, it is not clear that the ROK and U.S. nonnuclear forces now deployed in South Korea would lose a conventional war, unless massive forces from either the Soviet Union or the People's Republic of China were engaged at the outset in support of North Korean aggression—neither of which has seemed apparent at any time in recent decades.

In Korea the issue is not posed in light of obvious disparities of conventional military power to force an early U.S. decision on whether to use nuclear weapons. Similarly, although issues of nuclear weapons have been discussed publicly in the ROK at different times in its history (more in recent times), there is no established position of preferring that any conflict rapidly become nuclear as a means of lowering the nuclear threshold while raising the risks for North Korea and its potential allies. Thus, the actual conventional military balance is much more likely to be the principal determinant of the outcome of any hostilities, should they occur.

At the same time, however, in an actual conflict on the peninsula—determined by real rather than by fanciful circumstances—there would be a strong chance that a North Korean attack would have the backing, implicit if not explicit, of one of its nuclear-armed neighbors. The United States would certainly not easily contemplate the use of nuclear weapons in Korea, just as it would be circumspect elsewhere. The lack of an explicit Soviet (or Chinese) military role in North Korean security—certainly not in deployed personnel—means that there has not developed the same sort of calculations or doctrines regarding the role of nuclear weapons in a Korean conflict as there has been in Europe. Similarly, this whole range of issues, from the outset, does not necessarily impinge upon the central U.S.–Soviet political relationship. Such an impact there could be, but it is certainly notable that there is nothing in Korea like the regular debates about the nature of doctrine involving nuclear weapons that is a staple of the NATO alliance.

This discussion is important as a background to understanding the development of conventional arms control talks in Europe and the lessons that can be drawn for possible talks in Korea. In sum, the contexts, quite simply, are very different. At least six aspects need to be singled out. They are listed here not necessarily in order of importance.

- The role of the Soviet Union, and hence of U.S.–Soviet relations, is quite different in the two cases.
- The role of nuclear weapons is quite different in the two cases, both in Western allied doctrine and in the calculations the two sides make about each other.
- There is a basic asymmetry in the political–military equation in Korea, whereas there is far less of one in Europe (where each alliance has a closely involved nuclear superpower).
- In the Republic of Korea, there are no "decoupling" crises of the magnitude found in NATO, with their elaborate rituals for resolution, for at least two reasons: the lack of an explicit Soviet–Chinese connection and the greater likelihood of conventional defense.
- There is also less of an anti-nuclear problem in Korea for a variety of factors, including the fact that there is less discussion of nuclear issues and far less need than in Europe for deployments and doctrinal elaboration in order to reassure the ROK that the U.S. nuclear commitment is credible.
- The relationship of arms to calculations of stability and political evolution is quite different in the two circumstances.

This last point is particularly revealing, especially concerning the conditions that existed when conventional arms control talks began in Europe—conditions that have continued, in different form. Despite the extent to which the Western allies have felt the need to sustain robust conventional forces on the European Central Front, along with a nuclear doctrine (and associated forces) that will both deter Soviet aggression and reassure the allies of U.S. commitment to their security, there has been a widespread perception of a low likelihood of military conflict. Today, of course, the perception is that a deliberate Warsaw Pact attack on the West can be virtually ruled out. Ironically, there may be a higher risk of military conflict in central Europe—though still quite small—than at any other time in more than three decades because of the potential instabilities from change in Eastern Europe, which still sits along the most heavily fortified frontier in the world.

Thus the first set of formal East–West conventional arms control talks, the Mutual and Balanced Force Reductions (MBFR)—although the East resisted the use of the word "balanced"—began against the background of an implicit, though not acknowledged, understanding that war in Europe was most unlikely and had been for some time. This perception could have derived from several factors, all of which are consistent: Perhaps the Soviet Union and its allies had never intended to attack the West; perhaps the Soviets and their allies had been successfully deterred from moving westward; perhaps they (and especially the leaders in the Kremlin) had come to understand that even a minuscule risk of nuclear retaliation (by the United States, but also by either Britain or France) would not be worth anything they could reasonably hope to attain through aggression; perhaps Soviet leaders had simply mellowed; or perhaps there had been the growth of a mutual awareness (varying, perhaps, on the two sides) that there had developed a high degree of military stability, certainty, and predictability in central Europe, along with the acceptance of the political *status quo*. This last point is especially important. It implies that the military situation (effective stalemate) led to the recognition of a political standoff and thus to a willingness to move beyond sterile confrontation.[5] By this reasoning, manipulating the risks of asymmetry and uncertainty (posed by instabilities that still exist, especially regarding the role played by Western nuclear doctrine) was apparently seen by the Soviet Union as less valuable, at least in comparison with other goals.

Clearly, this picture is quite different from that which has appeared in Korea. Two levels are most important: At the superpower level, the basic relationship between the United States and the Soviet Union is not fundamentally affected by events in Korea, although neither superpower is indifferent to what happens in Korea and would be especially concerned if there were war. By contrast, Europe has been a central element—politically *the* central element—in the superpower relationship. Thus a general evolution of U.S.–Soviet relations and calculations made by the two superpowers on a global basis do not directly determine what happens, politically, on the Korean Peninsula. What North Korea does diplomatically with regard to the South is not totally divorced from broader global developments, but to a degree changes what many observers have seen as coincidental to the Gorbachev revolution.

At the local level, meanwhile, not only is the North Korean leadership less responsive to its neighboring nuclear powers than are the East European states to the Soviet Union (at least in terms of not pursuing potentially aggressive policies), but there is not the same history of political stability in Korea. As noted earlier, military stalemate was born of war, not of political standoff. There is a regime in North Korea that has used methods that go further than anything used by an East European state or the Soviet Union against the West (with the exception of the assassination attempt against the Pope). There is also far less of a solid, irreversible political evolution of relations between the two Koreas to underpin military negotiations, which are also fundamentally political.

There is, in fact, a triple difference, subtle but real. In Europe, the MBFR talks had to be seen against the background of nuclear weapons on both sides, and especially the U.S. commitment to the potential first use of these weapons on behalf of it allies. Thus, within limits, raising or lowering the level of conventional military forces on both sides would not, in and of itself, have a decisive impact on the military outcome of conflict. The nuclear weapons would still be there in the background. To be sure, U.S. nuclear weapons would still be there in the case of Korea, but they are not as explicitly integrated into the entire process and politics of defense on the peninsula—that is, they do not play the central role that such weapons do in calculations of the military and political aspects of security in Europe.

At the same time, the MBFR talks had less of an inherently political nature than would be true of conventional arms talks in Korea. Not only would the latter be unprecedented (whereas by the time the MBFR talks were convened, discussions between East and West were commonplace, as were diplomatic relations), but also the MBFR talks could take place without also necessarily raising the fundamental political relationship between the two sides or any country so engaged. This latter proposition, however, varied from country to country and could have changed if, indeed, the talks appeared likely to succeed. This is far less true of the new CFE talks, however, both because of the prospective size of cuts to be made on both sides and the political context within which they are now occurring—that is, in George Bush's words, as part of an effort to end the division of Europe.

In Korea, by contrast, not only would talks on conventional arms control break new ground politically between North and South, but any discussions about the military balance could not be separated from the fundamental political issues defining the relationship between, and the future of, the two countries. In Europe, up to a point, the MBFR talks could proceed almost outside of politics, based on tacit agreements already reached about the nature of the political and military relationship between East and West. In Korea, that would be impossible both because there is not yet such a tacit agreement about the nature of the political relationship and because the military balance is so intimately connected to the definition of Korea's future.

The third critical difference relates to the role of the United States. In theory, there could be a reconciliation between North and South Korea—perhaps even leading to reunification—that could lead to the withdrawal of U.S. military forces, an end to its nuclear commitment, and even an end to the underlying political commitment to the Republic of Korea's security. This could be possible if political, military, and associated conditions were correct for such a development on the peninsula. These conditions may not now be likely, but they are at least conceivable, and some observers believe that they will develop during the next few years. By contrast, in Europe, the United States will be needed as a European power even after critical changes take place in the structure of security on the Continent. Even a total "success" of the CFE talks—a major change in the nature of European security and a wholesale reduction of forces on both sides—would still not answer all the imponderables.

The lesson of this point is that the two Koreas could conduct much of the business of conventional arms reductions largely between themselves—certainly in the political aspects of their future on the peninsula—even though there would be issues related to other states that are part of the United Nations Command (that is, essentially the United States). In Europe, by contrast, the MBFR talks—and with stronger reason the CFE talks—of necessity are tied to the U.S. role in Europe and to U.S.–Soviet relations. Thus, a key U.S. role in these talks must be taken for granted; there can be no West European diplomatic independence such as there could be for the Republic of Korea.

Lessons of European Conventional Arms Talks

It is not necessary to review all that has happened in the two key sets of East–West talks on controlling and reducing conventional forces in Europe. That history can be found in many places, as well as commentary on ancillary efforts—especially through the so-called Helsinki process and instruments like confidence- and-security-building measures (CSBMs).[6] Indeed, the lessons from these political efforts may be more important than analyzing the talks on conventional force reductions. Two sets of points are worth emphasizing about MBFR and CFE, both on their own and in relationship to the possible negotiations in Korea.

Motives

From the beginning of the MBFR talks in 1973, there were a variety of motives by both East and West. For the former, there can only be inference: Military stalemate and emerging political stability provided a reason for codifying what had been achieved (especially if Eastern conventional force advantages could be preserved); there could be an opportunity to prevent force increases in Western Europe (if not to produce a decrease); there could be a kindling of hope in the United States for a reduction of involvement in Europe; and there would be a generally more positive view in the West (especially in Western Europe) of the Soviet Union and its allies.

In the West, motives for MBFR were more openly presented. There was certainly a concern about creating greater political stability through a mutual recognition of what had been achieved by military stalemate, and there was the possibility of increasing stability through discussions about potential risks to stability. In short, the process of talking was itself a spur to increased stability, both in content (military issues) and in the fact that the talks were taking place (the impact on East–West political relations). The MBFR talks also provided an East–West forum that included a wide variety of Western allies, as opposed to the Strategic Arms Limitation Talks (SALT) that were strictly bilateral. The MBFR talks provided a mechanism for determining how and what changes could take place to reduce forces on both sides so that there would continue to be a high degree of military, and hence political, stability. Of course, there was also the belief—right or wrong—that if the MBFR talks succeeded, there could be major savings in personnel and money.

When the MBFR talks began, there was also a further motive, especially on the part of the U.S. government. It was to place any arms reductions within the East–West context, thus reducing the likelihood of any unilateral Western reductions, especially by the United States. This was the time of the so-called Mansfield amendments, proposals by the Senate majority leader for cuts in U.S. forces by as many as 150,000 troops. The existence of the talks was used by the administration to ensure that no cuts should take place without a return for cuts by the East.[7] This political tactic worked: It can be argued that it continues to work today, at least regarding U.S. forces on the Continent.

Motives for the CFE talks, of course, have gone much further. With all the changes that have taken place in Europe, politically, CFE offers major promise of success. Thus, it is a genuine forum for deciding how reductions can take place—reductions providing for at least an equal, if not greater, degree of security and stability on the Continent. At the same time, the process surrounding the CFE talks is a mechanism for the Western allies to decide which states should take which cuts—in part a means for dealing with burden sharing—although economic pressures for reductions in virtually all allied states raise doubts about whether this process will be orderly, whatever happens at the Vienna talks. And CFE offers a positive role for political developments in East–West relations far beyond what was possible in the age of MBFR—indeed, in time, perhaps functioning as a key forum for restructuring the whole security system in Europe.

In Korea, motivation to talk would hardly be to prevent change, but to accelerate it. At one level, there could simply be an effort to create greater stability through constraints on North Korea. There could also be agreement about military relationships with external powers, which is unlike the situation in Europe, where the "external powers" (the United States and the Soviet Union) are both engaged in the structure of alliance forces and in the negotiations. Also, in Korea, a key motive would surely be to connect these particular negotiations to broader political issues (an analog better to CFE than to MBFR). Of course, there could also be a motive on the part of South Korea to have negotiations with the North while U.S. forces remain on the peninsula. The North is more likely to have incentives for codifying stability and advancing it while the United States continues to be such an important part of the military balance.

Process

Many aspects of the actual conduct of the MBFR and CFE talks have been important, but, for purposes of drawing parallels, certain issues are worth highlighting, of which five are most important: coalition issues, data, what to control or reduce, verification, and political will.

Coalition Issues. In Europe, both military structures are made up of several countries. That complicates a number of issues, including the relative quality of different military establishments (and, since late 1989, whether any East European states should even be properly counted in the Warsaw Pact balance); the states to be involved in negotiations; the apportioning, by nation, of any cuts that take place; zones of reduction and the political implications thereof (especially, in the West, for the Federal Republic and a reunified Germany); and the whole process of creating negotiating a position. The situation is clearly quite different in Korea, especially if there is the assumption that the United States would not be an active partner with South Korea in negotiations with the North; even if it were, the model is infinitely simpler to analyze and deal with, both in negotiations and in implementation.

Data. One of the thorniest problems at the MBFR talks, from beginning to end, which is related to the question of counting, is the number of forces and weapons there are on each side. Given the far-flung nature of the alliances, there have been difficulties because of the somewhat different roles played by deployed personnel in each alliance (noting, in particular, the garrison role played by Soviet and other East bloc forces, at least until the current changes), because of the difficulties of calibrating the course of combat, and because of the nature of the different military establishments that make up each overall alliance system. Further, the MBFR negotiations dealt essentially with the European Central Front as the area of most concern; even CFE—with its Europe-wide geographic mandate—will probably have to adopt a range of special rules to deal with individual cases.

The data issue was, however, only in part about the actual contribution that particular forces could make to conventional conflict. In part, it related to the question of relative military strength for political purposes—for example, to lend credence to diplomatic efforts—and the issue was always an effective means of slowing down negotiations or diverting them from central issues. The politics of data exchange can also be seen in terms of verification: At different times, debate centered on whether agreement on relative numbers had to be established at the beginning of any agreement or only after reductions had taken place. The latter method was one of the proposals made to try getting around Soviet assertions that the Warsaw Pact started out with fewer forces than NATO sources claimed. With basic agreement on intrusive verification, however, this issue is far less important—counting and counting rules should be much easier to agree upon, with at least one major exception: deciding what countries' forces should be counted as being part of the Warsaw Pact. Indeed, the Warsaw Pact in a very real sense has ceased to exist.

In Korea, there would also be difficulties with data. That must always be true in situations in which there is not complete congruity of military estab-lishments, training, doctrine, deployments, and weaponry. In practice, how-ever, data issues should not be as important, unless one side or the other chooses to make them so for political purposes.

A further issue related to data should also be understood. Once talks begin, with their definitions and disagreements about data, it can become politically difficult to make unilateral reductions, especially for nations in coalition. This point was underscored by the Mansfield amendments and a long history of debate in the United States about so-called bargaining chips. Such cuts can be a tactic, however, especially on the part of the Soviet Union and its allies. Examples are the unilateral cuts announced by Soviet President Gorbachev in December 1988, which, in this instance, were also an indication of political will to move the new CFE talks forward expeditiously.[8]

What to Control or Reduce. The data issue in talks on conventional arms control in Europe has always been closely tied to the question of what to control and what to reduce. In military terms, this is far from obvious, but it must take into account a wide range of difficult matters relating to the potential course of hostilities.

For most of the MBFR period, the NATO allies focused on personnel, and tended to do so in raw terms—that is, overall numbers—although particular deployments in particular regions and by particular allies (especially the United States and the Soviet Union) were also considered from time to time. The essence, however, was an overall approach to military stability and political perception of balance and of advantage, not a detailed analysis of what might actually happen in combat. To a degree, this was a measure of the relative seriousness of the talks: for many observers, dealing with forces in this way connoted a stage before the talks would become truly serious.

Near the end of the MBFR talks, there was a significant shift in the NATO position toward including various categories of military equipment and toward analyzing the actual and potential (after reductions) military balance in terms of what might happen in conflict. This approach has been especially evident at the CFE talks. Indeed, it is one of the hallmarks. Thus, the structure of the talks is much closer to military reality than was the conduct of the MBFR talks for most of their existence. Key elements include personnel, tanks, armored personnel carriers, and artillery—those likely to be the most important in defining a military balance in combat terms. From the Soviet point of view, helicopters and tactical aircraft are also important. In fact, in any long-range security regime, the United States and the West would probably want to have constraints on these weapons, but they had not included them before, in part because of Western advantages. The West continues to resist the inclusion of naval forces on the grounds that these are fungible—that is, they can be used for many purposes—and that the Soviets are trying to constrain U.S. military capabilities worldwide.

The issue of what to include is also important in terms of ceilings set on forces and whether they can be deployed. This issue has proved to be particularly important in Europe with regard to the pace at which an arms agreement could be reversed—that is, if there were a recrudescence of confrontation. The need for U.S. forces to withdraw across an ocean has been particularly important, not just in terms of moving forces back to Europe, but also in terms of the relative capacity of the United States and the Soviet Union to reintroduce forces to the European Central Front and the diplomatic "signals" that would be sent in a crisis by the movement of forces back to Europe.

Verification. As with all arms control negotiations, a prospective agreement on conventional forces in Europe will be only as good as the confidence that it will be carried out—that is, that there will be no militarily significant cheating. For many years, discussions centered on so-called national technical means of verification: what each side could tell about the other's military capabilities through independent means of intelligence. This method has considerable merit when relatively few items have to be counted and those items tend to stay put—in particular, nuclear missiles in fixed silos. Even in the context of a SALT or START agreement, verification problems intrude. They are much worse when dealing with conventional forces, major elements of which are, by definition, mobile, and that operate in a part of the world not known for sunny skies. Thus, for years, the West sought to include some form of intrusive verification, including on-site inspection.

It was only with the breakthrough at the U.S.–Soviet negotiations on intermediate-range nuclear forces that the Soviets were prepared, on a systematic and comprehensive basis, to accept the principle of onsite inspection. There had long been less-comprehensive examples of such inspection, including agreements concerning maneuvers covered by the Helsinki Final Act and its modifications, and even including the role of U.S. and Soviet military observers in the opposing parts of Germany.

On-site inspection, the stationing of observers at crossing points as forces and equipment are withdrawn, and random access to a variety of places where activities could indicate compliance or violation have been seen as critical to the prospects for a CFE agreement. This is true militarily and also politically, although political events in Europe—and especially in the Soviet Union—could reduce this requirement. In the West and especially the United States, the Soviets must not only be constrained from cheating, they must be seen to be constrained.

There are two types of verification—militarily significant verification, which means a high degree of confidence that cheating can be detected while there is still time to counter it effectively, and politically significant verification, which is a more absolute standard, especially during times of tension.[9] Regarding the latter, one device that has proved effective has been the Standing Consultative Commission (SCC) in Geneva, set up pursuant to the SALT I Agreement, under which each side's uncertainties, ambiguities, and anxieties can be presented for discussion and resolution.[10] Indeed, through most of the last 17 years, the SCC has worked effectively, and virtually all problems have been resolved. (The most difficult problem—the Soviet phased-array radar at Krasnoyarsk—was only resolved when Moscow admitted that this device did, indeed, violate the ABM Treaty.) Some such military–political mechanism will no doubt be needed for a CFE agreement.

One special issue applies to both Europe and Korea: residual military capabilities for defense. Following an agreement to reduce forces on both sides, what number of forces must the West retain to prevent a successful conventional attack? This is an issue expressed partly in terms of the ratio of forces to space. In Europe, there has long been a belief in the value of expanding CSBMs, such as constraints on maneuvers and the massing of forces, the elimination of bridge-building equipment, and petroleum, oil, and lubricants (POL) pipeline stocks, and perhaps the erection of passive defenses, such as permanent tank obstacles. In Korea, as well, special care would have to be applied to ensure that a thinning out of forces did not create new vulnerabilities.

Political Will. Finally, it is clear from the experience in Europe with talks on conventional arms control that the overriding element is political will. Do the two sides genuinely want to conclude an agreement? This political will was clearly absent, probably on both sides, through most, if not all, of the life of MBFR; yet, political will apparently exists now in the CFE talks. Thus, in May 1989, the U.S. president could talk of a timetable of six months to a year and have a reasonable expectation that something would be possible not too long after that. To be sure, many problems remain. If both sides continue to want this time to balance a Mansfield amendment against arms talks and produce stalemate, pressures for unilateral reductions—along with U.S. efforts to gain a better distribution of burdens from its European allies—argue for an orderly process that can best be done through East–West talks.

At another level, political will relates to the basic nature of confrontation, born of politics. Given that a profound change is taking place in the underlying nature of East–West relations, dealing with the CFE talks has become an instrument of those relations, not a factor in determining them. To be sure, there will continue to be problems of defining a new security structure for the Continent, a process that has critical political dimensions, but at least politics will not be driving toward military confrontation in the same manner as before and could, instead, be working toward a far higher degree of cooperative effort to ensure their mutual security.

Clearly, this concept can also be applied to the Korean Peninsula. Indeed, this could be the most important lesson of the conventional arms control process in Europe: Agreements will become possible when and if the underlying politics of the relationship argue for such a development.

Notes

1. Adam Ulam, *Expansion and Coexistence: Soviet Foreign Policy 1917—1973* (New York: Praeger, 1974), 611.

2. John Lewis Gaddis, *Strategies of Containment: A Critical Appraisal of Postwar American Security Policy* (New York: Oxford University Press, 1982), 191.

3. Robert Hunter, *Security in Europe* (Bloomington, Ind.: Indiana University Press, 1969), 87–89.

4. Lawrence Freedman, *The Evolution of Nuclear Strategy* (London: Macmillan Press Ltd., 1983), 235–236.

5. The conclusion of the Helsinki Accords in 1975 also underscores this Soviet perception.

6. See, for example, Uwe Nerlich and James A. Thomson, *Conventional Arms Control and the Security of Europe* (Boulder, Colo.: Westview Press, 1988) and the paper presented by Ambassador James Goodby to the Second Simulation and Workshop on Security Policies, sponsored by Korea Institute for Defense Analyses and CSIS, Seoul, South Korea, December 7–8, 1989.

7. Robert Blackwill and Stephen Larrabee, *Conventional Arms Control and East—West Security* (Durham, N.C.: Duke University Press, 1989), xxiii.

8. See Mikhail S. Gorbachev's address to the UN General Assembly as reported in *Foreign Broadcast Information Service (Soviet Union),* December 8, 1988, p. 11.

9. Carnegie Panel on U.S. Security and hte Future of Arms Control, *Challenges for U.S. National Security* (Washington, D.C.: Carnegie Endowment for International Peace, 1983), 36.

10. See Article XII of the SALT I Agreement as found in *Arms Control and Disarmament Agency* (Washington, D.C.: U.S. Arms Control and Disarmament Agency, 1980), 141.

15

The Unthinkable Thinking about the Korean Peninsula

Yang Sung-Chul

> Diverting huge resources from other priorities, the arms race is lowering the level of security, impairing it. It is in itself an enemy of peace. The only way to security is through political decisions and disarmament.[1]
>
> —*Mikhail Gorbachev*

Despite the revolutionary change in central Europe, the DMZ on the Korean Peninsula, the last remaining cold war emblem, persists. If the Berlin Wall epitomized, first and foremost, freedom or lack of it between East and West Germany, the DMZ primarily represents peace or lack thereof between North and South Korea. After 28 years, freedom has at last triumphed over the Berlin Wall, but the fortresses built around the DMZ by North and South Korea are as impregnable as ever 40 years after the Korean War. The West German *ostpolitik* has now plucked its major fruit, while South Korean *nordpolitik* has just begun its seeding.

The political cataclysm in Europe is not an overnight happenstance, but a cumulative product of a long and arduous piecemeal undertaking by many of foresight and perseverance. People like Willy Brandt and Mikhail Gorbachev represent only the tip of a "peaceberg" that has been building all these years by those with vision and conviction.

The dividing line between the two halves of Korea—first, the 38th Parallel, now the DMZ—has become more militarily fortified than ever. The DMZ is now the most militarized area in the world. The fact that more than 1.5 million troops face each other across the 155-mile DMZ in contrast with only 2 million across the 4,600-mile Sino–Soviet border dramatically illustrates this potentially explosive situation.

Worse still, the continuing arms race in North and South Korea is becoming increasingly anachronistic in light of the global trend toward peace and common security.[2] A serious consideration of arms control and disarmament on the Korean Peninsula should not be merely wishful thinking, but the first and foremost priority.[3] For Korean reunification cannot be realized by advocating seemingly attractive unification formulas or by appealing to the Korean people's nationalistic sentiment and zeal. Rather, it can be accomplished only when both sides cease to regard each other as "mortal enemies."

To put it another way, what Korea needs now more than ever are the political leaders who dare think the unthinkable and act accordingly. Ideas and machines are made by humans, and they remain useless until and unless those ideas are put into action and those machines are put into operation. By the same token, peace plans, unification formulas, or arms control proposals, no matter how well thought out and thoroughly researched, are worthless when decision makers fail to implement them with vision and firmness.

Bearing the above caveats in mind, three questions will be dealt with in this chapter. First, conventionally recognized constraining and contributing factors in the eventual realization of North and South Korean arms control will be identified. Second, the most crucial element for the implementation of a genuine arms control agreement on the Korean Peninsula will be pinpointed. Finally, a number of previously taboo notions will be introduced as alternatives to the present arms race on the Korean Peninsula.

Push and Pull Factors in Arms Control

Restricting itself to the military and political situations on the Korean Peninsula, the following discussion will identify the constraining ("pull") and contributing ("push") elements in any potential arms control negotiation.

Constraining Factors

Mutual Misunderstandings, Misperceptions, and Miscalculations. With the exception of a few intermittent dialogues, both Koreas have existed for more than 40 years with little or no contact, communication, or cooperation. The absence of such interaction was the result of each country's continuing hostility toward the other, which in turn has served to reinforce the existing animus.[4]

Mutual Distrust. From the very beginning, mutual distrust has been the norm, but this distrust was further aggravated by the outbreak of the fratricidal Korean War and concomitant sufferings and tragedies of the Korean people, not to mention the escalating arms race. In particular, North Korea's terrorist acts, such as the Rangoon bombing in 1983 and the destruction of KAL 858 in 1987, added fuel to such distrust.

The Four Major Powers' Policy of Status Quo. Although the roles and interests of the four major powers—the United States, the Soviet Union, Japan, and China—on the Korean Peninsula differ widely, they are in basic agreement that there should not be another Korean War, which is very likely to trigger World War III. This means that all four seek a peaceful solution to the Korean question. From a negative perspective, this means that a stalemate or the status quo will continue to exist until and unless a peaceful formula for the Korean question, agreeable to all four powers, is devised.

Arms Control Proposals as a Political Propaganda Tool. From 1948 to 1988, the North made 238 arms control proposals in 27 different areas. During the same period, the South advocated 64 arms control proposals in 17 areas. The three most frequent items in the proposals by North and South Korea are as follows. North Korea has demanded the withdrawal of U.S. troops (80 times), the conclusion of a peace treaty (28 times), and the reduction of force levels to 100,000 troops (22 times). South Korea has espoused a mutual nonaggression treaty (18 times), mutual tension reduction measures (12 times), and the abandonment of unification by force (8 times). On balance, it is evident that the North, far more than the South, tends to utilize arms control proposals as a political propaganda tool.[5] North Korea's duplicity, double-talk, and discrepancy between words and deeds is evidenced by its advocacy of a nuclear-free zone on the Korean peninsula despite its frenetic efforts to develop atomic weapons.[6]

Irreconcilability of the Unification Formula. As long as the Korean reunification approaches of South and North remain unchanged and irreconcilable, no serious arms control talks are feasible. North Korea contends that the reunification talks will not make any progress until and unless, *inter alia,* the question of foreign elements—that is, the U.S. troops in South Korea—is resolved satisfactorily. South Korea, on the other hand, demands a substantive and credible guarantee of peace on the Korean Peninsula before reunification can be dealt with in earnest. In essence, then, it is not the lack of a reunification policy or formula that has halted the reunification dialogue, but rather the absence of a mutually agreeable one.

Subversive Elements in the South. If subversive groups—be they radical students, workers, or farmers—try to overthrow the current government by violent means, especially when they are linked to the North's liberation strategy or are boosted by the North's propaganda, the existence of such groups would indeed be a serious hindrance to any genuine arms control talks.

Soviet and Chinese Military Support and Alliance with the North and U.S. Military Assistance and Alliance with the South. As long as the North maintains a military alliance with the Soviet Union and China and the South with the United States,[7] and as long as both continue to receive sophisticated military hardware from their respective allies,[8] arms control talks will be in vain, if not utterly meaningless.

A Lack of Genuine Willingness to Hold Successful Arms Talks. Although both sides are guilty of not pushing for mutually acceptable arms control, comparatively speaking, the North has been far more hypocritical than the South. The fact that the North continues to escalate offensive military preparedness by increasing its force levels, its offensive mode of deployment, and its offensive military force training, while concurrently advocating peace on the Korean Peninsula, speaks to that hypocrisy.

Contributing Factors

A High Degree of Cultural Homogeneity and Common Nationalistic Longing for Reunification. Few nations in the world today are as culturally homogeneous as are the Korean people who speak the same language and share the same ethnic and historical heritage. These factors should facilitate arms control and disarmament between the two as a prelude to their eventual reunification.

A Common Fear of Another Fratricidal War on the Korean Peninsula. The memory of the Korean War in the 1950s, with its accompanying destruction in human lives and the suffering of some 10 million separated families, is sufficient reason for people to seek an alternative to continuing hostility.

An Excess of Military Expenditures. The two sides should learn lessons from the deleterious effects that have ensued from the intense arms race between North and South Korea and between the two superpowers. Fifty years after the outbreak of the World War II, the two major victors of the war—the United States and the Soviet Union—which have been pursuing a military-first policy, are declining, while the two major vanquished nations—Japan and West Germany—which have been reorienting themselves toward an economy-first policy, are prospering.[9] In particular, North Korea, whose economy is shrinking compared with that of South Korea, is facing a crisis. If the size of the South Korean economy is five or even seven times larger than that of the North, the latter will be forced to spend some 25 to 35 percent of its GNP for military expenditures to simply match 5 percent of South Korea's GNP for such expenditures. Therefore, it is hoped that the leadership of North and South Korea would realize that the continuing arms race will lead to continuing stagnation, not to coprosperity. The North is far more desperate than the South in this regard.

North–South Contact, Communication, and Cooperation. North–South dialogue, which has been ongoing in four areas—the Red Cross talks, the preparatory meetings for the North–South parliamentary conference, the sports talks, and the preparatory meetings for the North–South prime ministerial conference—will facilitate the creation of the political and military milieu conducive to arms control talks.

The Global Trend toward Peace and Freedom. Although Gorbachev's peace move was initially regarded by the West merely as a "peace offensive," and Bush's freedom crusade was downgraded in the East simply as a "freedom offensive," daily there is evidence of the cataclysmic changes occurring, especially in the former Soviet bloc. The cold war is indeed in its final stages, and the new global paradigm is being ushered in. Although the Korean Peninsula still remains the lone island of the cold war, it would be increasingly difficult for the Korean Peninsula to remain isolated from such global changes.

The Big Powers' Tacit Agreement on the Peaceful Resolution of the Korean Question. It is quite evident that none of the four major powers—the United States, the Soviet Union, China, and Japan—support the idea of resolving the Korean question by military means, although their interests in the Korean Peninsula may be at odds. Accordingly, North Korea's designs on the South and its violent methods are increasingly becoming anachronistic.

Democratization Process in the South. If democracy reflects the demands of the people, the present democratization process begun in the Sixth Republic will be conducive to arms control talks. Although the father–son succession campaign transpiring in North Korea typifies an antithesis of democracy and democratization, some day soon the North may reverse its present course. For, if the people on the Korean Peninsula genuinely desire peace and reunification, then only the emergence of democratic governments on both sides of the DMZ can lead to real progress toward such goals.

Recent Arms Control Proposals

It is clear from the above discussion that some contributing and constraining factors overlap. The global trend, however, is self-evident: That is, even on the Korean Peninsula, the elements conducive to arms control are increasingly gaining momentum.

One positive sign in this direction is the increase in public and academic debates about arms control issues in South Korea today—a topic forbidden only a few years ago. A few examples suffice to illustrate this point. Song Dae-Sung, for example, recently proposed what he called a five-stage arms control formula for North and South Korea (see table 15.1).[10] Likewise, Park Young-Kyu proposed a multidimensional formula for North–South arms control talks. Park's model, unlike Song's formula, examines not only the North–South arms control equation, but also the dimensions for broader cooperation and North–South political relations, as well as the changing relations between South Korea and the United States.[11]

Table 15.1 Song Dae-Sung's Five-Stage Arms Control Formula on the Korean Peninsula

First Stage: *A North and South Korean Nonaggression Agreement to:*

1. abandon the use of mutual military force and invasion attempts
2. provide for noninterference in internal affairs
3. prohibit mutual vituperation

Second Stage: *Establishment of a North and South Korean Military*

Commission as a formal instrument of mutual CBMs

Third Stage: *Institution of the Following CBMs:*

1. mutual exchange of military personnel
2. advance notification of key military exercises and mutual exchange of military observers
3. establishment of friendship promotion facilities in the DMZ
4. establishment of communication links between North and South Korean top military decision makers
5. demilitarization of the DMZ

Fourth Stage: *Arms Control Proposals:*

1. a formula to stop the acceleration of the arms race
2. a formula to reduce military force levels
3. a formula to verify arms control implementation
4. a formula to punish arms control violations

Fifth Stage: *Implementation of Arms Control on the Korean Peninsula*

Choe Young, meanwhile, proposed a number of concrete agenda items for North–South arms control talks based on three key analytic principles: (1) confidence building measures (CBMs) and CSBMs such as the advance notification of military exercises and relocation; the mutual exchange of observers to these exercises; the mutual exchange of military intelligence, as well as military doctrines; and tactics based on openness and transparency;

(2) the reasonable sufficiency principle, which identifies the first and foremost targets for negotiation as those offensive weapons and offensive mode of deployments; and (3) follow-on forces attack (FOFA) strategy in support of early warning capabilities, such as the airborne warning and control system (AWACS). Further, he identified three key unresolved issues between South Korea and the United States: the U.S. forces' possession of the short-range nuclear forces (SNF); its restructuring of the CFC, especially the question of OPCON; and burden sharing.

Against the backdrop of the above relevant guidelines and unresolved U.S.–South Korean questions, Choe pinpointed five agenda items for the North–South arms control talks. They include the conclusion of a North–South basic peace treaty; the reduction of the North–South military force levels to 400,000; the gradual reduction of offensive weapons; the banning of nuclear weapons development; and on-the-spot inspection of mutual military and security facilities and other areas. In addition, he attempted to assess the feasibility scores for three options. First, the North accepts the reasonable sufficiency principle; second, the South removes the SNF in close consultation with the United States; and, third, the North accepts the first and the South the second, simultaneously.[12]

On the other hand, North Korea's most recent proposal called for "the comprehensive guarantee of [a] peace policy in order to expedite the independent peaceful unification of the fatherland," which was announced on November 8, 1988, in the name of the general conference of the DPRK Central People's Committee, the Supreme People's Assembly's Standing Committee, and the Administration Council.[13] The gist of this most recent proposal is as follows.

First, it proposes four principles for guaranteeing peace. They are: peace for unification, peace assured by the withdrawal of foreign forces (the code for the U.S. forces in the South), peace through North–South arms control, and peace through dialogue by those who are responsible for causing tension identified as the North, the South, and the United States. (Note here that the North is included as one of the three culprits for causing tension). On the basis of these four principles—*T'ongil chihyang, Oekun ch'olsu, Pukham kamch'uk,* and *Tangsaja hyopsang*—the following specific, though unrealistic and hardly new, proposals are spelled out.

1. *The Gradual Withdrawal of U.S. Forces.* The removal of nuclear weapons by two stages—first, the withdrawal of nuclear weapons above the latitude of 35°30 ' by the end of 1989; second, the rest of the nuclear weapons in the South should be removed by the end of 1990. The withdrawal of U.S. troops would occur in three stages: first, the withdrawal of the U.S. command headquarters and ground forces

above the latitude of 35°30 ' to the line below Pusan and Chinhae by
the end of 1989; second, the withdrawal of all U.S. ground forces from
the South by the end of 1990; third, the withdrawal of U.S. naval and
air forces from the South by the end of 1991. In addition, the United
States would be banned from supplying new weapons and other
military equipment. During the U.S. withdrawal phase, no U.S.-owned
military weapons or equipment could be transferred to the South.
2. *The Gradual Reduction of North and South Korean Military Forces.* The
reductions would be implemented in three stages: first, down to
400,000 on both sides by the end of 1989; second, to 250,000 by the
end of 1990; third, to 100,000 or less after 1992. During the first stage,
all special weapons—including nuclear and chemical weap-
ons—should be removed; no importing of new weapons from abroad
may occur during the first stage of military force reduction; finally,
within six months after the implementation of force reduction, all
civilian military organizations should be disbanded.
3. *Notification and Inspection of the U.S. Troop Withdrawal and
North–South Military Force Reductions.* The United States will withdraw its troops and notify the North. Then, the North and the South
will notify each other of their military force reduction. Finally, the
Neutral Nations' Inspection Commission in Panmunjom will inspect
both the U.S. troop withdrawal and the reduction of the North–South
military force levels, thereby expanding and strengthening the
Commission's power.
4. *Tripartite Conference among the North, the United States, and the South.*
A tripartite conference comprising representatives from the North, the
United States, and the South would be held. (Within this tripartite
framework, there would be North Korean–U.S., and North–South
bilateral conferences.) In the tripartite conference, the question of the
U.S. forces' gradual withdrawal and North–South military force reductions and the question of expanding and strengthening the Neutral
Nations' Inspection Commission power would be deliberated. The
representatives from the said Commission—Poland, Czechoslovakia,
Switzerland, and Sweden—would participate in the conference as
observers. At the conference, a North Korea–U.S. peace treaty and a
North–South nonaggression declaration would be confirmed.
5. *A Set of Formulas to Reduce the Political and Military Confrontation
between North and South.* All mutual vituperation should be halted;
any political rally attacking the other side should not occur; cooperation and exchange between the two should begin in all areas; the
DMZ should be converted to a peace zone; any large-scale military
exercise to aggravate the tension (the code for Team Spirit) should be

halted; any armed clashes along the DMZ should be avoided; a telephone hot line linking the top military leaders of the North and the South should be installed to reduce political and military tensions; and a high-level North–South military leaders' conference should be held.

As it is quite clear from the foregoing, the North Korean proposals are still essentially the same as before, although at a first glance they appear new. North Korea's first and foremost objective for the past several decades has been the removal of the U.S. forces from the South. This latest peace proposal, too, boils down to the same objective. Any additional points are merely window dressing. The hard choice now is whether the South should dismiss this old proposal or try to take it a step further—that is, to single out some useful items for talks. The global trend, the regional setting, and the North–South domestic political situation demand the latter. The situation calls for the South to take more initiative and develop a positive approach.

Conclusion and Some Unthinkable Thinking

Instead of the customary conclusion and summary, some unthinkable thinking about the Korean question, particularly in regard to arms control will be proposed here as food for thought, as well as for action in the foreseeable future.

Can the two halves of Korea declare war on pollution, poverty, uneven development, unequal distribution, disease, drugs, and other problems instead of wasting their energies and resources in preparing for war against each other?

Can Kim Il-Sung become a Gorbachev? If not a Gorbachev, what about becoming a Deng?

Can the North Korean ruling elites abandon their united front strategy of "the liberation of the South"? Can they stop practicing double-talk—holding an olive branch in one hand and lethal weapons in the other? Can they stop lying to their own people, to South Korea, to the rest of the world, and, above all, to themselves?

Can South Korea permit all information and material to flow in from North Korea and other socialist countries, including the North Korean radio and TV broadcasts, without any restrictions? Can South Korea allow those persons and groups who wish to visit or even settle in North Korea to leave without restrictions?

Can it permit all social and political organizations, including the Communist Party, to participate in the political process as long as those organizations do not act illegally or with violent tactics and strategy?

Can they cease to see each other as their mortal archenemies? Can they stop buying such prohibitively expensive lethal weapons from abroad? Can they pause a moment to think seriously about who has benefited most while both nations have been at odds with each other all these years? Can they stop contemplating building nuclear weapons? Finally, can they seriously think about alternative uses for the vast human energies and material resources that have been poured into mutual arms buildups during all these years?

Notes

1. Mikhail Gorbachev, *Perestroika: New Thinking for Our Country and the World* (New York: Harper & Row, 1987), 127.

2. Ibid., 192. Gorbachev coined the term "common security" to mean the security for the survival of humanity, but he credited Olaf Palme's idea of "security for all" as the origin of his concept.

3. Bowie defines arms control as "any agreement among several powers to regulate some aspect of their military capability or potential. The arrangement may apply to the location, amount, readiness, or types of military forces, weapons, or facilities." Schelling and Halperin included in their arms control concept any kind of military cooperation between potential enemies with the aim of "reducing the likelihood of war; its scope and violence if it occurs and the political and economic costs of being prepared for it." Although the two concepts—arms control and disarmament—are not easily distinguishable, the latter always involves arms reduction, while the former may not. See Robert R. Bowie, "Basic Requirements of Arms Control," *Arms Control, Disarmament and National Security,* Donald G. Brennan, ed. (New York: G. Braziller, 1961), 43; Thomas C. Schelling and Morton H. Halperin, *Strategy and Arms Control* (New York: The Twentieth Century Fund, 1961), 142. For a detailed discussion of the two concepts, see Michael Sheehan, *Arms Control: Theory and Practice* (London: Basil Blackwell, 1988), 1–22.

4. The most notable example of inter-Korean hostility was the resumption of their dialogue in August 1971 that led to the July 4th Joint Communique in 1972, which soon ended in stalemate. For details, see *A White Paper on the South-North Dialogue in Korea* (Seoul: National Unification Board, Republic of Korea, 1982), 63–192.

5. For a detailed analysis of arms control proposals in the North and South, see Yang Sung-Chul and Hyun Cho-Duk, "An Analysis and Appraisal of North and South Korean Arms Control Proposals" [in Korean] *Korean Political Science Review* 27, no. 1 (1987): 91–113. See also, Song Dae-Sung, "An Examination on the Relevance of the Disarmament Theory in the Korean Peninsula: The Possibility and Limitation of Disarmament in the

Korean Peninsula" [in Korean] *Korean Journal of International Relations* 29, no. 1 (1989): 71–110.

6. Lee Byung-Ho, a specialist, presented his review of North Korean efforts to develop nuclear weapons to a seminar arranged by the Peace Research Institute on November 9, 1989, Hyatt Regency Hotel, Seoul, South Korea. See also Ohn Chang-Il, "Nuclear Deterrence and Reunification of Korea" [in Korean] *Korean Journal of International Relations* 29, no. 1 (1989): 141–156.

7. For a detailed comparative discussion of North Korea's alliance system with the Soviet Union and China and that of South Korea with the United States, see Yang Sung-Chul, "The North and South Korean Military Forces and their Alliance Systems" [in Korean] *Sasang kwa Chongch'ek* (Summer 1989): 98–127; Kim Kye-Dong, "The ROK–US Mutual Defense Treaty Decision-Making Process and the Improvement Plan," [in Korean] *Sasang kwa Chongch'ek* (Summer 1989): 154–162.

8. According to *World Military Expenditures and Arms Transfer,* North Korea bought some $990 million worth of weapons, mostly from the Soviet Union and China during the 1981–1985 period, while South Korea purchased nearly $2 billion worth of weapons, almost all from the United States. For details, see Yang Sung-Chul, "North and South Korean Military Forces and Their Alliance Systems," 125.

9. A detailed analysis of the postwar Japanese peace economy model and the U.S.–Soviet militaristic interactive model, see Yang Sung-Chul, "Integration Model for Japan and the Asian NICs in the Pacific Era," *The Northeast Asian Era and the Roles of Korea, China and Japan in the 21st Century,* Choue Chung-Won ed. (Seoul: Kyunghee University, 1988), 23–40.

10. For details, see Song Dae-Sung, "An Examination of the Relevance of the Disarmament Theory in the Korean Peninsula," 71–110.

11. For details, see Park Young-Kyu, "The East–West Arms Control Negotiation Experiences and the Problem of Arms Control in the Korean Peninsula," [in Korean] Paper delivered at Korea University Peace Research Institute Seminar, October 30–31, 1989.

12. Young Choi, "Restructuring of the ROK-U.S. Security System and the North and South Korea Arms Control," [in Korean] Paper delivered at Korea University Peace Research Institute Seminar, October 30–31, 1989. See also Young Choi, "Korean Proposals for Adjusting ROK–U.S. Security Cooperation: Focusing on the Four Major Issues," Paper presented at the Fourth Annual Conference of Council on U.S.–Korean Security Studies, Honolulu, Hawaii, November 15–18, 1988, pp. 16–19.

13. The full text of North Korea's statement is available. [in Korean] Only the key points of this proposal are listed in this paper.

16

Conclusions and
Policy Implications

John Q. Blodgett

This book is the product of 17 accomplished strategists, all keen observers of current world affairs and most with specialized expertise on Northeast Asian security issues. Some have been senior architects of their nation's policies in that region. Each approaches the hub issue of this enterprise— prospects for peace and arms reduction on the Korean Peninsula—along the path of his own discipline and his own individual and national perspective. The editors made no effort to regiment the analysis toward a preconceived consensus.

The result is precisely the diversity of thought on the common issue that the editors were looking for. Well reflected here are the dichotomies in the U.S. and Korean appraisal of the health of the U.S.–ROK alliance, the challenges it confronts, and the timing of actions to bring about the peaceful outcome that both nations want. But equally well reflected is the remarkably high level of common understanding about the need for the U.S.–ROK relationship to adapt to, and exploit, global change.

The purpose of this final chapter is to glean from what precedes a near-term strategy for the alliance that will accommodate the differing perceptions and circumstances of both parties, while simultaneously keeping the alliance flexible enough to build on the fast-evolving global environment.

The Dichotomies

A salient phenomenon of the maturing ROK–U.S. relationship is the impact of South Korea's remarkable economic takeoff on the atmospherics

253

of the partnership. There is a new Korean self-assertiveness, encouraged by democratization, that finds expression at both the official and popular levels. But there is reciprocally a new American toughness about the ROK—and also at both levels. While Seoul asks for greater military OPCON, Washington presses for greater economic burden sharing. Though these opposing considerations are by no means incompatible, they inject unhelpful heat and frustration into the dialogue.

There are also some differences in perceptions of the North Korean threat and the correlation of forces. Seoul, in the shadow of an overarmed and unpredictable dictatorship, will not feel safe short of full military parity. Washington, under a budgetary gun 12,000 miles away, suggests that given the South's enormous economic edge, there is already effective parity and thus an opportunity for the United States to shift more toward a supportive role in the alliance. This dichotomy, among other things, inhibits a meeting of the minds on the depth and timing of U.S. force reductions, which will inevitably have a bearing on the OPCON shift. The Korean authors resist deep reductions; the Americans set timetables for a much smaller U.S. ground presence.

Finally, there is perhaps a greater impatience in Washington than in Seoul for early North–South negotiations that could break the deadlock and begin a process of arms reduction. The South Koreans appear to set a higher priority (and who can blame them) on entering peace and reunification talks from a position of still greater relative strength.

Areas of U.S.–ROK Agreement

There is a common awareness between the allies of the largely favorable implications for Korea of current global events. In particular, Washington doubtless applauds Seoul's readiness to emulate Tokyo in exploiting opportunities for economic cooperation with China and the Soviet Union. This cements North Korean isolation while providing yet another demonstration of what North Korea might hope to gain from a changed policy. It also gives Moscow and Beijing a stake in a secure and functioning South Korea.

Both allies recognize that time is on their side on the Korean Peninsula, but that to make time work they must remain strong and united. If there are fears in the ROK that the United States will falter in its commitment to the common goal, they are unjustified. A strong, peaceful, and democratic South Korea is more vital to U.S. interests than ever before.

Both agree that the ROK–U.S. relationship is now—and should remain—fraternal, not paternal. Any forward alliance strategy must accommodate and advance, in balanced fashion, the vital interests of both partners. But chief among them will remain a shared interest in the prosperous tranquility of the Northeast Asian region.

The Underpinnings of Alliance Strategy for the 1990s

Strategy must start from the situation as it stands. These are the realities of the situation in Northeast Asia as of mid-1990:

- The ROK–U.S. alliance has contained North Korean ambitions, but has not prevented the strengthening of the North Korean military. (See chapters 5, 6, and 12.)
- The relative strength of North Korea, however, continues to deteriorate in both the military and economic dimensions (chapters 8 and 15).
- Soviet forces confronting Northeast Asia remain far superior to defensive needs and are not being reduced (chapters 4 and 5).
- There is abundant evidence, however, that no outside power, including China and the Soviet Union, is prepared to support North Korean aggression against the South (chapter 4).
- Despite the foregoing, North Korea remains powerful and capricious; a high-intensity attack on the South cannot be precluded (chapter 6).
- The DPRK remains a Communist dictatorship; until that changes, any serious discussion of reunification is hypothetical (chapter 15).
- Though U.S. vital interests in the western Pacific continue to rise, declining defense budgets will require force reductions and restructuring in that theater and an increased dependence on indigenous security inputs (chapter 8).

Of the foregoing factors in the current equation, all but the last-listed have been fully discussed in the preceding chapters of this book. For an authoritative clarification of how the defense budget crunch could affect the U.S. Pacific Command out to the year 2000, I refer readers to *A Strategic Framework for the Asian Pacific Rim: Looking Toward the 21st Century*, a Department of Defense concept paper delivered to the Congress in April 1990.

Prepared in accordance with the Nunn–Warner amendment to the FY 1990 Defense Authorization Act, the DOD paper starts from the premise that because of the uniquely volatile and complex military environment in the region, "a continued, substantial air and naval presence in East Asia is required" along with a sustained nuclear umbrella. The paper acknowledges, however, that "measured reductions of ground and some air forces in Korea, Japan, and the Philippines can take place." The paper puts forward a three-phase process to accomplish those reductions regionwide by 2000, with some country-specific detail for each phase.

With specific regard to Korea, DOD proposed to cut 2,000 air force and 5,000 army personnel in Phase I (1990–1992) and essentially to play it by ear in Phase II (1993–1995) and Phase III (1995–2000), depending on the levels of threat, ROK force improvement, and burden sharing.

In a final section on arms control and confidence-building measures, the DOD paper calls primarily for Soviet and North Korean initiatives, with virtually no speculation about what might be an appropriate ROK or U.S. response to such initiatives. DOD argues with some cogency that countering the Soviet and North Korean threats in Northeast Asia is only one of many CINCPAC concerns in the region.

It is no criticism of the Pentagon to suggest that its proposals fall far short of a U.S. governmentwide, or ROK–U.S. alliancewide, strategy for a peaceful solution on the Korean Peninsula. DOD's business is peacekeeping, not peacemaking. It is basing its planning—as it must—on an assumption of continued confrontation on the Korean Peninsula.

The basic premise of this book, by contrast, is that the global environment in 1990 may offer opportunity to resolve the dangerous and expensive Korean impasse once and for all. Its authors have sought to show how the atmosphere of detente and arms reduction in Europe can provide a platform for proactive peacemaking in Northeast Asia. By and large, they come out in favor of ROK–U.S. pump-priming to get the peace process off dead center. By and large, they reject the premise that North Korea, even under Kim Il-Sung, can long resist the rising economic, military, and diplomatic pressures it faces. By and large (though not unanimously) they want to at least make a start on the process *now,* before Pyongyang's embattled leaders make a tragic miscalculation.

A precondition to any effective ROK–U.S. strategy for a Korean settlement is a full, binational meeting of the minds on its key elements. Whichever party appears publicly to take an initiative, for example, a U.S. force reduction or an ROK proposal for freer travel across the DMZ, it should be publicly endorsed by the other party. Any semblance of alliance disunity will encourage the risk-takers in Pyongyang.

To contribute to this crucial unity, the allies must abstain for a time from government-to-government bickering, at least in public, about peripheral economic issues. An understanding between the White House and the Congress on this need should be negotiable.

The pivotal reality in all peacemaking—a reality demonstrated time and again in Europe and well understood by UN negotiators—is that the process cannot begin unless all parties have a political will to move at least part of the way down the road toward a negotiated solution. (See chapter 13.) The first step—confidence building—alone requires a major commitment of political will because to some degree it deprives each party of the weapon of secrecy. A nation with even a lingering proclivity for launching a surprise attack will resist that first step because, once taken, it cannot be undone without sending a clear signal of hostile intent. Thus if North Korea agrees to an exchange of CSBMs, it implies a readiness to explore the modalities of peace. If it demurs, we are back to square one, but at least we know where we stand.

The ROK–U.S. alliance thus needs two concurrent strategies at this juncture—one for negotiation and the other for continued containment. Both the carrot and the stick must be openly displayed, for Pyongyang may reject the carrot if the stick is ambiguous or loses credibility.

A Strategy for Peace

The carrot (the strategy for peace) might take the form of declared alliance readiness to launch serious negotiations with Pyongyang on CSBMs as soon as two preconditions are met by the North Koreans: a categoric and public rejection of first use of force, including terrorism, and a public expression of DPRK readiness to negotiate with South Korea as an equal and sovereign partner. These preconditions would merely establish a level playing field. South Korea is already committed on both points. But they are crucial in demonstrating North Korean political will.

The next step is to establish a tripartite forum for the CSBM talks, perhaps at Panmunjom. Ideally, the forum should be bilateral—between the two Koreas—but with ample provision for interrelated U.S.–DPRK and Soviet– ROK talks on issues involving the superpowers. Though neither Korea is yet a UN member, it might be useful to have a senior UN official present as observer or arbitrator, if only because some of the CSBMs might entail undertakings by outside powers (e.g., China, Japan, or the Soviet Union).

It would seem vital that the CSBM talks be conducted in secrecy. The parties must communicate directly—not, as in the past, through the media. This promotes sincerity and constructive trade-offs. The negotiators should go public only when there is an agreement to announce.

I will not attempt to catalogue here the array of CSBMs that could come under discussion. I would suggest only the obvious wisdom of starting with the relatively easy ones—reopened communication links, joint cultural events, joint studies on such common problems as the environment and tourism promotion, and prenotification of major military movements or exercises. At some early point, in my view, it would be constructive to discuss the establishment of U.S.–DPRK diplomatic relations—a logical sequel to the ROK–Soviet agreement of June 6, 1990 (though it may not seem so to the North Koreans).

Predictable attempts by the North to demand the withdrawal of U.S. troops and nuclear weapons under the rubric of confidence building should be rejected. That is more properly a component of arms reduction talks, which should await clear evidence that the CSBM process is solidly on track.

The strategy for peace should not be seen as a one-time alliance campaign—"take it now or leave it forever"—but rather as a standing offer to the North Koreans to come to the table when they are ready. In that light, it becomes a new element of time pressure on the Pyongyang leadership—an ROK diplomatic manifesto that the DPRK's allies (China and the Soviet Union) might find it in their interest to rally behind. It exploits the dynamics of the North Korean dilemma. When a nation is on a downward slope, it is best to apply the brakes as near the top as possible.

It is useful for ROK and U.S. planners to flesh out a peace strategy that might take us from CSBMs through arms reduction and peace treaty, projecting at the end a unified Korea that is democratic, less militarized, economically integrated, and a free world bastion in the Northeast Asian quadrant. Such a projection is, in fact, the purpose of chapter 8 of this book as covered by alternative scenarios in chapter 15. The planners must recognize, however, that such scenarios are academic unless and until the immovable object in Pyongyang begins to yield to the irresistible force of North Korea's growing isolation and erosion, coupled with a beckoning alliance and global economic mainstream. In my view, leadership attention in Seoul and Washington today should be focused on that first vital breakthrough that can only come from a successful CSBM process. It was, after all, the Helsinki Process, essentially CSBMs, that helped set the stage for a CFE negotiation, though one cannot carry the analogy too far. (See chapter 13.)

A Strategy for Containment

As I have suggested, the carrot needs a stick—and it must be strong, open ended, and credible.

To be strong, the alliance should continue the ROK force improvement program, though the tempo of that program may now be less important than its steady direction. A relocation of USFK headquarters and units within Korea and the DOD-proposed reduction of 7,000 support troops by 1992 should not materially compromise the alliance's deterrent posture.

To be open ended, the alliance must be understood as a permanent arrangement—one that will guarantee ROK defense, whatever it requires and as long as needed. In particular, Washington should be planning now for the alliance role after the North Korean threat has been erased. In that context, the DOD plan to keep its USFK options open after 1992 is totally unassailable. Korea remains far and away the most impelling contingency in the Pacific theater, and perhaps the world. It would be folly at this juncture—just when a serious negotiation may be in the offing—to change the signals by announcing a timetable for substantial U.S. force reductions in South Korea. Those reductions may come with peace on the peninsula, but to mandate them now would jeopardize that peace.

To be credible, the alliance must be seen as a reflection of a long-term and indestructible confluence of national interest between its partners. This is arguably the greatest challenge facing the ROK–U.S. alliance today. But despite all the tensions in the partnership over political, economic, and command issues, there is a commonality of strategic interest—peace, growth, and democracy in Northeast Asia—that should provide a rationale for alliance unity well into the 21st century.

Implications for U.S. Policy

An ROK–U.S. alliance strategy to initiate a call for early and serious CSBM negotiations with North Korea would entail the following U.S. government actions and policy directions:

1. Develop, in coordination with the ROK government, a list of CSBMs or "operational arms control" accommodations that the alliance is prepared to negotiate reciprocally with the DPRK on the sole condition that Pyongyang first publicly renounce the first use of force and declare its readiness to negotiate with South Korea as an equal partner.
2. Publish the list jointly as an official alliance invitation to negotiate.
3. Announce plans to withdraw 7,000 U.S. troops from South Korea by 1992, but make it clear that further withdrawals would depend on significant progress in the CSBM talks.
4. Seek public (or at least private) PRC and Soviet endorsement of the CSBM process as a step toward peace on the Korean Peninsula.
5. If the DPRK agrees to the negotiation and its preconditions, announce U.S. readiness to establish full diplomatic relations with North Korea.
6. Seek a private understanding with U.S. congressional leaders on a moratorium on legislative or policy proposals affecting South Korea that could give an appearance of alliance disunity.
7. Take all feasible steps in South Korea that might help to defuse anti-Americanism there, including the expeditious relocation of USFK headquarters from Yongsan, increased ROK OPCON in CINCCFC, and a formal announcement that the United States has no nuclear weapons deployed on South Korean soil.

About the Contributors

JOHN Q. BLODGETT is a fellow in international security studies at CSIS. As a career foreign service officer, he specialized in economic, military, and political affairs serving at nine overseas posts in Europe, Asia, and Africa for 32 years. He also served as deputy director of plans for policy, U.S. Air Force Staff.

CHA YOUNG-KOO, director of policy planning at KIDA, is a graduate of the Korea Military Academy and holds a Ph.D. from the University of Paris. Cha is an adviser to the Korean National Unification Board and a former visiting fellow at CSIS.

PARRIS CHANG is director of East Asian Studies at Pennsylvania State University. Born in Taiwan, Chang has written extensively on contemporary Chinese history.

YANG SUNG-CHUL teaches political science and is dean of the Graduate School of Peace Studies at Kyunghee University in Seoul. He earned his Ph.D. from the University of Kentucky in 1970 and is the author of *Korea and Two Regimes* (Cambridge: Schenkman, 1981).

GERRIT W. GONG, director of Asian studies at CSIS, served as special assistant to the U.S. ambassador to China and the under secretary of state for political affairs. A Rhodes scholar, Dr. Gong has taught at Johns Hopkins and Oxford Universities.

JAMES GOODBY is a Distinguished Service Professor at Carnegie Mellon University's Program on International Peace and Security. After serving as U.S. ambassador to Finland in 1980–1981, he played a leadership role as a U.S. negotiator in the arms control process in Europe.

ROBERT E. HUNTER, vice president for regional programs at CSIS, has served in the White House under Presidents Johnson, Ford, and Carter as both a Middle East and European expert. With a Ph.D. from the London School of Economics, Hunter is a widely published authority on international security issues.

AMOS A. JORDAN is vice chairman of the board of CSIS and president of the Pacific Forum of CSIS in Honolulu. A Rhodes scholar and retired U.S. army brigadier general, Jordan has held senior policy positions in the Departments of State and Defense and was a consultant to the National Security Council, the Joint Chiefs of Staff, and the Agency for International Development, among others.

NORMAN D. LEVIN is a Rand Corporation expert on East Asian security affairs with an extensive background in Japanese and Soviet relations with the two Koreas. He was a member of the State Department's Policy Planning Staff from 1984 to 1987.

KIM YU-NAM is a professor of international relations in the Department of Political Science at Hankook University, Seoul, and a Russian linguist. Kim received his B.A. and M.A. from San Francisco State University and his Ph.D. from the University of North Texas, Denton in 1973.

ROBERT MARTIN, with a Ph.D. from Harvard University, is an internationally known authority in the field of international and strategic studies with special expertise on the U.S. defense relationship with the People's Republic of China. He is currently director of Asia operations at the Systems Planning Corporation.

MICHAEL J. MAZARR is a fellow in political–military studies at CSIS. His research centers on U.S. nuclear and conventional policies, U.S.–South Korean security relations, and Cuba. He holds an M.A. from Georgetown University.

THOMAS H. MOORER has recently retired as senior adviser at CSIS. Former chairman of the Joint Chiefs of Staff, chief of naval operations, and commander in chief of the U.S. Pacific and Atlantic fleets, Admiral Moorer also commanded the NATO Allied Command, Atlantic, and the U.S. Unified Atlantic Command.

OH KWAN-CHI, chief researcher and director of the force development directorate at KIDA, is a former president of the Korea Institute for Economics and Technology and a former associate professor at Soongsil University. He holds a Ph.D. in economics from Vanderbilt University.

OHN CHANG-IL is a professor of Military History and Strategy at the Korea Military Academy (KMA). He received bachelor's degrees from KMA (1967) and at Seoul National University (1971), finished the U.S. Army

Command and General Staff College in 1977, and earned a Ph.D. in diplomatic history and international relations from the University of Kansas in 1983. He is now director of the Division of Humanities and Social Sciences at KMA.

PARK PONG-SHIK is a professor of political science at Seoul National University. He graduated from that institution in 1955 and received his Ph.D. in Political Science there in 1975. Park was director of the Center for International Studies at Seoul National University from 1972 to 1975 and served as its president from 1985 to 1987.

PARK TONG-WHAN is currently a visiting resarch fellow and associate professor of political science at Northwestern University. He received an M.A. in international law and a Ph.D. in political science at the University of Hawaii in 1969.

WILLIAM J. TAYLOR, JR., is vice-president for public policy programs at CSIS. A retired U.S. army colonel, Taylor is the author or editor of numerous books and articles on U.S. defense policy, including many on ROK–U.S. security relations. Taylor is a member of the Council on Foreign Relations.

Index